Lecture Notes in Computer Science 11557

Commenced Publication in 1973
Founding and Former Series Editors:
Gerhard Goos, Juris Hartmanis, and Jan van Leeuwen

More information about this series at http://www.springer.com/series/7411

Éric Renault · Selma Boumerdassi ·
Cherkaoui Leghris · Samia Bouzefrane (Eds.)

Mobile, Secure, and Programmable Networking

5th International Conference, MSPN 2019
Mohammedia, Morocco, April 23–24, 2019
Revised Selected Papers

 Springer

Editors
Éric Renault
Télécom SudParis
Évry, France

Selma Boumerdassi
Conservatoire National des Arts et Métiers
Paris, France

Cherkaoui Leghris
Hassan II Mohammedia University
Mohammedia, Morocco

Samia Bouzefrane
Conservatoire National des Arts et Métiers
Paris, France

ISSN 0302-9743 ISSN 1611-3349 (electronic)
Lecture Notes in Computer Science
ISBN 978-3-030-22884-2 ISBN 978-3-030-22885-9 (eBook)
https://doi.org/10.1007/978-3-030-22885-9

LNCS Sublibrary: SL5 – Computer Communication Networks and Telecommunications

This Springer imprint is published by the registered company Springer Nature Switzerland AG
The registered company address is: Gewerbestrasse 11, 6330 Cham, Switzerland

Preface

The rapid deployment of new infrastructures based on network virtualization and cloud computing triggers new applications and services that in turn generate new constraints such as security and/or mobility. The International Conference on Mobile, Secure, and Programmable Networking (MSPN) aims at providing a top forum for researchers and practitioners to present and discuss new trends in networking infrastructures, security, services, and applications while focusing on virtualization and cloud computing for networks, network programming, software defined networks (SDN), and their security. In 2019, MSPN was hosted by the Faculté des Sciences et Techniques (FST) of Mohammedia, a member of Hassan II University, one of the most important universities in Morocco.

The call for papers resulted in a total of 48 submissions from all around the world: Algeria, France, Germany, India, Mauritania, Morocco, Saudi Arabia, Senegal, Tunisia. All submissions were assigned to at least three members of the Program Committee for review. The Program Committee decided to accept 23 papers. Five intriguing keynotes from Antoine GALLAIS, Inria Lille, France, Awatif HAYAR, Hassan II University of Casablanca, Morocco, Bruno STEVANT, IMT Atlantique, France, Guy PUJOLLE, University of Paris 6, France, and Mohammed ACHOUR, Cisco Inc., France, completed the technical program.

We would like to thank all who contributed to the success of this conference, in particular the members of the Program Committee and the reviewers for carefully reviewing the contributions and selecting a high-quality program. Our special thanks go to the members of the Organizing Committee for their great help.

We hope that all participants enjoyed this successful conference, made many new contacts, engaged in fruitful discussions, and had a pleasant stay in Mohammedia, Morocco.

April 2019

Cherkaoui Leghris
Selma Boumerdassi
Éric Renault

Organization

MSPN 2019 was jointly organized by the Faculty of Sciences and Techniques (FST) of Mohammedia, Hassan II University, Morocco, the Wireless Networks and Multimedia Services (RS2M) Department of Télécom SudParis (TSP), a member of Institut Mines-Télécom (IMT) and University Paris-Saclay, France, and Conservatoire National des Arts et Métiers (CNAM), France.

General Chairs

Cherkaoui Leghris	FSTM, UH2C, Morocco
Selma Boumerdassi	CNAM, France
Éric Renault	IMT-TSP, France

Steering Committee

Selma Boumerdassi	CNAM, France
Éric Renault	IMT-TSP, France
Samia Bouzefrane	CNAM, France

Publicity Chair

Rahim Haiahem	ENSI, Tunisia

Organizing Committee

Abdellah Adib	FSTM, UH2C, Morocco
Habib Ayad	FSTM, UH2C, Morocco
Lahcen El Bouny	FSTM, FSTM, UH2C, Morocco
Fouad Elhajji	FSTM, FSTM, UH2C, Morocco
Ali Elksimi	FSTM, FSTM, UH2C, Morocco
Lamia Essalhi	ADDA, France
Mustapha Jebbar	University Hassan II, Morocco
Mohammed Khalil	FSTM, UH2C, Morocco
Feddoul Khoukhi	FSTM, UH2C, Morocco
Mouad Mansouri	FSTM, FSTM, UH2C, Morocco
Lahcen Mchaara	FSTM, FSTM, UH2C, Morocco
Noureddine Moukine	FSTM, UH2C, Morocco
Said Raddouche	FSTM, FSTM, UH2C, Morocco
Mouad Riyad	FSTM, FSTM, UH2C, Morocco
Sara Sekkat	FSTM, FSTM, UH2C, Morocco

Technical Program Committee

Abdellah Adib	FSTM, UH2C, Morocco
Abdeslam Annaque	EMI, UM5, Morocco
Mounir Arioua	Abdelmalek Essaadi University, Morocco
Habib Ayad	FSTM, UH2C, Morocco
Khalid Baamrani	ENSA, UCA, Morocco
Mohamed Belaoued	University of Constantine, Algeria
Assia Belbachir	IPSA, France
Aissa Belmeguenai	University of Skikda, Algeria
Hassan Berbia	ENSIAS, UM5, Morocco
Indayara Bertoldi Martins	PUC Campinas, Brazil
Luiz Bittencourt	University of Campinas, Brazil
Naïla Bouchemal	ECE Paris, France
Nardjes Bouchemal	University Center of Mila, Algeria
Selma Boumerdassi	CNAM, France
Ahcene Bounceur	University of Brest, France
Luca Caviglione	National Research Council, Italy
Driss Chana	EST, UMI, Morocco
De-Jiu Chen	KTH, Sweden
Yeh-Ching Chung	National Tsing Hua University, Taiwan
Domenico Ciuonzo	Network Measurement and Monitoring (NM2), Italy
Sanae El Filali	FSB, UH2C, Morocco
Raja Elassali	ENSA, UCA, Morocco
Paul Farrow	BT, UK
Hacène Fouchal	Université de Reims Champagne-Ardenne, France
Aravinthan Gopalasingham	NOKIA Bell Labs, France
Jean-Charles Grégoire	INRS, Canada
Viet Hai Ha	Hue University, Vietnam
Awatif Hayar	ENSEM, UH2C, Morocco
Alberto Huertas Celdran	University of Murcia, Spain
Noureddine Idboufker	ENSA, UCA, Morocco
Mohammed Khalil	FSTM, UH2C, Morocco
Feddoul Khoukhi	FSTM, UH2C, Morocco
Donghyun Kim	Kennesaw State University, GA, USA
Adam Krzyzak	Concordia University, QC, Canada
Mohammed Lahby	EST, UH2C, Morocco
Cherkaoui Leghris	Hassan II University, Morocco
Zoltán Mann	University of Duisburg-Essen, Germany
Natarajan Meghanathan	Jackson State University, USA
Saurabh Mehta	Vidyalankar Institute of Technology, Mumbai, India
Abdeltif Mezrioui	INPT, Morocco
Redha Mili	University of Constantine, Algeria
Ruben Milocco	Universidad Nacional del Comahue, Argentina
Pascale Minet	Inria, France
Noureddine Moumkine	FSTM, UH2C, Morocco

Paul Mühlethaler	Inria, France
Benayyad Nsiri	ENSET, UM5, Morocco
Frank Phillipson	TNO, The Netherlands
Éric Renault	IMT-TSP, France
Abdallah Rhattoy	EST, UMI, Morocco
Rachid Saadane	EHTP, Morocco
Hamida Seba	University of Lyon, France
Abderrahim Sekkaki	FSAC, UH2C, Morocco
Augustin Solanas Gomez	Universitat Rovira i Virgili, Spain
Patrick Sondi	Université du Littoral, France
Mounir Tahar Abbes	University of Chlef, Algeria
Van Long Tran	Hue Industrial College, Vietnam
Vinod Kumar Verma	Sant Longowal Institute of Engineering and Technology, India
Martine Wahl	IFSTTAR, France
Lei Zhang	East China Normal University, China

Sponsoring Institutions

CNAM, Paris, France
FST, Hassan II University, Mohammedia, Morocco
IMT-TSP, Évry, France
IT Innov Research Development, Mohammedia, Morocco

Contents

Deep Generative Models for Image Generation: A Practical Comparison Between Variational Autoencoders and Generative Adversarial Networks

Mohamed El-Kaddoury[1]([✉]), Abdelhak Mahmoudi[2],
and Mohammed Majid Himmi[1]

[1] LIMIARF, Faculty of Sciences, Mohammed V University, Rabat, Morocco
mh.kadouri@gmail.com, himmi.fsr@gmail.com
[2] LIMIARF, École Normale Supérieure, Mohammed V University, Rabat, Morocco
abdelhak.mahmoudi@um5.ac.ma

Abstract. Deep Learning models can achieve impressive performance in supervised learning but not for unsupervised one. In image generation problem for example, we have no concrete target vector. Generative models have been proven useful for solving this kind of issues. In this paper, we will compare two types of generative models: Generative Adversarial Networks (GANs) and Variational Autoencoders (VAEs). We apply those methods to different data sets to point out their differences and see their capabilities and limits as well. We find that, while VAEs are easier and faster to train, their results are in general more blurry than the images generated by GANs. These last are more realistic but noisy.

Keywords: Generative adverserial networks ·
Variational Autoencoders · Image generation · Unsupervised learning

1 Introduction

Unsupervised learning from large unlabeled datasets is an active research area. In practice, millions of images and videos are unlabeled and one can leverage them to learn good intermediate feature representations via approaches in unsupervised learning, which can then be used for other supervised or semi-supervised learning tasks such as classification. One approach for unsupervised learning is to learn a generative model. Two popular methods in computer vision are variational auto-encoders (VAEs) [1] and generative adversarial networks (GANs) [2].

Variational auto-encoders are a class of deep generative models based on variational methods. With sophisticated VAE models, one can not only generate realistic images, but also replicate consistent "style". For example, DRAW (Deep Recurrent Attentive Writer) [5] was able to generate images of house numbers with number combinations not seen in the training set, but with a consistent style/color/font of street sign in each image. Additionally, as models learn to

© Springer Nature Switzerland AG 2019
É. Renault et al. (Eds.): MSPN 2019, LNCS 11557, pp. 1–8, 2019.
https://doi.org/10.1007/978-3-030-22885-9_1

generate realistic output, they learn important features along the way, which potentially can be used for classification; we consider this in the Conditional VAE and semi-supervised learning [11] models. However, one main criticism of VAE models is that their generated output is often blurry.

In the generative adversarial networks [2], a generator model and a discriminator model both built by multilayer perceptrons are the basic modules. The goal of GANs is estimating generative models that can capture the distribution of real data with the adversarial assistance of a paired discriminator based on minimax game theory. After the birth of GANs, many variants have been widely researched to generate effective synthetic samples, such as image generation [2], image inpainting [12], image translation [13], super-resolution [14], image de-occlusion [15], natural language generation [16], text generation [17], Medical Image Analysis [10], etc. Though the powerful learning capabilities have gained great success in many fields.

In this paper, we want to compare VAEs and GANs in image generation, on different data sets. In Sects. 2 and 3, we will present the theory and architecture of these models and in Sect. 4, we will compare the two methods on MNIST, CIFAR-10 and CelebA datasets.

2   Variational Auto-Encoders

Let x be a vector of D observable variables and $z \in \mathbb{R}^M$ a vector of stochastic latent variables. Further, let $p_\theta(x, z)$ be a parametric model of the joint distribution. Given data $X = \{x_1, ..., x_N\}$ we typically aim at maximizing the average marginal log-likelihood, $\frac{1}{N} \ln(p(X)) = \frac{1}{N} \sum_{i=1}^{N} \ln(p(x_i))$, with respect to parameters. However, when the model is parameterized by a neural network (NN), the optimization could be difficult due to the intractability of the marginal likelihood. One possible way of overcoming this issue is to apply variational inference and optimize the following lower bound:

$$
\begin{aligned}
\mathbb{E}_{x \sim q(x)}[\ln(p(x)] \geq \mathbb{E}_{x \sim q(x)}[\mathbb{E}_{q_\phi(z|x)}[\ln p_\theta(x|z) \\
+ \ln p_\lambda(z) - \ln q_\phi(z|x)]] \\
\triangleq \mathcal{L}(\phi, \theta, \lambda)
\end{aligned}
\tag{1}
$$

where $q(x) = \frac{1}{N} \sum_{n=1}^{N} \delta(x - x_n)$ is the empirical distribution, $q_\phi(z|x)$ is the variational posterior (the encoder), $p_\theta(x|z)$ is the generative model (the decoder) and $p_\lambda(z)$ is the prior, and ϕ, θ, λ are their parameters, respectively.

There are various ways of optimizing this lower bound but for continuous z this could be done efficiently through the re-parameterization of $q_\phi(z|x)$ [3,4], which yields a VAE architecture. Therefore, during learning we consider a Monte Carlo estimate of the second expectation in (1) using L sample points:

$$
\tilde{\mathcal{L}}(\phi, \theta, \lambda) = \mathbb{E}_{x \sim q(x)}[\frac{1}{N} \sum_{l=1}^{L} (\ln p_\theta(x|z_\phi^{(l)})
\tag{2}
$$

$$+ \ln p_\lambda(z_\phi^{(l)}) - \ln q_\phi(z_\phi^{(l)}|x))], \tag{3}$$

where $z_\phi^{(l)}$ are sampled from $q_\phi(z|x)$ through the re-parameterization trick.

The first component of the objective function can be seen as the expectation of the negative reconstruction error that forces the hidden representation for each data case to be peaked at its specific MAP value. On the contrary, the second and third components constitute a kind of regularization that drives the encoder to match the prior (see Fig. 1).

We can get more insight into the role of the prior by inspecting the gradient of $\tilde{\mathcal{L}}(\phi, \theta, \lambda)$ in (2) with respect to a single weight ϕ_i for a single data point x, see Eq. (4) for details. We notice that the prior plays a role of an "anchor" that keeps the posterior close to it, i.e., the term in round brackets in Eq. (5) is 0 if the posterior matches the prior.

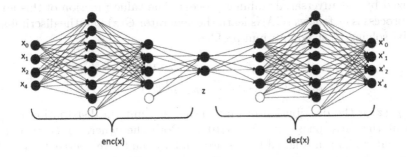

Fig. 1. VAE architecture.

$$\frac{\partial}{\partial \phi_i} \tilde{\mathcal{L}}(x; \phi, \theta, \lambda) = \frac{1}{L} \sum_{l=1}^{L} [\frac{1}{p_\theta(x|z_\phi^{(l)})} \frac{\partial}{\partial z_\phi} p_\theta(x|z_\phi^{(l)}) \frac{\partial}{\partial \phi_i} z_\phi^{(l)}$$
$$- \frac{1}{q_\phi(z_\phi^{(l)}|x)} \frac{\partial}{\partial \phi_i} q_\phi(z_\phi^{(l)}|x) \tag{4}$$

$$+ \frac{1}{p_\lambda(z_\phi^{(l)}) q_\phi(z_\phi^{(l)}|x)} (q_\phi(z_\phi^{(l)}|x) \frac{\partial}{\partial z_\phi} p_\lambda(z_\phi^{(l)})$$
$$- p_\lambda(z_\phi^{(l)}) \frac{\partial}{\partial z_\phi} q_\phi(z_\phi^{(l)}|x)) \frac{\partial}{\partial \phi_i} z_\phi^{(l)}] \tag{5}$$

Typically, the encoder is assumed to have a diagonal covariance matrix, i.e., $q_\phi(z|x) = \mathcal{N}(z|\mu_\phi(x), diag(\sigma_\phi^2(x)))$, where μ_ϕ and $\sigma_\phi^2(x)$ are parameterized by a NN with weights ϕ, and the prior is expressed using the standard normal distribution, $p_\lambda(z) = \mathcal{N}(z|0, I)$. The decoder utilizes a suitable distribution for the data under consideration, e.g., the Bernoulli distribution for binary data or the normal distribution for continuous data, and it is parameterized by a NN with weights θ.

3   Generative Adversarial Nets

The GANs [2] framework is composed of a generator $G(z)$ and a discriminator $D(x)$, where z is random noise. The generator $G(z)$ tries to generate more and more likely data to 'fools' the discriminator $D(x)$, while the discriminator $D(x)$ aims to tell apart the fake data from the real data. These two adversarial opponents are optimized to overpower each other and play a zero-sum game (also called the min-max game) in the whole training process (see Fig. 2). The random noises $z \in \mathcal{R}^N$ (usually normal distribution or Gaussian distribution) are provided as the input of the generator $G(z)$. And then, the generator $G(z)$ will generate synthetic data, $\tilde{x} = G(z)$. The real data x and fake data $\tilde{x}$ will be both fed to the discriminator $D(x)$, and then the discriminator $D(x)$ will output a scalar which represents the probability of input data are from the real data distribution $p(x)$ rather than the generator $G(z)$. The two adversarial players are optimized by the adversarial training process. The value function of this adversarial process is as follows (GANs learn the generator $G(z)$ and the discriminator $D(x)$ by solving Nash equilibrium problem):

$$min_G max_D V(D,G) = \\ \mathbb{E}_{x \sim p_{data}(x)}[log D(x)] + \mathbb{E}_{z \sim p_z(z)}[log(1 - D(G(z)))] \tag{6}$$

where $p_z(z)$ is the distribution of random noises (uniform distribution in most GANs at the early phase, $p_z(z) = \mathcal{U}(0,1)$. Both the generator $G(z)$ and the discriminator $D(x)$ in original GANs are built by multilayer perceptrons. They are both trained using stochastic gradient descent (SGD) [6] according to the Eq. 6.

From the Generator's perspective $G(z)$:

$$min_G V_G(D,G) = \mathbb{E}_{z \sim p_z(z)}[log(1 - D(G(z)))] \tag{7}$$

- $x_G = G(z)$ represents that the generator is modelled to transforms a random vector z into target sample x_G.
- $p_{data}(x_G)$ is maximized for training G (The probability that the generated samples belong to the distribution of real data).
- $p_z(z)$ is a fixed, easy sample prior distribution that GANs assumed.

From the Discriminator's perspective $D(z)$:

$$max_D V_D(D,G) = \\ \mathbb{E}_{x \sim p_{data}}[log(D(x))] + \mathbb{E}_{z \sim p_z(z)}[log(1 - D(G(z)))] \tag{8}$$

- GANs framework uses a sigmoid neuron at the last layer of Discriminator $D(x)$, so its output is in $[0,1]$.
- The discriminator tries to assign a high value (the upper limit is 1) to real data, while assigning a low value (the low limit is 0) to fake data from the generator.

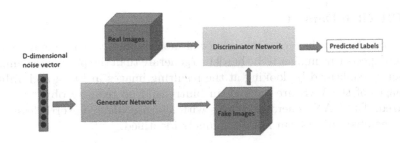

Fig. 2. GAN architecture.

4 Experiments and Results

The described methods were applied to three different data sets, namely MNIST [8], CIFAR10 [7] and CelebA [9]. To reduce the required computational effort we resized to images to have a maximum size of 72×72 pixels.

4.1 MNIST Dataset

As the MNIST data set has the least variance of the examined datasets, one expects the two models to generate realistic images. Therefore, this data set is the first one to be examined. Some exemplifying images, generated by a conditioned VAE and an auxiliary GAN, can be seen in Fig. 3 and Table 1. Both models generate images which can easily be recognized as digits. While the GAN generates sharper images, the VAE tends to smooth the edges of the digits.

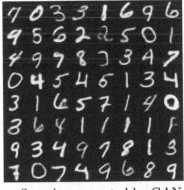

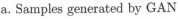
a. Samples generated by GAN   b. Samples generated by VAE

Fig. 3. Comparison of sampled images of the two models based on the MNIST dataset.

4.2   CIFAR10 Dataset

The Cifar10 data set has a great variance of motives and camera angles. There-fore, one expects this images to be harder to generate than the previous examples. This can be confirmed by looking at the resulting images in Fig. 4 and Table 1. The images of the VAE are once again blurry and no realistic objects can be recognized. The GAN generates images with sharper edges; nevertheless, most of the generated objects can not be uniquely identified.

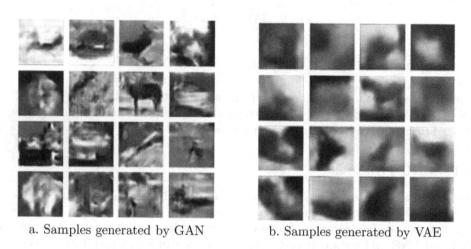

a. Samples generated by GAN   b. Samples generated by VAE

Fig. 4. Comparison of sampled images of the two models based on the CIFAR10 dataset.

Table 1. Comparison of Insception scores of the two models based on a different dataset.

Dataset	Method	Inception score [18]
MNIST	VAEs	3.32
	GANs	**9.05**
CelebA	VAEs	2.78
	GANs	**7.02**
CIFAR-10	VAEs	3.0
	GANs	**6.8**

4.3   CelebA Dataset

Lastly, the generative models have been used to generate portrait images of humans using the CelebA dataset. Figure 5 shows exemplary portraits of the data set and generated images. Here GAN has been compared to the results of VAE.

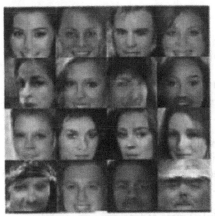

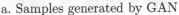

a. Samples generated by GAN   b. Samples generated by VAE

Fig. 5. Comparison of sampled images of the two models based on the CelebA dataset.

The GAN produces again much sharper images than the VAE. Nevertheless, the faces produced by the VAE own a more natural appearance. Apart from the blurry earth-colored background, some VAE-generated images resemble to realistic faces. In Fig. 5a and b and Table 1, the condition between male and female persons is demonstrated.

5   Conclusion

The main difference between VAEs and GANs is their learning process. VAEs are minimizing a loss reproducing a certain image, and can, therefore, be considered as solving a semi-supervised learning problem. GANs, on the other hand, are solving an unsupervised learning problem because they do not use labeled pixels. The most important difference found in this work was the training time for the two methods. GANs took longer time to train (in terms of number of epochs, as well as in terms of running time). Another advantage of VAEs is their stability. For GANs highly oscillating image quality could be observed in the course of training. Clear pictures turned into purely grey images within only a few epochs of training. Therefore the use of GANs was considered and proved a lot more stable. The problem with VAEs is, that with the increasing diversity of the data set generated images to become more and more blurry and a lot of details get lost (see CIFAR10 results). With GANs this does not necessarily occur. Eventually, we conclude, that for low-diversity datasets like MNIST, both methods give sufficiently realistic images. For more complex data sets this was not the case in this work, but prior work like [1,2] shows, that it is possible to generate realistic images with both the techniques used here.

Finally, using VAEs one can achieve results in less time, but with decreased image quality compared to results of GANs.

References

1. Goyal, P., Hu, Z., Liang, X., Wang, C., Xing, E.: Nonparametric variational autoencoders for hierarchical representation learning. arXiv:1703.07027 (2017)
2. Goodfellow, I., et al.: Generative adversarial nets. In: Advances in Neural Information Processing Systems, pp. 2672–2680 (2014)
3. Kingma, D.P., Welling, M.: Auto-encoding variational bayes. arXiv:1312.6114 (2013)
4. Rezende, D.J., Mohamed, S., Wierstra, D.: Stochastic backpropagation and approximate inference in deep generative models. In: ICML, pp. 1278–1286 (2014)
5. Gregor, K., Danihelka, I., Graves, A., Rezende, D.J., Wierstra, D.: DRAW: a recurrent neural network for image generation. arXiv preprint arXiv:1502.04623 (2015)
6. Bordes, A., Bottou, L., Gallinari, P.: SGD-QN: careful quasi-Newton stochastic gradient descent. J. Mach. Learn. Res. **10**, 1737–1754 (2009)
7. Krizhevsky, A., Hinton, G.: Learning multiple layers of features from tiny images. Technical report, University of Toronto (2009)
8. LeCun, Y., Cortes, C.: MNIST handwritten digit database (2010)
9. Liu, Z., Luo, P., Wang, X., Tang, X.: Deep learning face attributes in the wild. In: Proceedings of International Conference on Computer Vision (ICCV), December 2015
10. Gu, X., Knutsson, H., Nilsson, M., Eklund, A.: Generating diffusion MRI scalar maps from T1 weighted images using generative adversarial networks. CoRR (2018)
11. Abbasnejad, M.E., Dick, A., van den Hengel, A.: 2017 IEEE Conference on Computer Vision a (2017)
12. Yeh, R.A., Chen, C., Lim, T.Y., Schwing, A.G., Hasegawa-Johnson, M., Do, M.N.: Semantic image inpainting with deep generative models. In: Proceedings of the IEEE Conference on Computer Vision and Pattern Recognition, pp. 5485–5493 (2017)
13. Isola, P., Zhu, J.-Y., Zhou, T., Efros, A.A.: Image-to-image translation with conditional adversarial networks. arXiv preprint arXiv:1611.07004 (2016)
14. Ledig, C., et al.: Photo-realistic single image super-resolution using a generative adversarial network (2016)
15. Zhao, F., Feng, J., Zhao, J., Yang, W., Yan, S.: Robust lstmautoencoders for face de-occlusion in the wild. IEEE Trans. Image Process. **27**(2), 778–790 (2018)
16. Press, O., Bar, A., Bogin, B., Berant, J., Wolf, L.: Language generation with recurrent generative adversarial networks without pre-training. arXiv preprint arXiv:1706.01399 (2017)
17. Yu, L., Zhang, W., Wang, J., Yu, Y.: SeqGAN: sequence generative adversarial nets with policy gradient. In: AAAI 2017, pp. 2852–2858 (2017)
18. Barratt, S., Sharma, R.: A note on the inception score. In: ICML Workshop (2018)

A Game Stochastic Model for Data Dissemination Between Ferries and Cluster Head in Delay Tolerant Networks Routing Hierarchical Topology

El Arbi Abdellaoui Alaoui[1,3](✉) (iD), Mustapha El Moudden[2] (iD), Khalid Nassiri[1], and Said Agoujil[1]

[1] E3MI Research Team, Department of Computer Science,
Faculty of Sciences and Techniques at Errachidia,
University of Moulay Ismaïl, Meknès, Morocco
abdellaoui@ieee.org, nasskhalid@gmail.com, agoujil@gmail.com
[2] Department of Mathematics, Faculty of Sciences,
University of Moulay Ismaïl, Meknès, Morocco
muelmoudden@gmail.com
[3] EIGSI, 282 Route of the Oasis, Maârif, 20140 Casablanca, Morocco

Abstract. Ferries play an important role in data dissemination in delay tolerant networks (DTN). The DTN routing hierarchical topology (DRHT) includes three fundamental concepts: ferries messages, ferries routes and clusters. We use ferries in DRHT to improve network performance. In the DRHT, the intra-cluster routing is managed by the cluster head, while the inter-cluster routing is managed by the ferries messages. In this work, we analyse the behavior of ferries' problem of data dissemination in the DRHT. More specifically, in order to analyse the inter-cluster communication in the DRHT, we formulate game stochastic which models the behavior of the ferries.

Keywords: Delay Tolerant Networks · DRHT · Message ferry · Cluster Head (CH) · Game stochastic

1 Introduction

In recent years, Delay Tolerant Network (DTN) hase become very popular lately and are receiving an increasing amount of attention by the research community. Compared to wired networks, routing in DTN hase two fundamental characteristics. The first one is the intermittent connectivity due to the difficulty of maintaining end-to-end communication and connections between the nodes is opportunistically and referred to as "contact". As a consequence, packet delivery

© Springer Nature Switzerland AG 2019
É. Renault et al. (Eds.): MSPN 2019, LNCS 11557, pp. 9–24, 2019.
https://doi.org/10.1007/978-3-030-22885-9_2

probabilities is different for every contact in DTN which leads to use "store-and-forward" mecanisme for data transmission [9]. The second one is the long delivery delay due to the high mobility of nodes, the asymmetric flow and the high error rate. These factors lead to a large-scale network, and therefore the delivery delay is very long and the delivery rate is potentially low. Thus, the choice of a technique for transmitting messages is essential to ensure a great autonomy to these networks which are typically deployed in hostile or inaccessible areas [1,2,5].

To overcome these challenges and increase the chances of successful delivery with a reasonable delay delivery, we proposed in this paper a DRHT approach which ensures a reliable data transmission during an optimal delivery delay.

The main objective of the DRHT is to optimise the delivery delay and the delivery rate [6,7]. For this purpose, the DRHT integrates the ferries messages which aim to ensure the information exchange between the different clusters. This information exchange must be optimized in order to avoid the overloading of the ferries routes which causes network paralysis. Thus, to ensure the information forwarding from a cluster to all the others, our goal here is to optimize the number of ferries messages circulating in the DRHT and to avoid the redundancy.

Clearly, in order to improve the quality of service (QoS) and the resources use in the DRHT, a ferry message must take account of two related issues. At the operational level, what should be the transmission routes to manage the flow of bundles between clusters? At the strategic level, how should the ferries messages circulate between the different clusters, while considering their number in the DRHT, so that the overall service level of the system is optimized? The study presented in this paper was motivated by the need of analytical tools to model the behavior of the system and to obtain the optimal decision rules with regard to the two previously mentioned questions.

The main objective of this paper is to characterize the behavior of information exchange between ferries and CHs in the DRHT by adopting stochastic games [3], in the sense of finding a strategy for the circulation of ferries which optimizes the delivery rate and the delivery time. In our model, each ferry is aware of its own state, but unconscious of the state of the other ferries. In addition, it does not know if the bundle has already been delivered to the $CH_{destination}$ or not. Our game is therefore a stochastic game with partial information [4].

2   Related Works

Hierarchical routing has been used in DTN [10–12], as well as in the Internet, in order to provide hybridization of proactive and reactive routing protocols. It consists of deciding on routing path taking into account different types of nodes with different level of responsibility. A network is said clustered when it involves at least three-level of hierarchy. A DTN Routing Hierarchical Topology (DRHT) [13] has been introduced on the basis of three fundamental concepts: clustering, message ferrying, and ferry-based routing. Within this topology, each region is considered as an independent cluster where the communication is managed

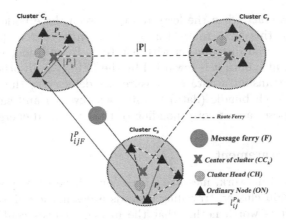

Fig. 1. Diagram of the DRHT.

proactively by means of a principal node called cluster head. The clusters are connected by means of ferry nodes that move according to a certain movement scheme. The ferry nodes are assumed to be able to store huge amount of data in order to assure the store-carry-forward communication paradigm. Figure 1 illustrates an example of the DRHT topology over a network with three regions, where three main entities are identified: (i) cluster head (CH), a principal node responsible for managing the communication inside the cluster, (ii) message ferry (MF), a node acting a gateway between clusters and responsible for carrying and forwarding data over clusters, and (iii) cluster centre (CC), a geographical position at which ferry nodes may exchange data with cluster heads.

Considering a hypothetical transmission from a node i to a node j, the routing process would consists of two possible cases, namely intra-cluster routing and inter-cluster routing. If both i and j are inside the same cluster, the transmission would follow a classical local routing mechanism. That is, the cluster head would decide on the route relaying i to j. If i and j belong to two different clusters, the transmission would be performed by means of a ferry node that can rely the cluster containing i to the one containing j. DRHT uses multiple message ferries to enhance the network performance, particularly in terms of transmission delay.

3   Problem Statement and Notations

3.1   Network Model

In our study, we consider a DTN with a CH_{source}, a $CH_{destination}$, and a set of ferries n implicated in the transmission process of inter-clusters communication in the DRHT. We suppose that there is no direct path between CH_{source} and $CH_{destination}$, in this case, the n ferries are used to forward a data from CH_{source} to $CH_{destination}$ by a two-hop routing. In a DTN, the ferry route between two nodes is called *contact* when the ferry route between these nodes is up. In the case of a lack of this ferry route, this is called *inter-contact* [8]. This latter follows an exponential distribution with a rate λ. In addition, when the ferry accepts to transmit a data it is rewarded by the CH_{source}. In other words, each ferry accepts to transmit a data and ensures its delivery to the destination, it earns a reward (each bundle (data) has its own reward) and each attempt of transmission imposes a cost corresponding to the consumed energy.

3.2 Problem Statement

Within a clustered network, message ferries could have three possible options: staying at a certain cluster, travelling towards a destination cluster, or getting out of service. It is worth noting that the message ferries could serve in the networking process as additional responsibilities; they could consists of transportation vehicles for example. message ferries would encounter different delays depending on the options allowed. Thus, ferry behaviour should be controlled in regard to delivery time, message rate, and data loss rate. Furthermore, the number of involved message ferries should be reasonably determined.

4 Behavior of Data Dissemination Between Ferries and CH

After having analyzing the distribution of ferries through game theory, we will focus in this subsection on the transmission of information between the ferry and the CH in the DRHT, by adopting stochastic games. Suppose now that a CH_{source} of the cluster C_k wants to transmit an information (bundle) to a $CH_{destination}$ while respecting the TTL of the information. To do this, the ferry will intervene to accomplish this mission before the expiry of the information life to be sent in order to obtain a reward. When a ferry responds to the CH_{source}, at this stage, the ferry may decide to either accept or reject the bundle. If he decides to accept it, at this time the ferry can drop the bundle or keep it during a period of time until its delivery to the final destination.

The main objective of this subsection is to characterize the behavior of information exchange between ferries and CHs in the DRHT by adopting stochastic games [3], in the sense of finding a strategy for the circulation of ferries which optimizes the delivery rate and the delivery time. In our model, each ferry is aware of its own state, but unconscious of the state of the other ferries. In addition, it does not know if the bundle has already been delivered to the $CH_{destination}$ or not. Our game is therefore a stochastic game with partial information [4].

We assume a multi-hop routing policy in the DRHT. A ferry that accepts the message has a receipt cost C_r, then a storage cost C_s per unit of time incurred to store the message, and a delivery cost C_d to transmit the bundle to the destination. To model our system with stochastic games, the following must be identified:

We define the following elements of the game. Obviously, it is a stochastic game with partial information

- τ: time horizon (bundle deadline (TTL), in our case)
- $\mathcal{R} = \{1, 2, \ldots, N\}$ set of players (ferries)
- $\mathcal{E}_j$, $j \in \mathcal{R}$ state space of ferry j. We denote by X_n^j the state of player j at time n.
- $\mathcal{A}_j$, $j \in \mathcal{R}$ action space of ferry j. We denote by $\mathcal{A}_n^j$ the action taken by player j at time n.
- $\mathcal{E} := \bigotimes_{j \in \mathcal{R}} \mathcal{E}_j$.
- $\mathcal{A} := \bigotimes_{j \in \mathcal{R}} \mathcal{A}_j$.
- $\mathcal{B}_j : \mathcal{E}_j \times \{0, 1, \ldots, \tau - 1\} \to \mathcal{D}(\mathcal{A}_j)$, where $\mathcal{D}(\mathcal{A}_j)$ is the set of probability measures on $\mathcal{A}$. The set $\mathcal{B}_j(t)$ is the set of mixed strategies available to ferry j at every time instants. In other words, an element $\sigma_n^j(x)$ is the probability distribution over the set of actions $\mathcal{A}_j$ used by player j to choose its action when it is in state x at time n.
- $\mathcal{P}_j$, $j \in \mathcal{R}$ transition probability matrix of ferry j on the space of its state-action pairs.
- $\mathcal{E}_0$: state space of the bundle. This can be 0 or 1 which indicates whether the bundle has been delivered or not.
- $g_j : \mathcal{E}_j \times \mathcal{A}_j \times \mathcal{E}_0 \to \mathbb{R}, j \in \mathcal{R}$ cost function for ferry j.

Fix $\sigma =: (\sigma^j)_{j \in \mathcal{R}} \in \bigotimes_{j \in \mathcal{R}} \mathcal{B}_j$. Let $\left\{ \mathbf{Z}_n^\sigma := (X_n^j, A_n^j)_{j \in \mathcal{R}}^{(\sigma)} \right\}_{n=0,\ldots,\tau-1}$ be the stochastic process of state-action pairs generated by σ. Assume that the process $X_n^0 \geqslant 1$ is adapted to the natural filtration of $\mathbf{Z}_n^\sigma$. By this we mean that, at every instant, X_n^0 is measurable with respect to the history of the state-action pairs.

Denote by $\mathbf{b}_{-j} \in \mathcal{D}(\varepsilon_{-j})$ the distribution of the initial state of the ferries other than j. We define the expected cost of ferry j for σ as follows:

$$V_j(\sigma^j, \sigma^{-j}; x_0^0, x_0^j, \mathbf{b}_{-j}) = \mathbb{E}_{\mathbf{x}_0, \mathbf{b}_{-j}} \sum_{n=0}^{\tau-1} \beta^n g_i(X_n^j, A_n^j, X_n^0) \tag{1}$$

where β is the discount factor in every state, the terminal cost is assumed to be zero.

The main goal of ferry j is to minimize its cost given the strategy of the others. In other words

$$W_j(\sigma^{-j}; x_0^0, x_0^j, \mathbf{b}_{-j}) = \min_{s \in \mathcal{B}_j} V_j(s, \sigma^{-j}; x_0^0, x_0^j, \mathbf{b}_{-j}), \tag{2}$$

and calculate

$$h_j(\sigma^{-j}; x_0^0, \mathbf{b}_{-j}) = \arg\min_{s \in \mathcal{B}_j} V_j(s, \sigma^{-j}; x_0^0, x_0^j, \mathbf{b}_{-j}), \tag{3}$$

which is the best-response of ferry to σ^{-j} given the initial conditions.

A policy σ is called to be an *equilibrium* if:

$$h_j(\sigma^{-j}; x_0^0, \mathbf{b}_{-j}) = \sigma^j, \forall j. \tag{4}$$

Based on the big picture described above, we define the elements of our stochastic game as follows:

State and Action Spaces
On arrival at the multi-cluster system, ferry can take one of the five states summarizing in Table 1. In states 0 and 2 the ferry does not have a non-trivial action. In state 0 it is waiting to meet the CH_{source}, while in state 2 it has already quit the game.

Table 1. States of ferries

Value	Significance	Action set
0	Ferry does not have the bundle	$\emptyset$
m_{CH_s}	Ferry meets the CH_{source}	*(accept; reject)*
1	Ferry has the bundle	*(drop; keep)*
m_{CH_d}	Ferry meets the $CH_{destination}$	$\emptyset$
2	Ferry quits the game	$\emptyset$

4.1   Transition Matrix

Regarding the contact process that keeps track of the contacts of the ferry with the CH_{source} and the $CH_{destination}$, we shall assume i.i.d. contact times. Consequently, a ferry needs to know only the current state of the contact process, and not its entire history to take its decision.

Denote by p the probability that a ferry encounters the $CH_{destination}$ at the next time step and by q the probability that it encounters the CH_{source}. The transition probability matrix of the Markov model for our model is expressed, as a function of the action chosen in each state, as follows:

$$P_j = \begin{array}{c} \\ 0 \\ m_{CH_s} \\ 1 \\ m_{CH_d} \\ 2 \end{array} \begin{array}{c} \begin{array}{ccccc} 0 & m_{CH_s} & 1 & m_{CH_s} & 2 \end{array} \\ \left(\begin{array}{ccccc} 1-q & q & 0 & 0 & 0 \\ \mathbb{1}_{reject} & 0 & \mathbb{1}_{accept} & 0 & 0 \\ \mathbb{1}_{drop} & 0 & (1-p)\mathbb{1}_{keep} & p\mathbb{1}_{keep} & 0 \\ 0 & 0 & 0 & 0 & 1 \\ 0 & 0 & 0 & 0 & 1 \end{array} \right) \end{array}$$

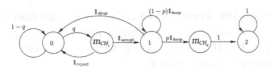

Fig. 2. Transition diagram for the Markov chain governing the state of each ferry

In Fig. 2, we show the transition diagram of the Markov chain.

State of the Bundle
The state of the bundle in our stochastic game can be one of the following two states:

$$x = \begin{cases} 0 \text{ (it has not been delivered);} \\ 1 \text{ (it has been delivered).} \end{cases} \tag{5}$$

The transition probabilities between these two states depends upon the state of the ferries

$$P(X^0_{n+1} = 1 \mid X^0_n = 0, \mathbf{X}_n)$$
$$= P((\cup_{j \in \mathcal{R}} \{X^j_n = 2\} = \emptyset) \cap (\cup_{j \in \mathcal{R}} \{X^j_n = m_{CH_d}\} \neq \emptyset))$$
$$= 1.$$

Cost Function
Each ferry accepts to transmit bundle has must to pay a cost for the usage of the route ferry. This cost depends on the current state and the action it takes. A cost C_r is allotted when a ferry is accept the receipt of bundle, whereas a cost C_s is inflicted when the ferry keep the bundle. C_d is a cost of delivery bundle to destination. Thus, we describe three cost functions associated with the considered objectives as follows:

$$\begin{cases} g(m_{CH_s}, accept, \cdot) & = C_r \\ g(1; keep, \cdot) & = C_s \\ g(m_{CH_d}, \cdot, 0) & = R - C_d. \end{cases} \tag{6}$$

4.2 The Single Player Case

In order to facilitate understanding our model, we consider the single player setting of our stochastic game that models the interactions among ferry and the $CH_{destination}$. Since no other ferry can deliver the bundle, the state of the bundle is $X^0_n = 0$ until the ferry encounters the $CH_{destination}$,. Thus we can simplify notation by writing $g(x, a)$ instead of $g(x, a, 0)$.

Dynamic Programming Formulation. Let us assume that the ferry encounters the CH_{source} at instant $t \in [0; \tau]$. Thus, for times $0, \ldots, t-1$, there are no decisions to be made. For the resting times, the optimal policy in our model can be obtained by dynamic programming.

Denote by $V_n(x)$ the optimal cost-to-go starting in state $x \in \{0, m_{CH_s}, 1, m_{CH_d}, 2\}$ at instant n. From the dynamic programming, it is given by:

$$V_n(X_n) = \min_{a \in \mathcal{A}(X_n)} g(X_n, a) + \beta \mathbb{E} V_{n+1}(X_{n+1}), \tag{7}$$

where β is the discount factor $(0 \leqslant \beta < 1)$.

If the ferry meets the $CH_{destination}$ at time n, the terminal cost is given by the following expression:

$$V_n(m_{CH_d}) = C_d - R, \quad n = 1, 2, \ldots, \tau. \tag{8}$$

Particularly, at time τ we have $V_\tau(m_{CH_d}) = C_d - R$. If at that instant the ferry has the bundle and is not in meeting with the $CH_{destination}$, then it is optimal to drop the bundle since it is no longer useful, so that $V_\tau(1) = 0$. If the ferry does not have the bundle at time τ, then it incurs no costs, so that $V_\tau(0) = V_\tau(m_{CH_s}) = 0$. In summary, the terminal costs at the time $n = \tau$ are as follows:

$$V_\tau(m_{CH_d}) = C_d - R. \tag{9}$$

$$V_\tau(x) = 0, \quad \forall x \neq m_{CH_d}. \tag{10}$$

The optimal policy at different decision times and states can be calculated from the expression (7). In the case where the contact process is history dependent, the optimal policy is usually calculated numerically. In fact, under the hypothesis of an i.i.d. contact process allows the determination of properties of the optimal policies, as we shall see below.

Drop or Retain. Le us assume that the ferry 1 is in state 1 at time $\tau - 1$, i.e. it has the bundle but it is not in contact with the $CH_{destination}$. The relay has to choose whether to drop the message or not. We have

$$
\begin{aligned}
V_{\tau-1}(1) &= \min_{a \in \{keep, drop\}} [(1, a) + \beta \mathbb{E} V_\tau(X_\tau)] \\
&= \min(0, C_s + \beta(p V_\tau(m_{CH_d})) + \bar{p} V_\tau(1))), \\
&= \min(0, C_s + p\beta(C_d - R)), \tag{11}
\end{aligned}
$$

where $\bar{p} = 1 - p$, and the last equation is from (9)–(10). Hence, if the first term is the minimum, it is optimal to drop the bundle at $\tau - 1$, else it is optimal to keep it.

In view of Eq. (11), we can calculate the optimal policy at time n given that the ferry has the bundle and has not yet met the $CH_{destination}$. For $n = \tau - 2$, the optimal policy is:

$$
\begin{aligned}
V_{\tau-2}(1) &= \min\{0, C_s + \beta(pV_{\tau-1}(m_{CH_d}) + \bar{p}V_{\tau-1}(1))\} \\
&= \min\{0, C_s + p\beta(C_d - R), C_s(1 + \bar{p}\beta) \\
&\quad + (C_d - R)\beta(p + \bar{p}p\beta)\},
\end{aligned}
\tag{12}
$$

where the second and the third terms in the minimum correspond to the cost of taking the bundle at time $\tau - 2$. Otherwise, it is optimal to drop the bundle at instant $\tau - 2$.

The ith component in the min corresponds to the cost can be determined under the action *keep* is played i successive times starting from the current decision time n, until the ferry encounters the $CH_{destination}$ or decides to drop the bundle. This i^{th} component can be given as:

$$
\begin{aligned}
U_{n,i} &= \sum_{j=1}^{i}(\beta\bar{p})^{j-1}(C_s + (C_d - R)\beta p) \\
&= (C_s + p\beta(C_d - R))\frac{1 - (\beta\bar{p})^i}{1 - \beta\bar{p}}.
\end{aligned}
\tag{13}
$$

The Eq. (11) can be rewritten in terms of $U_{n,i}$ as

$$
V_n(1) = \min(0, U_{n,1}, U_{n,2}, ..., U_{n,\tau-n}).
\tag{14}
$$

Note that the optimal policy at time n is to keep the bundle if either $U_{n,i}$ is negative. Else, it is optimal to drop the bundle at time n. According to (14), if $(C_s + (C_d - R)\beta p) < 0$, then $U_{n,i} < 0, \forall n$, and $\forall i$, and the sequence decreases with i. Again according to (14), if $(C_s + (C_d - R)\beta p) < 0$, then the ferry will keep the bundle before the expiration of the TTL, otherwise, the ferry will drop the bundle immediately, and so:

$$
R > \frac{C_s}{\beta p} + C_d
\tag{15}
$$

is a necessary condition for the ferry to attempt the delivery of the bundle.

Accept or Reject. Let us assume that the ferry is in state m_{CH_s} at time t, in other words, the ferry is in contact with the $CH_{destination}$. The ferry has to choose either to accept the bundle or not. The optimal cost at time t can be expressed as:

$$
\begin{aligned}
V_t(m_{CH_s}) &= \min(0, g(m_{CH_s}, accept) + \beta V_{t+1}(1)) \\
&= \min(0, C_r + \beta V_{t+1}(1)),
\end{aligned}
\tag{16}
$$

where $V_{t+1}(1)$ can be calculated from (14). So, if at time t the second term is negative, then it is optimal to accept the bundle from the CH_{source}. Otherwise, it is optimal to reject it. In particular, if condition (15) is satisfied, $U_{n,i}$ is a decreasing function of i and Eq. (14) implies

$$V_n(1) = U_{n,\tau-n}$$

$$= (C_s + p\beta(C_d - R)) \frac{1 - (\beta\bar{p})^{\tau-n}}{1 - \beta\bar{p}}. \tag{17}$$

Therefore, the expected cost for the ferry if it accepts the bundle can be obtained as follows:

$$g(m_{CH_s}, accept) + \beta V_{t+1}(1) = C_r + U_{t+1,\tau-t-1}. \tag{18}$$

According to (17) and (18), we conclude that if the ferry encountered the $CH_{destination}$ at time t, it will accept the bundle if the following condition is satisfied:

$$C_r + U_{t+1,\tau-t-1} < 0. \tag{19}$$

According to (17), $U_{t+1,\tau-t-1}$ increases with t. As $U_{t+1,\tau-t-1}$ is negative and increases with t. there exists a threshold t^* such that $t \leqslant t^*$, hence the ferry will accept the bundle, and it will reject the bundle after t^*. We can easily calculate the threshold by using the following:

$$t^* = \tau - 1 - \frac{ln\left(1 + \dfrac{C_r(1 - \beta\bar{p})}{C_s + \beta p(C_d - R)}\right)}{ln(\beta\bar{p})}. \tag{20}$$

4.3   Game with Two Ferries

Consider now the network with two ferries. We shall restrain our study to threshold type policies, in particular, we consider policies such $\sigma_n^j(m_{CH_s}) = accept$ if $n \leqslant \theta_1$ and *reject* otherwise, and $\sigma_n^j(1) = drop$ if $n \geqslant \theta_2$ and *keep* otherwise. Notice that the threshold θ_2 could depend on the meeting time with the $CH_{destination}$.

Thus, we shall suppose that one of the two ferries, for example ferry 2, follows a threshold type policy. Namely, there exist φ_1^2 and $\varphi_2^2 > \varphi_1^2$ such that:

$$\sigma_n^j(m_{CH_s}) = \begin{cases} accept & \text{if } n \leqslant \varphi_1^2, \\ reject & \text{if } n > \varphi_1^2, \end{cases} \tag{21}$$

and

$$\sigma_n^j(1) = \begin{cases} keep & \text{if } n \leqslant \varphi_2^2, \\ drop & \text{if } n > \varphi_2^2. \end{cases} \tag{22}$$

In order to derive the best response policy of the first player to the above policy of ferry 2, we are going to use dynamic programming as in Sect. 4.2. Let $V_n^1(x)$ denote the optimal cost-to-go starting in state $x \in \{0, m_{CH_s}, 1, m_{CH_d}, 2\}$ at time n.

Expected Costs When the Destination Is Reached. If at time n, the ferry 1 has the bundle and is in contact with the $CH_{destination}$, then, the expected cost is given by:

$$V_n^1(m_{CH_d}) = \frac{1}{2}(m_{CH_d} - R)\mathbb{P}(X_n^2 = m_{CH_d})$$
$$+ (C_d - R)\mathbb{P}(X_n^0 = 0, X_n^2 \neq m_{CH_d}), \tag{23}$$

for all $n \in \{1, 2, \ldots, \tau\}$, where it is accepted that if the two ferries meet the $CH_{destination}$ at the same time, then every one wins the reward with probability $\frac{1}{2}$.

We define $1 - \delta_n$ as the probability that ferry 2 delivers the bundle at a time $t \leqslant n$, as evaluated by ferry 1. Notice that $\delta_{n-1} - \delta_n$ represents the probability that the second relay is in contact with the $CH_{destination}$ with the bundle precisely at time n. The expression of $V_n^1(m_{CH_d})$ can be rewritten as follows:

$$V_n^1(m_{CH_d}) = \frac{1}{2}(C_d - R)(\delta_{n-1} - \delta_n) + (C_d - R)\delta_n$$
$$= \frac{\delta_{n-1} + \delta_n}{2}(C_d - R). \tag{24}$$

In order to establish the structure of the optimal policy of ferry 1, we states two fundamental properties of the sequence $V_1^1(m_{CH_d}), V_1^2(m_{CH_d}), \ldots$ in the following lemma.

Lemma 1. *The sequence $V_1^1(m_{CH_d}), V_1^2(m_{CH_d}), \ldots$ satisfies the following properties:*

(a) it is non-decreasing with n,
(b) it is constant for all $n \geqslant \varphi_2^2 + 1$.

Proof. (a) First, observe that since $\delta_{n-1} - \delta_n$ is the probability was defined before, we have $\delta_{n-1} \geqslant \delta_n$. Consequently, the sequence $\delta_1, \delta_2, \ldots$ is non-increasing. This together with (24) yields that

$$V_{n+1}^1(m_{CH_d}) - V_n^1(m_{CH_d}) = \frac{1}{2}(C_d - R)(\delta_{n+1} - \delta_{n-1}) \geqslant 0.$$

(b) As at time $\varphi_2^2 + 1$, the second ferry drops the bundle if it has it, the probability that it delivers the bundle after that time is 0, yielding that $\delta_n - \delta_{\varphi_2^2+1}$ for all $n > \varphi_2^2$. For $k > \varphi_2^2 + 1$, we obtain

$$V_{n+1}^1(m_{CH_d}) = \frac{\delta_{k-1} - \delta_k}{2}(C_d - R)$$
$$= \delta_{\varphi_2^2+1}(C_d - R)$$
$$= V_{\varphi_2^2+1}^1(m_{CH_d}). \tag{25}$$

Thus, the proof is completed.

Drop or Retain. Assume that ferry 1 is in state 1, i.e. it has the bundle but it is not in contact with the $CH_{destination}$. Thus, this ferry needs to choose whether to hold it or to drop it. Proceeding backward in time, we have

$$V_{\tau-1}^1(1) = \min_{a \in \{keep, drop\}} [g(1,a) + \beta \mathbb{E} V_\tau^1(X_\tau^1)]$$
$$= \min(0, C_s + \beta p V_\tau^1(m_{CH_d}) + \beta \bar{p} V_\tau^1(1))$$
$$= \min(0, C_s + \beta p V_\tau^1(m_{CH_d})) \tag{26}$$

and

$$V_{\tau-2}^1(1) = \min_{a \in \{keep, drop\}} [g(1,a) + \beta \mathbb{E} V_{\tau-1}^1(X_{\tau-1}^1)]$$
$$= \min(0, C_s + \beta p V_{\tau-1}^1(m_{CH_d}) + \beta \bar{p} V_{\tau-1}^1(1))$$
$$= \min(0, C_s + \beta p V_{\tau-1}^1(m_{CH_d}), C_s$$
$$+ \beta p V_{\tau-1}^1(m_{CH_d}) + \beta \bar{p}(C_s + \beta p V_{\tau-1}^1(1))). \tag{27}$$

In general, we have

$$V_n^1(1) = \min(0, U_{n,1}, U_{n,2}, \ldots, U_{n,\tau-n}), \tag{28}$$

where

$$U_{n,i} = \sum_{j=1}^i (\beta \bar{p})^{j-1}(C_s + \beta p V_{n+j}^1(1)). \tag{29}$$

The optimal policy at time n is to keep the bundle if $\min_{i=1,\ldots,\tau-n} U_{n,i} < 0$. Else, it is optimal to drop the bundle at time n.

Two proprieties of $U_{n,1}$ are established.

Lemma 2. *The sequence $\{U_{n,1}\}_{n=1,2,\ldots}$ is a non-decreasing sequence. Furthermore, it is constant starting from $n = \varphi_2^2$.*

Proof. We first prove that the sequence is a non-decreasing. From (29), we have

$$U_{n+1,1} - U_{n,1} = C_s + \beta p V_{n+2}^1(m_{CH_d}) - C_s - \beta p V_{n+1}^1(m_{CH_d})$$
$$= \beta p(V_{n+2}^1(m_{CH_d}) - V_{n+1}^1(m_{CH_d})).$$

This together with Lemma 1 yields that $U_{n+1,1} \geqslant U_{n,1}$, and the first assertion of the lemma is proved. Now, we prove that $U_{n,1} = U_{\varphi_2^2,1}$ for all $n \geqslant \varphi_2^2$. Using Lemma 1(b), we obtain that

$$U_{n,1} = C_s + \beta p V_{n+1}^1(m_{CH_d})$$
$$= C_s + \beta p V_{\varphi_2^2+1}^1(m_{CH_d})$$
$$= U_{\varphi_2^2,1}.$$

Lemma 3. *For all $n \in \{1, 2, \ldots, \tau\}$, if $U_{n,1} \geqslant 0$, then $\min\limits_{i=1,\ldots,\tau-n} U_{n,i} = U_{n,1}$.*

Proof. Assume that $U_{n,1} \geqslant 0$ for a fixed $n \in \{1, 2, \ldots, \tau\}$. It suffices to show that the sequence $U_{n,1}, U_{n,2}, \ldots$ is a non-decreasing sequence. From (29), we can observe that $U_{n,i}$ can be rewritten as follows

$$U_{n,i} = \sum_{j=0}^{i-1} (\beta \bar{p})^{j-1} U_{n+j,1}. \tag{30}$$

This together with Lemma 2 yields that

$$U_{n,i+1} - U_{n,i} = (\beta \bar{p})^i U_{n+i,1} \geqslant (\beta \bar{p})^i U_{n,1}.$$

Hence, we conclude that $U_{n,1} \geqslant 0$ implies that $U_{n,1}, U_{n,2}, \ldots$ is a non-decreasing sequence. The proof is completed.

We now state the following result.

Proposition 1. *At time n, $V_n^1(1) < 0$ if and only if $U_{n,1} < 0$.*

Proof. Using (28), it is easy to check that $U_{n,1} < 0$ implies $V_n^1(1) < 0$. By contraposition, to prove that the converse is true, it suffices to prove that $U_{n,1} \geqslant 0$ implies that $V_n^1(1) \geqslant 0$, which is an immediate result of Lemma 3.

From Lemma 2, $U_{n,1}$ is non-decreasing with n. Hence, Proposition 1 infers that ferry 1 will retain the bundle as long as $U_{n,1} < 0$, and will drop it once $U_{n,1}$ becomes positive. Now, we are in position to prove that once ferry 1 has the bundle, it uses a threshold type policy to decide whether to retain it or to drop it.

Proposition 2. *If $U_{\varphi_2^2,1} \geqslant 0$ then there exists threshold $\varphi_2^1 \leqslant \varphi_2^2$ such that ferry 1 holds the bundle until φ_2^1 and drops it at time $\varphi_2^1 + 1$. Else, if $U_{\varphi_2^2,1} < 0$, ferry 1 holds the bundle until it meets the $CH_{destination}$ or the TTL expires.*

Proof. Consider the case $U_{\varphi_2^2,1} \geqslant 0$. We denote by t the time at which ferry 1 accepts the bundle from the CH_{source}. As

$$V_t^1(m_{CH_s}) = \min(0, C_r + V_{t+1}^1(1))$$

must to be negative for ferry 1 to accept the bundle, this yields that $V_{t+1}^1(1) < -C_r$. In view of Proposition 2, $V_{t+1}^1(1) < 0$, which in turn implies that $U_{t+1,1} < 0$.

As the sequence $U_{1,1}, U_{2,1}, \ldots$ is non-decreasing (see Lemma 2), $U_{t+1,1} < 0$ and $U_{\varphi_2^2,1} \geqslant 0$ yield that there exists $\varphi_2^1 \in [t+1, \varphi_2^2]$ such that $U_{n,1} < 0$ for all $n \leqslant \varphi_2^1$ and $U_{\varphi_2^1+1,1} \geqslant 0$. Thus, we obtain that $V_n^1(1) < 0$ for all $n \leqslant \varphi_2^1$ and $V_{\varphi_2^1+1}^1(1) \geqslant 0$. In other words, ferry 1 retains the bundle until time φ_2^1, and drops it at time $\varphi_2^1 + 1$.

Consider now the case $U_{\varphi_2^1+1,1} < 0$. In view of Lemma 2, the sequence $U_{1,1}, U_{2,1}, \ldots$ is non-decreasing and constant starting from $n = \varphi_2^2$. Hence, we obtain that $U_{n,1} < 0$ for all $n \in \{1, 2, \ldots, \tau\}$. This together with Proposition 1 implies that $V_n^1(1) < 0$ for all $n \in \{1, 2, \ldots, \tau\}$, yielding that the optimal policy for ferry 1 is to hold the bundle until it meets the $CH_{destination}$ before the TTL expired.

From Proposition 2, the best-reaction of policy of ferry 1 to the policy of ferry 2 is consequently as follows:

$$\sigma_n^1(1) = \begin{cases} keep \text{ if } n \leqslant \varphi_2^1 \\ drop \text{ if } n > \varphi_2^1 \end{cases} \tag{31}$$

with the threshold φ_2^1 can be higher than τ.

Accept or Reject. We denote by t the time at which ferry 1 encounters the CH_{source}. Then the optimal expected cost at t is given by:

$$\begin{aligned} V_t^1(C_s) &= \min[0, g(C_s, accept) + \beta V_{t+1}^1(1)] \\ &= \min[0, C_r + \beta V_{t+1}^1(1)] \end{aligned} \tag{32}$$

with $V_{t+1}^1(1)$ can be calculated from (28). Hence, if at time t the second term is negative, then it is optimal to accept the bundle from the CH_{source}. Moreover, it is optimal to reject it.

Proposition 3. *There exists φ_1^1 such that ferry 1 rejects the bundle if it meets the CH_{source} at a time $n > \varphi_1^1$.*

Proof. First, note that (32) can be rewritten as:

$$V_t^1(C_s) = \min(0, C_r + \min_{i=1,\ldots,\tau-t-n} U_{t+1,i}).$$

As Lemma 2 yields that $\min_{i=1,\ldots,\tau-t-n} U_{t+1,i}$ increases with t, we can affirm that if at time φ_1^1 the ferry rejects the bundle, in other words, if $\min_{i=1,\ldots,\tau-\varphi_1^1} U_{\varphi_1^1,i} \geqslant 0$, then it will also reject it at all subsequent contact times $k > \varphi_1^1$ with the CH_{source}.

Notice that the threshold φ_1^1 can be larger than τ, in which case ferry 1 always accepts the bundle when it meets the CH_{source}. In the same way, the threshold φ_1^1 can be smaller than 1, in which case ferry 1 never accepts the message when it meets the CH_{source}.

5 Conclusion

DRHT aims at finding an efficient scheme that minimize the delivery delay and maximize the delivery rate. It involves message ferries that ensure information exchange between the different network regions. Information exchange efficiency allows avoiding overloading of the message ferries routes. A model allowing to obtain an efficient visiting schedule for message ferries in DTN network with hierarchical routing structure has been proposed.

References

1. Fall, K.: A delay-tolerant network architecture for challenged internets. In: Proceedings of the 2003 Conference on Applications, Technologies, Architectures, and Protocols for Computer Communications, Karlsruhe, Germany, pp. 27–34. ACM (2003)
2. Azzuhri, S.R., Ahmad, H., Portmann, M., Ahmedy, I., Pathak, R.: An efficient hybrid MANET-DTN routing scheme for OLSR. Wirel. Pers. Commun. (2016). https://doi.org/10.1007/s11277-016-3323-8
3. Shapley, L.S.: Stochastic games, vol. 39, pp. 1095–1100 (1953)
4. Goush, M.K., McDonald, D., Sinha, S.: Zero-sum stochastic games with partial information. J. Optim. Theory Appl. **121**, 99–118 (2004)
5. Abdellaoui Alaoui, E.A., Agoujil, S., Hajar, M., Qaraai, Y.: The performance of DTN routing protocols: a comparative study. WSEAS Trans. Commun. **14**, 121–130 (2015)
6. Abdellaoui Alaoui, E.A., Agoujil, S., Hajar, M., Qaraai, Y.: Improving the data delivery using DTN routing hierarchical topology (DRHT). In: The International Conference on Wireless Networks and Mobile Communications (WINCOM 2016), Fez, Morocco, 26–29 October 2016. IEEE (2016)
7. Abdellaoui Alaoui, E.A., Nassiri, K.: Maximizing the delivery rate for DTN networks. In: Abraham, A., Haqiq, A., Ella Hassanien, A., Snasel, V., Alimi, A.M. (eds.) AECIA 2016. AISC, vol. 565, pp. 10–17. Springer, Cham (2018). https://doi.org/10.1007/978-3-319-60834-1_2
8. Zhu, H., Fu, L., Xue, G., Zhu, Y., Li, M., Ni, L.M.: Recognizing exponential inter-contact time in VANETs. In: Proceedings of the 29th Conference on Information Communications (INFOCOM), pp. 101–105. IEEE (2010)
9. Chuah, M.C., Yang, P., Davison, B.D., Cheng, L.: Store-and-forward performance in a DTN. In: IEEE 63rd Vehicular Technology Conference, VTC 2006-Spring, Melbourne, Victoria, vol. 1, pp. 187–191, 7–10 May 2006
10. Hua, D., Du, X., Qian, Y., Yan, S.: A DTN routing protocol based on hierarchy forwarding and cluster control. In: 2009 International Conference on Computational Intelligence and Security, vol. 2, pp. 397–401 (2009). https://doi.org/10.1109/CIS.2009.150

11. Liu, C., Wu, J.: Scalable routing in cyclic Mobile networks. IEEE Trans. Parallel Distrib. Syst. **20**(9), 1325–1338 (2009)
12. Tao, Y., Wang, X.: Adaptive clustering hierarchy routing for delay tolerant network. J. Central S. Univ. **19**(6), 1577–1582 (2012). https://doi.org/10.1007/s11771-012-1179-y
13. Abdellaoui Alaoui, E.A., Agoujil, S., Hajar, M., Qaraai, Y.: Improving the delivery rate of data with: DTN Routing Hierarchical Topology (DRHT). Int. J. Commun. **10**, 95–101 (2016)

Delay-Bandwidth Optimization Method Based on Ant Colony Algorithm Applied to Transport Network Using SDN Paradigm

Mounir Azizi[⊠], Redouane Benaini[⊠], and Mouad Ben Mamoun[⊠]

Department of Computer Science, Mohammed V University, Rabat, Morocco
mounir.azizi@gmail.com,
{benaini,ben_mamoun}@fsr.ac.ma

Abstract. New Transport Technologies are being developed to support the fast growing of IP based services like video and voice, mobile broadband and Cloud. Multiprotocol Label Switching Transport Profile (MPLS-TP) is an emerging transport technology aimed to satisfy requirements of these new technologies. It is characterized by its strong Operation, Administration and Maintenance (OAM) toolbox. MPLS-TP can take advantage of Software Defined Network (SDN) which is an emerging network paradigm allowing network virtualization and offering flexibility for more innovations. Our work is based on existing Ant colony Algorithm which will be modified to fulfil MPLS-TP's requirements which are different from IP/MPLS technology. The present paper shows how we can take benefit from classical optimization methods in order to optimize resources inside a SDN based transport network using modified Ant Colony Algorithm.

Keywords: MPLS-TP · SDN · Openflow · Ant colony algorithm

1 Introduction

Transport networks are subject of big transformation during the last few years. New emerging technologies are being adopted to satisfy the huge demand of bandwidth and new services. MPLS-TP is one of new transport technologies which take benefit from MPLS notoriety [1]. The way MPLS-TP operates, in term of Label Switched Path (LSP) establishment, can be dynamic using GMPLS as it is the case in MPLS, or, in the most of cases, static using manual provisioning, using Network Management Service NMS, like it is done in legacy transport circuit switched networks. Provisioning manually LSP can lead to situations where network resources are under-used and therefore to an optimization problem. Applications can be developed on top of NMS which execute optimization's tasks, but the multi-vendor character of NMS makes this kind of solution not suitable for operators and very expensive. An optimization solution should than be scalable and suitable for multi-vendor MPLS-TP networks. Software Defined Network (SDN) is answering to those two questions [2]. The way SDN is constructed makes it easy to be adapted to MPLS-TP networks.

© Springer Nature Switzerland AG 2019
É. Renault et al. (Eds.): MSPN 2019, LNCS 11557, pp. 25–36, 2019.
https://doi.org/10.1007/978-3-030-22885-9_3

In this paper we will first start by explaining how SDN paradigm can be applied for MPLS-TP use case and in the next section we present how an optimization application can operate. Two algorithms are used for the optimization approach: the first one is Depth First Search (DFS) [3] and the second one is based on the Ant Colony Optimization approach [4] which should be modified in order to fulfil MPLS-TP's requirements such as multi-pathing is not allowed, and forward path should be the same as backward one.

2 SDN Paradigm Applied to MPLS-TP Networks

2.1 MPLS-TP Concept

The MPLS-TP is subset of IP/MPLS technology where some new extensions, such as inheriting OAM from SONET/SDH world, have been added to meet transport network requirements.

The principals MPLS-TP technology attributes are shown in Fig. 1 [5]:

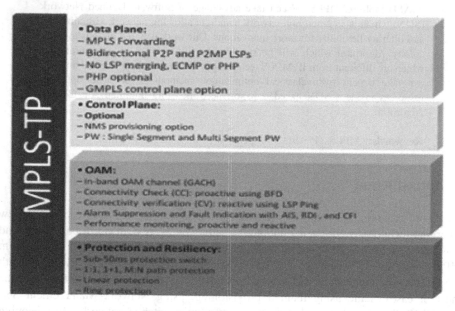

Fig. 1. MPLS-TP components

- Data Plane: is the same as in the MPLS technology to facilitate interoperability and Interworking;
- Control Plane: can be static based on management platform or dynamic based on IP based protocols. It is optional;
- OAM tools: are transport-like OAM, and are used for performance and monitoring;
- Protection and Resiliency: are likely the same as those used on SDH;

When static control plane is used, the Network Management System (NMS) plays a central role on MPLS-TP network. NMS is then used for pro-visioning and monitoring tasks using some protocols like Netconf, Command Line Interface (CLI) Scripting, Simple Network Management Protocol (SNMP) and syslog.

However, there are still some points that MPLS-TP and actual Transport Net-works are still missing [6]:

- Complexity when adding or moving devices which makes it time-consuming and risky.
- Scalability problem due to rigidity of software running on switch-es/routers which codes are not open source. This implies that Vendors are the only responsible for adding new features via software up-grade.
- Vendor dependency traduced by lack of standard and limitation: Vendor-specific interfaces and Software bundled with hardware.
- Very high Cost regarding building, operating, scaling networks when delivering innovative services.

2.2   SDN Concept

The concept of SDN is based on decoupling control functionality from forwarding functionality which allows to create a network-wide abstraction while keeping data plane as simple as possible [7]. As consequence, thanks to SDN, the network became programmable.

Apart from the network abstraction, the SDN architecture provides a range of Application Programming Interfaces API (northbound, southbound and East/Ouest API) which simplify actions like implementation of common network services. In SDN, the network intelligence is located on the Network Operating System NOS and network applications (e.g. security, load balancing, routing, switching, etc.). The NOS communicate with SDN controllers using northbound API. Network devices become the simple packet forwarding devices (e.g. SDN Switch) that can be programmed via an open interface: Southbound API. OpenFlow is the most popular protocol used as southbound interfaces [2]. SDN controller communicate with SDN Switches using OpenFlow as shown in Fig. 2. The meaning of applications here can be used either for network or for service-related functions.

2.3   Using SDN in MPLS-TP Networks

MPLS-TP provides connection-oriented transport for both packet and time division multiplexing services over optical networks taking profit from the widely deployed MPLS technology. It supports the same OAM definition and implementation, and same resiliency features to ensure the capabilities needed for carrier-grade transport networks [1]. However, as seen before, MPLS-TP is suffering from the same drawbacks as MPLS networks.

SDN comes to overcome such kind of limitations and permit to offer:

- Abstraction: Software decoupled from hardware and Standard interface (e.g. OpenFlow),

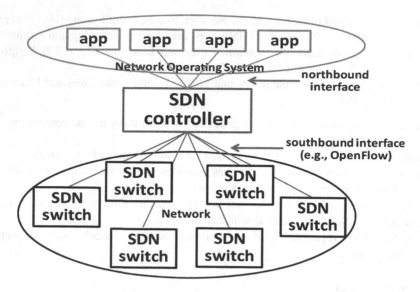

Fig. 2. SDN overall architecture

- Programmability: makes innovation and introduction of new features/services easier by using open APIs,
- Centralized intelligence: Simplify provisioning; Performance optimization and granular policy management.

In this paper, we are studying the case of an MPLS-TP network using SDN paradigm and especially how can application run on the top of SDN controller makes life easier for those who would make network optimization and traffic engineering based on constraints. These constraints can be "classical" like bandwidth, packet losses… or can also be unusual scheduled by OAM performance measurement method. Our proposed framework allows Delay based measurement to be used as constraint when setting up an LSP path. Classical Traffic-Engineering protocols like OSPF-TE and RSVP-TE don't support that kind of constraint.

The organization of this paper is as follows: In Sect. 3, we explain what two optimization methods using Ant colony and DFS algorithm, and we present results of each test scenario. Finally, concluding remarks are given in Sect. 4.

3   Optimization

A fundamental optimization problem of MPLS-TP networks is how we can find several LSP Paths answering to Service Level Agreements SLAs which are declined under constraints committed between the service provider and its customer. As an example of constraints, we can find: minimum requirement of bandwidth and/or maximum tolerated end to end delay. This kind of QOS routing problem in multi-constraint use cases is known as an NP-complete problem [10]. The objective is not to find the best path but to find one of the paths which is satisfying the constraints. Meta-heuristic algorithms like Ant Colony Optimization algorithm ACO can provide acceptable solution. In the following sections, we study one of those algorithms which is based on ACO. ACO algorithm uses the same process that ants use to join its food, as shown in Fig. 3. Ants deposit pheromone to indicate the path they took from nest to food. The next coming ants choose their way based on the concentration of pheromone they smell using a probabilistic manner. Each ant iterates this process and the quantity of pheromones are updated each time a path is chosen, and then shortest path contains high concentration of pheromone. A special variety of ACO treating multi-constraint issue is AnNet [11].

Fig. 3. Ant's behavior to join their food

4   The Proposed Ant Colony Algorithm Variance

AntNet attempted to solve the multi-constraints problem by making Nodes sending Ant agents following periodic intervals to their neighbors, randomly, assigning a quantity of pheromone when going through them. The quantity of pheromones is updated when a neighbor node is more solicited and increase to probability to take this node as next-hop within the LSP Path. AntNet is very suitable for IP/MPLS network but MPLS-TP has some requirements related to transport network like not allowing multi-path and also like taking same path for backward and forward direction. We are proposing a modified version of AntNet which is based on ACO algorithm in order to satisfy MPLS-TP technical constraints.

An MPLS-TP network is represented as a undirected graph G = (V, E), where V represents nodes and E represents links connecting Nodes. We consider that if there is a link e = (u, v) from node u ∈ V to node v ∈ V, then the link from v to u exists and is e = (u, v) = (v, u).

Each link e has two QOS parameters: bandwidth B(e) and delay D(e). B(e) refers to available bandwidth on the link e. D(e) refers to the concatenated delays caused by processing, transmission, propagation and queuing operations. For simplification purpose, we assume that for each link e their related QOS parameters are equal for both backward and forward direction.

The path p = p(s, d) represents the path from source node s to destination node d. the delay of the path p is equal to the sum of delays of all its link e:

$$D(p(s,d)) = \sum_{e \in p(s,d)} D(e) \tag{1}$$

And the bandwidth of the path p is the minimum of bandwidth of all its link e:

$$B(p(s,d)) = Min\{B(e), e \in p(s,d)\} \tag{2}$$

The objective is to find a path p or set of paths (working and backup path) which satisfy delay and bandwidth constraints where:
The total delay of path should not exceed Dmax:

$$D(p(s,d)) \le D_{max} \tag{3}$$

And the minimum bandwidth should be bellow Bmin:

$$B(p(s,d)) \ge B_{min} \tag{4}$$

We start first by a phase of coding, where several possible solutions are presented as individuals of a finite population. Because the individual might violate the constraints, a fitness function will assign bad value to this kind of individuals and they will be removed from the population. Therefore, the QOS routing problem uses the fitness function f(e) to evaluate the quality of a link. We define the fitness function as:

$$f(e) = \begin{cases} 0 & if\,[(B(e) < B_{min})\,or\,(D(e) > D_{max})], \\ \alpha \times e^{-D(e)} + \beta \times e^{-B(e)} & otherwise \end{cases} \tag{5}$$

Where α and β are coefficients to influence which of delay or bandwidth criteria is the most important and are equal to:
$\alpha + \beta = 1$ where $\alpha, \beta \in [0,1]$
For the rest of this paper, α and β will be given respectively a value of 0.7 and 0.3. The fitness of the path f(p) will be calculated as follow:

$$f(p) = 0.7 \times e^{-D(p)} + 0.3 \times e^{-B(p)} \tag{6}$$

The ACO algorithm indicates that every search period t, every ants k = 1, ..., m randomly select a path from a source i to destination j depending on the probability of the path. The probability p that an ant k will move from node i to a node j, where those nodes belong to the set of nodes S_i^k that ant k have not yet been visited:

$$p_{ij}^k(t) = \frac{[\tau_{ij}(t)]^a \times [\eta_{ij}]^b}{\sum_{l \in S_i^k} \left[[\tau_i(l)]^a \times [\eta_{il}]^b \right]} \tag{7}$$

τ_{ij} is the intensity of pheromone which is equal to τ_0 at t = 0 and η_{il} is a statistical information called also the "visibility" which allow to guide ants for "nearest" nodes. a and b are factor of influence such away if a = 0 then the "visibility" is selected and if b = 0 then only pheromone traces are taking into consideration when moving from a node to another node.

The pheromone update is executed by an ant k during each iteration along with link within the path following this formula:

$$\Delta \tau_{ij}^k(t) = \frac{Q}{L^k(t)} \tag{8}$$

where $L^k(t)$ is the length of the path covered by kth ant during one cycle. And Q is a constant (= 1 in our case).

In general, the rule to update pheromone for each iteration is:

$$\tau_{ij}(t+1) = (1 - \rho) \times \tau_{ij}(t) + \Delta \tau_{ij}(t) \tag{9}$$

where $\Delta \tau_{ij}(t) = \sum_{k=1}^{m} \Delta \tau_{ij}^k(t)$

Where ρ is pheromone's vaporization coefficient and "m" is number of ants that are updating pheromone information.

The process of making pheromone update and path decision is described as bellow:

(1) First, we collect bandwidth information of each link inside the network by collecting statistics [10].
(2) Then the delay measurement function is executed on the top of SDN controller to collect delay of each link [11].
(3) We create a black list containing all link not satisfying constraints of Eq. (4), start the Algorithm.
(4) The cycle started and set default pheromone quantity to τ_0 which is equal to 0.25. Fitness function is initialized to 0. Other value is fixed such as the maximal search cycle.
(5) The formula (6) is used to calculate probability to choose the next node by until ants found a path to destination or time is exceeded (Tmax value is fixed to limit a time of search).
(6) Calculate the fitness function using formula (5) and select the path with the maximum $f(e)$ while updating pheromone.
(7) We start again a new iteration (t + 1) and go back to step 4 until maximal search cycle is reached.
(8) The process ends by providing founded path.

4.1 Depth First Search Algorithm

The DFS algorithm is well-known algorithm which allows to discover path. The idea of DFS is to explore nodes deeper whenever possible. During each iteration, the algorithm verifies the unvisited vertex that is adjacent to the one it is currently in. Once the vertex is reached with no adjacent unvisited vertices (dead end), the algorithm will back up on edge to the parent and will tries to continue visiting unvisited vertices from that point. The algorithm ends execution after backing up to the starting vertex, with the latter being a dead end.

5 Experiments and Evaluation

5.1 Experiment Set-up

To get a clear picture if our contribution is justified and efficient, we evaluate the modified ACO Algorithm and we compare it to a classical algorithm which is DFS. We run test under different conditions (bandwidth and delay) while increasing for each test the number of nodes and the way they are connected each other.

Two machines are used for the experimental testing, Fig. 4. The first one is quadruple Intel Core mobile i5 2, 5 GHz running Ryu as SDN controller and applications (topology discovery, statistics collector for bandwidth, delay Measurement function and ACO/DFS Algorithms). The second machine is Octal Intel core i7 3 GHz running Mininet with multiple instance of Openvswitch and emulating hosts [12].

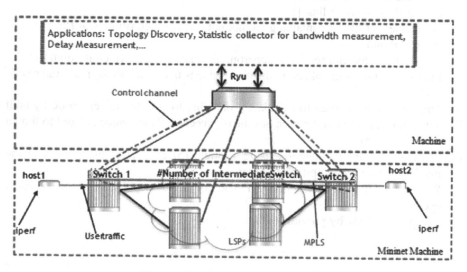

Fig. 4. General set-up of our test bed

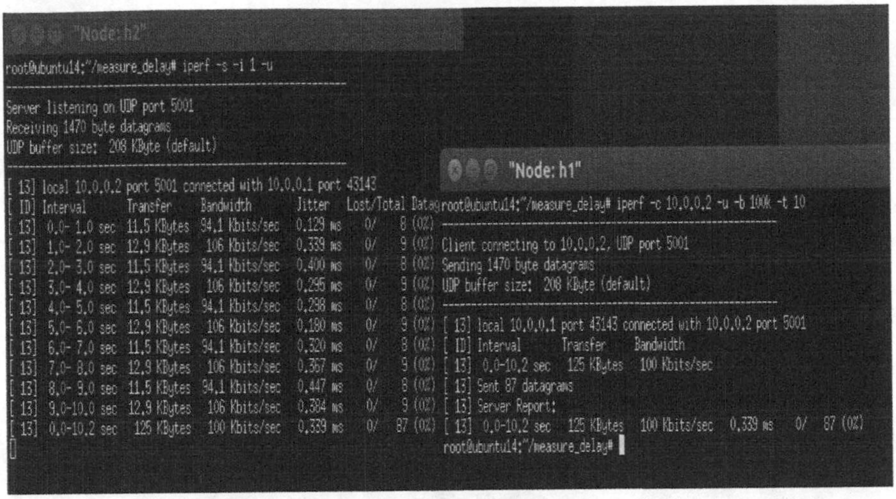

Fig. 5. iperf client & server

Iperf is used to increase bandwidth of links and is set to a maximum of 40 Mb, Fig. 5. Linux "tc commands" are used to vary delay over Linux interfaces. All applications are wrote in python.

h2.cmd('iperf -s –i 1 -u &') where the options "-s" means acting as server, and "-u" specify UDP protocol.

The client h1 generates traffic using iperf by setting desired bandwidth using « -b » option and setting frequency using « -u » option:

h1.cmd('iperf -c ' + h2.IP() + ' -u -t 100 -b 1 M &')

5.2 Simulation Results

Different topologies are launched, Fig. 6, to check the behavior and to measure the performance of our proposed model.

When the number of nodes is still lower (15 nodes) both algorithms have almost same performance, Fig. 7. But once we increase the number of nodes the modified ACO algorithm is much better and converge faster than DFS Algorithm.

These results are also confirmed by studying the complexity of each algorithm. DFS has a complexity of $O(|V| + |E|)$.

The complexity of modified ACO algorithm in the worst case scenario is $O(|V|Log|V| + |E|)$.

Simulations clearly demonstrate, Figs. 8 and 9, that when increasing the number of links inside the network, the bandwidth available is also increasing in case of modified ACO algorithm because number of neighbors increases so more of alternative paths from a source to a destination are available. In case of DFS, the increase of Bandwidth is not as high as ACO, because the most of time the same path is chosen.

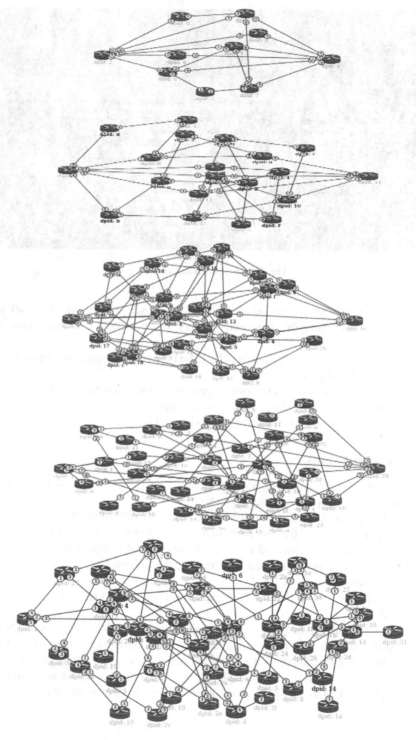

Fig. 6. Different set-up topologies of respectively 10, 20, 30, 40 and 50 nodes, and 20, 30, 62, 70 and 80 links

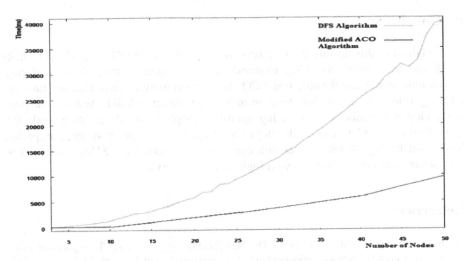

Fig. 7. Execution time of both algorithms

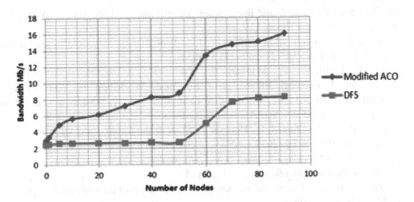

Fig. 8. Available bandwidth for each algorithm

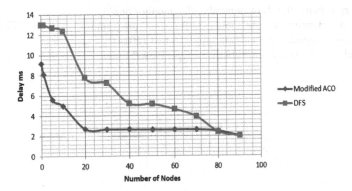

Fig. 9. Calculated delay for each algorithm

6 Conclusion

As explained in this document, we proposed to modify the AntNet algorithm to help the Transport Network to satisfy requirements. The running time, observed during simulations, shows that the modified ACO algorithm is more efficient than the classical DFS algorithm. More than that, we showed how it is easier to build a test bed and how to develop new applications resolving optimization problems. As a future work, the QOS Routing problem can be developed to support other constraint such as packet losses and latency. Transport Network can take then profit from SDN innovation to support and deliver new service with high quality of service.

References

1. Beller, D., Sperber, R.: MPLS-TP – The New Technology for Packet Transport Networks. In: DFN-Forum Kommunikationstechnologien, volume 149 of LNI, pp. 81–92. GI (2009)
2. Azodolmolky, S.: Software Defined Networking with Openflow. Packt Publishing, ISBN 978-1-84969-872-6, October 2013
3. Tarjan, R.: Depth-first search and linear graph algorithms. In: 12th Annual Symposium on Switching and Automata Theory (1971)
4. Deneubourg, J.L., Pasteels, J.M., Verhaeghe, J.C.: Probabilistic behaviour in ants: a strategy of errors. J. Theor. Biol. 105(2), 259–271 (1983)
5. Jarschel, M., Lehrieder, F., Magyari, Z., Pries, R.: A flexible openflow-controller benchmark. In: Proceedings of the 2012 European Workshop on Software Defined Networking, EWSDN 2012, pp. 48–53. IEEE Computer Society, Washington (2012). http://dx.doi.org/10.1109/EWSDN.2012.15
6. Hubbard, S., Perrin, S., Chapell, C., Hodges, J.: SDN & the future of the telecom ecosystem. Heavy Reading 10(8), 9–10 (2012)
7. https://www.opennetworking.org/images/stories/downloads/sdn-resources/onf-specifications/openflow/openflow-spec-v1.3.0.pdf
8. Wang, Z., Crocroft, J.: Quality of service routing for supporting multimedia applications. JSAC 14, 1228–1234 (1996)
9. Di Caro, G., Dorigo, M.: AntNet: distributed stigmergic control for communications networks. J. Artif. Intell. Res. 9, 317–365 (1998)
10. http://osrg.github.io/ryu-book/en/html/traffic_monitor.html
11. Azizi, M., Benaini, R., Mamoun, M.B.: The programmable cloud network: delay measurement application. In: SITIS, pp. 687–693 (2014)
12. http://yuba.stanford.edu/foswiki/bin/view/OpenFlow/Mininet

CCN Context-Naming for Efficient Context-Aware Service Discovery in IoT

Mohamed Labbi$^{(\boxtimes)}$ and Mohammed Benabdellah

ACSA Laboratory, Faculty of Sciences, Mohammed First University,
Oujda, Morocco
med.labbi@gmail.com, med_benabdellah@yahoo.fr

Abstract. The emergence of the Internet of Things (IoT) offers great potential for the development of new services and applications connecting the physical world to the virtual world. Due to the rapid growth and heterogeneity of connected objects, it is difficult for users to acquire precise knowledge about IoT services that can interact with. In order to effectively help end-users acquire services and data generated in the IoT, search and discovery mechanisms are crucial.

In this paper, we propose an efficient context-aware service discovery mechanism based on Content Centric Networking (CCN) naming feature which creates high level abstraction access to IoT devices. This solution provides a location-identity binding where content can be accessed quickly and accurately.

Keywords: Service discovery · Internet of Things · Context-aware · Content-Centric Networking · Naming

1 Introduction

The Internet of Things (IoT) [1] is a novel paradigm that converts the physical objects around us to an information ecosystem which quickly change for better our daily activities. It has evolved at an exceptional speed, connecting a large number of heterogeneous objects (sensors, actuators, smartphones, applications, etc.). All objects in the real world ranging from cars, robots, fridges, television, mobile phones, to shoes, plants, watches, and so on could be identified by a code and connected to others and communicate with them via the internet. Some estimates predict more than 26 billion connected IoT devices by 2020[1]. These kinds of things will generate data in various formats using totally different vocabularies. IoT applications are reflected in many concrete uses - new or improved - significantly impacting the daily lives of people, companies and communities. It finds applications in almost all major economic sectors, from health to education, agriculture, transport, manufacturing industry, smart grids and many more.

As part of the future internet, IoT aims to collect information and provide the proper services to the right user, at the right time, in the right place, and

---

[1] http://tinyurl.com/le-monde-informatique-IoT.

© Springer Nature Switzerland AG 2019
É. Renault et al. (Eds.): MSPN 2019, LNCS 11557, pp. 37–50, 2019.
https://doi.org/10.1007/978-3-030-22885-9_4

on the right device based on the available contexts. The user will therefore be surrounded by a large number of services offered by their connected objects and will need to find them to interact with them. However, the Internet of Things environments are characterized by the large number of connected objects, their mobility and heterogeneity. These characteristics make it difficult to find their adjacent services.

The search mechanism must meet certain requirements to be effective. Indeed, with a large volume of IoT services, it would be difficult for the user to know the characteristics of all the services around him that can meet his needs. Thus, the search mechanism must be flexible in the sense that it would be possible for the user to give a vague description of the service sought and that on the basis of this description, the search system would be able to return services that correspond exactly or partially to the expressed request.

Context-awareness will play a critical role in deciding what data needs to be processed and reduce the number of retrieved services by returning only the subset of potentially relevant services that conforms to the context of the request. Traditional context-aware web service discovery approaches are not ideal for service discovery in IoT, due to the distinctions between real-world services and traditional web services.

On the basis of the above, the paramount question is: how to set up an effective search mechanism that meets these requirements while taking into account the constraints of IoT environment?

To answer these problems, we introduce in this article a solution for the service discovery in IoT based on Content Centric Networking (CCN) [2] naming feature to meet the requirements of both IoT environment and IoT services. We take advantage of the CCN naming scheme to provide a high-level abstraction access to IoT devices. Moreover, CCN built in features allow a distributed and intelligent data distribution platform to support heterogeneous IoT services that are difficult to achieve over traditional network (TCP/IP).

The remainder of this paper is structured as follows. Section 2 introduces the Internet of things paradigm and the features provided by Content-Centric Networking (CCN) that are relevant for our proposal. In Sect. 3, the previous relevant works will be reviewed. Section 4 presents the architecture of our solution for IoT service discovery based on CCN context-naming feature. Section 5 concludes the paper.

2   Background

2.1   The Internet of Things Paradigm

The term "Internet of Things" was created in 1999 by Kevin ASHTON [1] to refer to the existing link between RFID and the Internet. Later, IoT was formally introduced by the International Telecommunication Union (ITU) by the ITU Internet report in 2005 [3]. It defined the Internet of Things as *"a global infrastructure for the information society, enabling advanced services by inter-connecting (physical and virtual) things based on existing and evolving interoperable information and communication technologies".* In fact, there aren't any standard definitions for IoT.

From a conceptual standpoint, the internet of things refers to connected physical objects with their own digital identity and able to communicate with each other. This network creates a bridge between the physical and virtual world. On the other hand, from a technical standpoint, Iot consists of direct and standardized digital identification of a physical object thanks to a wireless communication system which may be an RFID chip, Bluetooth or WiFi.

Several application areas are affected by IoT. In their paper, [4] classified the applications into four domains: 1. personal domain, 2. transport domain, 3. environment and 4. Infrastructure and public services. Connected objects produce large amounts of data whose storage and processing fall within the scope of the so-called big data. Nowadays, connected objects become a part of life. We already have connected objects in several fields including industrial sector. Supply chain management [5], transportation and logistics [6], aerospace, aviation, and automotive are some of the industry focused applications of IoT. It is also highly visible in health and welfare with the development of connected watches, bracelets and other sensors monitoring vital signs.

2.2 Content-Centric Networking

CCN (also called Named Data Networking [7]) is a new paradigm for the future internet where the communication model no longer relies on a server, cache or other network element, but rather, as its name suggests, on the content. CCN started as a research project at the Palo Alto Research Center (PARC) in 2007 to address the inadequacies of the present IP-based Internet design. Unlike current IP networks, CCN presents an exchange model allowing access to the content independently of the establishment of communication between the end nodes. It offers certain flexibility by using names rather than IP addresses. In other word, CCN focuses on finding and delivering named contents, instead of maintaining end-to-end communications between hosts. Table 1 compares the basic concepts of the CCN with those of the current Internet.

Table 1. Comparison between CCN and the current internet

	CCN	TCP/IP
Routing	Location-independent	Using IP address
Security	Secure content itself	Secure the pipe
Naming	Addresses content by name instead of location	Related to host location
Caching	In any node of the network	In specific servers

The goal of CCN is to provide a secure, flexible and scalable network that meets the requirements of the future internet (Internet of things). Due to its intrinsic features, common communication patterns of the IoT are easily accommodated by CCN and can benefit significantly from several functionalities (security [8], naming, data aggregation, etc.). The CCN features that meet the IoT requirements are summarized in Table 2.

Table 2. IoT requirements and native CCN support.

	Named data	Name-based routing	In-network caching	Mulicast	Anycast
QoS		√	√	√	√
Scalability	√		√	√	√
Heterogeneity	√				
Energy efficiency			√	√	
Security	√				
Mobility	√	√			√

Indeed, CCN has the potential to enhance the scalability and effectiveness of data dissemination in IoT for many reasons. The paper [9] presents key motivations of considering CCN for IoT.

Node Model. In CCN, there is no need to route the source/destination addresses through the network to retrieve data. Packets have a name rather than addresses, which has a fundamental impact on the operation of the network. CCN is based on two main types of packets. Interest and Data as seen in Fig. 1. The Interest packet represents a content request and the Data packet represents the response to this first packet.

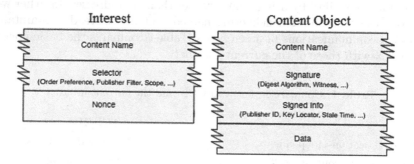

Fig. 1. CCN message formats

A consumer who wants to retrieve a certain content broadcasts its Interest, specifying the name of the content over all available interfaces. On receipt of an Interest by a node, if the latter can 'satisfy' the Interest, it sends out the corresponding Data packet onto the face from which it received the Interest, otherwise, Interest will be forwarded to the interfaces leading to the data in question. By definition, CCN nodes are stateful and only send Data if there was an Interest beforehand. Once the Interest reaches a node that has the requested data, a Data packet is sent back following the reverse path taken by the Interest.

To carry out the Interest and Data packet forwarding functions, three main table structures are used at each node:

- *Content Store(CS)*: In this database, content objects are preserved based on a specific policy (LRU, LFU, FIFO ..etc) to enable fast content retrieval.
- *Pending Interest Table (PIT)*: This table keeps record of Interests and corresponding interfaces from which Interests have been received.
- *Forwarding Information Base (FIB)*: is similar to the forwarding table in IP routers. It keeps record of potential content source(s), performing the mapping between content names and one or more output interfaces, allowing multiple source routing [10].

In-Network Caching. One of the most remarkable advantages obtained by using this novel paradigm. In-network caching mechanisms can be leveraged in order to boost the content distribution capabilities of the network. content replicated and cached in nodes closer to the users implies a large reduction in network traffic, improving service quality level. Moreover, Caching strategies are crucial to provide reliability, scalability and robustness to IoT ecosystems. It makes data available to different applications, without the need to query the original device. The impact of in-network caching on energy aspects with CCN has been studied by [11]. In the IoT, the paper [12] demonstrated by experiment that savings in terms of energy consumption are possible thanks to in-network caching.

Name-Based Routing. In CCN, routing is based on the names associated with the content instead of content physical location as in current networks. The contents are divided into "chunks"; each chunk is identified by a unique hierarchical human readable name. A maximum Content Object size (MTU) for CCN had not been specified, and there is some expectation that it may be larger than the MTU in IP networks. The comparison between IP stack and CCN stack is shown in Fig. 2.

The objective of the CCN architecture is to simplify research processes. Information is exchanged only in response to a request specifying the name of the data to retrieve. Content names are directly used to communicate, without the need to be resolved into network addresses. A user requests a content object by its name by sending Interest packet to its access router. If the data cannot be found in the content store (CS) of this router, the latter forward it to the next hop router. It is also possible in CCN to concurrently forward the same Interest on multiple faces (multicast), and this choice will be performed by the Forwarding Strategy Layer.

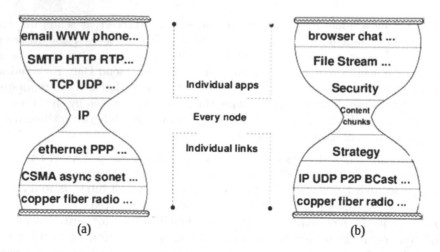

Fig. 2. Comparison between the current Internet stack (a) and the CCN stack (b)

Naming. CCN does not address specific hosts, but content object itself. CCN design assumes hierarchically structured names. This structure allows a fast and efficient prefix-based lookup similar to the IP lookup currently used. There are different naming schemes that can be used to identify content including hierarchical, flat and attribute-based. The authors in [13] discuss the issues related to each of these schemes. However, here we focus on hierarchical scheme which used by the CCN architecture.

The form of the name is similar to URI. It allows names to be context dependent i.e. $/Build.ma/1^{st}floor/Room2/thermometer$ references a thermometer in Room2. In the following section, we will see how this context-naming could make an efficient context-aware service discovery in IoT.

3   Related Work

The issue of service discovery in the IoT world has been the subject of several researches. Current service discovery protocols (SDP) including Jini[2], Service Location Protocol (SLP) [14], UPnP [15], UDDI and Salutation do not make use of contextual information in discovering services. Moreover, they are not directly applicable to 6LoWPAN [16]. Therefore, they don't give the most proper and pertinent services for users [17,18].

The paper [19] proposes a modular approach to IoT context-aware applications. by breaking down monolithic applications into an equivalent set of functional units, or context engines, Authors demonstrate that it increases reusability, reduces complexity at a minor cost in accuracy, and facilitates general data transformation.

---

[2] https://river.apache.org/release-doc/2.2.2/specs/html/discovery-spec.html.

The paper [20] presents a service discovery architecture that is based on directory proxy agent (DPA) that acts as a proxy to the directory agent (DA) in SSLP inside the 6LoWPAN. However, translating messages by Translation Agent (TA) to or from SLP is complex and takes a lot of time.

Authors in [21] propose a multi-modal context-aware reasoner to provide knowledge at the edge for each IoT application. Authors verified their approach with two different reasoning techniques namely rules-based and Bayesian reasoning for three IoT applications, SmartHome, SmartGardening and SmartHealth, on a raspberry pi.

In [22], the authors present an Efficient SemAntic Service DiscoverY (EASY) to support semantic, context and QoS-aware service discovery on top of existing SDPs in pervasive environments. EASY provides a language Easy-L for semantic service description covering both functional and non-functional service characteristics.

The paper [23] presents the design and implementation of a generic discovery service framework called POrtable Discovery Services (PODS). PODS utilises existing middleware abstractions to support heterogeneity in so far as such abstractions relate to the discovery process. Authors demonstrated that such an approach is tractable.

The paper [24] proposes a decentralized semantics-based service discovery framework, which can effectively locate trustworthy services based on requester's quality of service demands and changing context requirements.

After analyzing these works and many others, we observe that the research conducted to date is very modest in the face of an increasing presence of data and services that are not being exploited to their full potential.

4   CCN Naming-Based Service Discovery in IoT

Context-aware (CA) techniques are widely used for searching in IoT, such as information retrieval and extraction. The context-aware service discovery can play an important role in improving the quality of the discovery result: recall and precision rates become higher when including context in the service discovery process. The contextual information makes the user's query more information-rich and, thereby, provides means for high precision of the retrieved results. In the Context-Aware service discovery, an association between the service requester, service provider and context provider need to be created.

Using CCN is beneficial in fulfilling the general requirements of the IoT including service discovery. Energy efficiency, heterogeneity, mobility, quality of service, scalability and security IoT requirements are handled with CCN features.

In this architecture (Fig. 3), CCN acts as a networking layer that Provide a high-level abstraction layer to access sensor devices. Naming feature facilitates tasks such as efficient routing, storage and event detection taking into account energy consumption and availability. Figure 4 presents an overview of our proposed model.

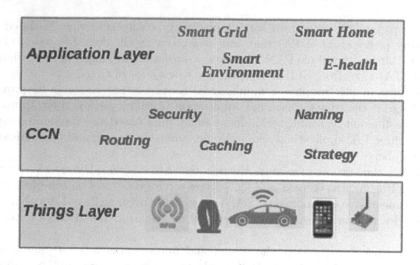

Fig. 3. 3-Layered IoT-CCN architecture

4.1 Context Types

The use of context is very important in IoT service discovery, it can play the role of a filtering mechanism deciding what information and services need to be presented to the user based on user's context. Different researchers have identified context types differently based of different perspectives. [25] classified context in two different perspectives:

Conceptual Perspective: Any information retrieved that can be directly measured such as temperature, humidity, voltage..etc without performing any fusion operations.

Operational Perspective: is defined as combinations of conceptual contexts e.g computing the average temperature of a building(installation of several thermometers in a building to estimate an average value).

However, some services require actuator command to operate. For example, a user can generate an actuator message to regulate the air-conditioner or to switch lights on or off. In this type of context, instead of retrieving information from the sensor device we request it to perform an action.

4.2 CCN Context-Naming

Instead of identifying machines as in today's Internet, CCN identifies data objects with names. Names are mainly formed by three parties. Each part contains one or more readable components, delimited by the character '/'. The first part of the names provides global routing information (Domain name). The second part contains organizational routing information and the last part gives information about the version and segment number.

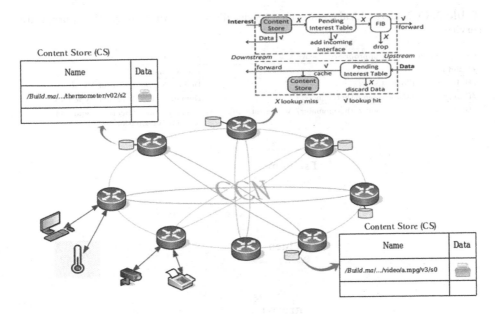

Fig. 4. Overview of proposed architecture

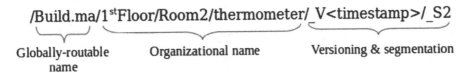

Globally-routable name   Organizational name   Versioning & segmentation

Fig. 5. Example of content name

In this example (Fig. 5), */Build.ma* represents the routable part, $/1^{st}Floor/Room2/$ thermometer reflects the organizational part and $/\_V <$ $timestamp > /\_S_{id}$ indicates the version (the time when the data is acquired, expressed as a timestamp) of the segment (data packet) identifier. This naming scheme provides a location-identity binding where content can be accessed rapidly and accurately.

This naming scheme offers a good quality of context (QoC) [26] that resolve context data conflicts. It provides the idea of presenting information based on context such as location, time, etc (example shown in Table 3). Data's integrity and authenticity is ensured using the publisher's public key.

4.3 Name-Based Service Discovery

The service discovery mechanism in our approach is based jointly on the propagation of the query (Interest packet) and response (Data packet) pair between the objects. In CCN, a content object is represented by a unique hierarchical name such as /fso.ump/video/intro.avi (Fig. 6). This video is composed of a set

Table 3. CCN hierarchical naming for a service discovery request to get the appropriate service.

CCN name queries for appropriate discovery	Matching criteria
/Build.ma/	Domain name
/Build.ma/1stFloor/Room2/	Domain name, Location
/Build.ma/1stFloor/Room2/thermometer/	Domain name, Location, type based
/Build.ma/1stFloor/Room2/thermometer/_V<timestamp>/_S2	Domain name, Location, type and relevant information based

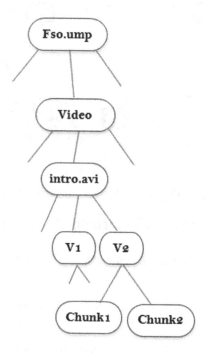

Fig. 6. Hierarchical tree

of segments, where the fact that a content object holds this identity proves that they are in fact created by /fso.ump.

Service Request. Once the service has been published, the consumer can then launch a request containing all the information necessary to invoke the service. Instead of announcing IP prefixes, a CCN router announces the prefixes of the content names that the router can serve. This announcement spreads across the network via a routing protocol, and each router builds its own FIB. Routers process names as opaque component sequences. They use these names to search for the longest prefix match between the content name of the Interest packet and the FIB entries. Routers have a dual responsibility: they transfer packets and they can also behave as distributed caches.

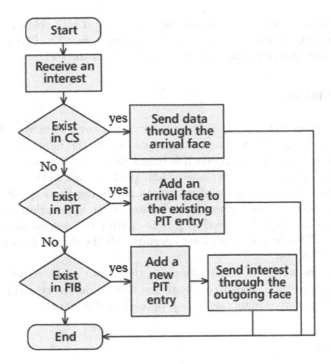

Fig. 7. Interest processing

Query Processing. As shown in Fig. 7, when an Interest packet arrives at a router, the search for the longest prefix match between the name and the entries of these three data structures is done. If the content exists in the Content Store (CS), a Data packet with the same name as the Interest packet will be sent through the interface that received the Interest. The latter will then be eliminated. If there is no exact match between the CS entries and the name, the PIT is consulted. If it contains an exact match between one of its entries and the content name, the requester interface of the packet is added to the list of interfaces. If the CS and PIT do not provide any information, the FIB is consulted. If a match between one of the FIB entries and the prefix of the Interest packet name is found, this packet is passed to the interfaces specified in the FIB for this prefix. The selected FIB entry is found by performing a Longest Prefix Matching (LPM) search using the prefix of the content name requested by the Interest. The PIT table will be updated with a new entry for the content in question. If no match is found, the Interest packet is eliminated.

Response of the Request. Once an Interest packet can be satisfied from a network node holding a copy of the desired content, the corresponding Data packet is sent to the requester following the reverse path of Interests. On receipt of the data packet, a name search is performed in the PIT. If a match is found, this Data packet is sent to all requesting interfaces. This packet is also stored in the CS (managed with a standard replacement policy, i.e. LRU, RND, etc.) [27–29] and the corresponding entry is removed from the PIT.

5   Conclusions

In this work we presented a context-aware service discovery based on CCN Naming feature able to give the proper Data and services to the right user. The service discovery mechanism in our approach is based jointly on the propagation of the query (Interest packet) and response (Data packet) pair between the objects. The first step is to launch a set of information forming the request to the network. The processing phase allows the selection of the appropriate service based on the context-naming. The third step is to deliver the service as described to the right user. This response takes into account all the details prescribed in the content of the request.

In the future work, we will continue to detail our architecture and design experiments on real use cases to evaluate the service discovery architecture, the context model and reasoning methods proposed in this paper.

References

1. Ashton, K.: That 'internet of things' thing. RFID J. **22**(7), 97–114 (2009)
2. Jacobson, V., Mosko, M., Smetters, D., Garcia-Luna-Aceves, J.: Content-centric networking. Whitepaper, Palo Alto Research Center, pp. 2–4 (2007)
3. Peña-López, I.: ITU Internet report 2005: the internet of things (2005)
4. Gubbi, J., Buyya, R., Marusic, S., Palaniswami, M.: Internet of things (IOT): a vision, architectural elements, and future directions. Future Gener. Comput. Syst. **29**(7), 1645–1660 (2013)
5. Chaves, L.W.F., Decker, C.: A survey on organic smart labels for the internet-of-things. In: 2010 Seventh International Conference on Networked Sensing Systems (INSS), pp. 161–164. IEEE, June 2010
6. Yuqiang, C., Jianlan, G., Xuanzi, H.: The research of internet of things' supporting technologies which face the logistics industry. In: 2010 International Conference on Computational Intelligence and Security (CIS), pp. 659–663. IEEE, December 2010
7. Zhang, L., et al.: Named data networking (NDN) project. Relatório Técnico NDN-0001, Xerox Palo Alto Research Center-PARC, pp. 157–158 (2010)
8. Labbi, M., Kannouf, N., Chahid, Y., Benabdellah, M., Azizi, A.: Blockchain-based PKI for content-centric networking. In: Ben Ahmed, M., Boudhir, A.A., Younes, A. (eds.) SCA 2018. LNITI, pp. 656–667. Springer, Cham (2019). https://doi.org/10.1007/978-3-030-11196-0_54
9. Labbi, M., Kannouf, N., Benabdellah, M.: IoT security based on content-centric networking architecture. In: Security and Privacy in Smart Sensor Networks, pp. 179–199. IGI Global (2018)
10. Labbi, M., BenSalah, N., Kannouf, N., Douzi, Y., Benabdellah, M., Azizi, A.: A game theoretic approach to multipath traffic control in content-centric networking. In: International Conference on Advanced Communication Systems and Information Security (ACOSIS), pp. 1–7. IEEE, October 2016

11. Choi, N., Guan, K., Kilper, D.C., Atkinson, G.: In-network caching effect on optimal energy consumption in content-centric networking. In: 2012 IEEE International Conference on Communications (ICC), pp. 2889–2894. IEEE, June 2012

12. Baccelli, E., Mehlis, C., Hahm, O., Schmidt, T.C., Wählisch, M.: Information centric networking in the IoT: experiments with NDN in the wild. In: Proceedings of the 1st ACM Conference on Information-Centric Networking, pp. 77–86. ACM, September 2014

13. De Brito, G.M., Velloso, P.B., Moraes, I.M.: Information-Centric Networks: A New Paradigm for the Internet. Wiley, Hoboken (2013)

14. Kaushik, S., Poonia, R.C.: Evolutionary Study of Service Location Protocol (2018)

15. Hakim, M.A., Aksu, H., Uluagac, A.S., Akkaya, K.: U-PoT: A Honeypot Framework for UPnP-Based IoT Devices. arXiv preprint arXiv:1812.05558 (2018)

16. Butt, T.A., Phillips, I., Guan, L., Oikonomou, G.: Adaptive and context-aware service discovery for the internet of things. In: Balandin, S., Andreev, S., Koucheryavy, Y. (eds.) NEW2AN/ruSMART -2013. LNCS, vol. 8121, pp. 36–47. Springer, Heidelberg (2013). https://doi.org/10.1007/978-3-642-40316-3_4

17. Zhu, F., Mutka, M.W., Ni, L.M.: Service discovery in pervasive computing environments. IEEE Pervasive Comput. 4, 81–90 (2005)

18. Cuddy, S., Katchabaw, M., Lutfiyya, H.: Context-aware service selection based on dynamic and static service attributes. In: IEEE International Conference on Wireless And Mobile Computing, Networking and Communications, WiMob 2005, vol. 4, pp. 13–20. IEEE, August 2005

19. Venkatesh, J., Chan, C., Akyurek, A.S., Rosing, T.S.: A modular approach to context-aware IoT applications, pp. 235–240. IEEE (2016)

20. Chaudhry, S.A., Do Jung, W., Hussain, C.S., Akbar, A.H., Kim, K.-H.: A proxy-enabled service discovery architecture to find proximity-based services in 6LoWPAN. In: Sha, E., Han, S.-K., Xu, C.-Z., Kim, M.-H., Yang, L.T., Xiao, B. (eds.) EUC 2006. LNCS, vol. 4096, pp. 956–965. Springer, Heidelberg (2006). https://doi.org/10.1007/11802167_96

21. Rahman, H., Rahmani, R., Kanter, T.: Multi-modal Context-Aware reasoNer (CAN) at the edge of IoT. Procedia Comput. Sci. 109, 335–342 (2017)

22. Mokhtar, S.B., Preuveneers, D., Georgantas, N., Issarny, V., Berbers, Y.: EASY: Efficient semAntic Service discoverY in pervasive computing environments with QoS and context support. J. Syst. Softw. 81(5), 785–808 (2008)

23. Görgü, L., Kroon, B., O'Grady, M.J., Yılmaz, Ö., O'Hare, G.M.: Sensor discovery in ambient IoT ecosystems. J. Ambient Intell. Humanized Comput. 9(2), 447–458 (2018)

24. Li, J., Bai, Y., Zaman, N., Leung, V.C.: A decentralized trustworthy context and QoS-aware service discovery framework for the internet of things. IEEE Access 5, 19154–19166 (2017)

25. Perera, C., Zaslavsky, A., Christen, P., Georgakopoulos, D.: Context aware computing for the internet of things: a survey. IEEE Commun. Surv. Tutor. 16(1), 414–454 (2014)

26. Bellavista, P., Corradi, A., Fanelli, M., Foschini, L.: A survey of context data distribution for mobile ubiquitous systems. ACM Comput. Surv. (CSUR) 44(4), 24 (2012)

27. Chai, W.K., He, D., Psaras, I., Pavlou, G.: Cache "less for more" in information-centric networks (extended version). Comput. Commun. 36(7), 758–770 (2013)

28. Rosensweig, E.J., Kurose, J.: Breadcrumbs: efficient, best-effort content location in cache networks. In: IEEE INFOCOM 2009, pp. 2631–2635. IEEE, April 2009

29. Saino, L., Psaras, I., Pavlou, G.: Icarus: a caching simulator for information centric networking (ICN). In: Proceedings of the 7th International ICST conference on Simulation Tools and Techniques, pp. 66–75. ICST (Institute for Computer Sciences, Social-Informatics and Telecommunications Engineering), March 2014

Efficient Distributed Authentication and Access Control System Management for Internet of Things Using Blockchain

Hadjer Benhadj Djilali[1]([✉]) and Djamel Tandjaoui[2]

[1] LSI, USTHB: University of Sciences and Technology Houari Boumediene,
Algiers, Algeria
h.benhadjdjilali@usthb.dz
[2] Computer Security Division,
CERIST: Research Center on Scientific and Technical Information, Algiers, Algeria
dtandjaoui@cerist.dz
http://www.usthb.dz, http://www.cerist.dz

Abstract. Internet of things (IoT) enables a huge network of connected devices inter-working and collaborating to provide relevant services and applications. This technology entered the market and is expected to grow in the upcoming years, as the critical questions related to the management and communication security continue to be challenging research problems. Current solutions of access control system management that enables communication between devices depend mainly on the use of digital certificates for authentication. However, such an approach imposes significant overhead on IoT devices since it is computationally demanding and requires validation of the certificate within a limited period. In addition, relying on a central node for deciding on issuing and revoking certificates introduces a single point of failure and could even risk the safety of personal information or physical damages related to IoT services. In this paper, we propose a new distributed authentication and access control system management for IoT by the use of Blockchain technology to keep track of the certificate of each IoT device (valid or revoked) in distributed and immutable records. In essence we replace certificate verification with a lightweight blockchain-based authentication approach. In addition, we propose a fully distributed IoT admission/revocation scheme. We show that our scheme could alleviate the computation overhead and enhance the response time while improving the overall system security.

Keywords: Internet of Things · Access control system management · Authentication · Blockchain · Security

1 Introduction

Today security and access control standards recommend the use of a Public-Key Infrastructure (PKI) with a centralized management for the creation, distribution and revocation of the digital certificates built around the notion of trust.

© Springer Nature Switzerland AG 2019
E. Renault et al. (Eds.): MSPN 2019, LNCS 11557, pp. 51–60, 2019.
https://doi.org/10.1007/978-3-030-22885-9_5

Typically, a PKI is mainly based on Certificate Authority (CA) that acts as a trusted third party to issue/revoke digital certificates. However, the use of a CA introduces a single point of failure in the IoT. Indeed, dramatic consequences could happen when the CA is compromised. Over the last decade, several cybersecurity attacks have been launched against CA networks [1,2] resulting into breaches, the inflicted damage includes hacking user accounts, issuing fake certificates and carrying out successful man-in-the-middle attacks [2]. Moreover, the inclusion of the certificate does not only introduce major computation overhead for performing the verification procedure but also imposes high communication overhead in terms of bandwidth. Additionally, it causes increased medium access contention and consequently longer message delivery delays. Basically, in order to include a certificate in a message an additional 145 bytes are required in every message sent as a result heavy traffic, network congestion and resource exhaustion.

To overcome the above-mentioned shortcomings, several schemes have been proposed; most of these schemes have focused on reducing the computation and communication overheads and only very, few of them have considered the single point of failure vulnerability. Although one may argue that the certificate authority can be equipped with redundant resources to make it continuously available, it may still become unreachable due to the instability of wireless links, especially when IoT devices are in motion. In this paper, we opt to overcome the shortcomings of existing solutions using the Blockchain technology.

Blockchain is one of the most revolutionizing technologies that can tremendously influence the future of various computer and communication systems [3]. Blockchain provides a secure shared database, ledger or log of transactions, without requiring a central trusted third party for its management. The consistency of the blockchain is guaranteed through a distributed consensus protocol where a set of participants (validators), in a trust-less peer-to-peer network, collaborate in a completely transparent way to accept only valid transactions. By design, every transaction is cryptographically encoded into a permanent record and it is almost impossible to modify any of them without being detected [3]. The full history of all performed transactions can be easily retrieved and checked by any entity in the network without requiring additional security mechanisms.

In this paper, we propose the use of blockchain as a mean to build a secure lightweight access control system of internet of things network, i.e., valid or revoked, in order to: (i) mitigate the single point of failure (central authority) vulnerability, and (ii) reduce the overhead of the authentication process (certificates exchanges and verification). In our proposed system, the admission/revocation of IoT device is performed in a completely distributed fashion. A set of blockchain validators, e.g., road side units, smart traffic lights panels, smart base transceiver station, smart light panels...etc any fixed smart objects that have processing and storage power, apply a distributed consensus protocol to decide about the admission/ revocation of a IoT device based on a set of predefined rules. For instance, to decide about the admission of IoT device, both the full IoT device's history that is already stored in the blockchain as well as certificates from the corresponding authorities such as the department of smart city, motor vehicle, manufacturer, insurance company, government etc. can be used. Similarly, the revocation of a particular IoT device, IoT_i, is performed by the validators based, for instance, on misbehaviour reports sent by the neighbours of such IoT device. Because the integrity and validity of the device state information in the blockchain is ensured and can be simply and securely accessed from anywhere, IoT devices no longer need to include a certificate in their messages to be authenticated by the receivers. To authenticate a sender of a message, the receiver can simply check if the sender's public key used to sign the message is already recorded in the blockchain with a valid status. This considerably reduces both the communication and computation overheads associated with the use of certificates.

The remaining of this paper is organized as follows. Section 2 provides a summary of the related work. Section 3 describes our proposed blockchain-based authentication and access control system scheme for IoT in detail. In Sect. 4, we discuss the system efficiency and evaluate its performances in comparison to traditional systems. Finally, Sect. 5 concludes the paper.

2 Related Work

Many researchers and company labs are coupling IoT technology with the blockchain technology to take advantage from each technology in purpose to improve their solutions. Indeed, a way to enhance the security of IoT networks and applications is the use of blockchain technology that is known for its high security and robustness.

Conoscenti et al. [4] conducted a systematic literature review on the blockchain for the Internet of Things. The survey described several papers that manage data collected by IoT devices. As an example, [5] describes a system to verify the identity of the data and [6] describes a method to preserve the data ownership of the IoT devices.

Cha et al. [7] proposed a design and a privacy-aware blockchain connected Gateway for Bluetooth low energy IoT devices, where the blockchain network is adopted as the underlying architecture for management of privacy preferences of the users from being tampered.

Zhang et al. [8] proposed a design of an access control policy framework based on XCAML language based on blockchain for IoT. Xu and Yu et al. [9] proposed a decentralized lightweight capability-based access scheme based on blockchain.

Reference [10], describes a cryptocurrency blockchain-based access control framework called FairAccess, a token-based access control model.

In [11], the authors propose an architecture for electronic commerce explicitly designed for IoT devices, based on the Bitcoin protocol. Distributed Autonomous Corporations (DAC) was used as a transaction entity to deal with data from IoT devices. In this model, the users can negotiate with DACs, using cryptocurrencies. Filament [12] it is a system designed to allow devices have unique identities and can discover, communicate, and interact autonomously with each other. Also, the devices involved can directly exchange value.

IOTA [13] it is a cryptocurrency explicitly developed for the selling of data from devices IoT. Instead of using a global Blockchain, the IOTA uses a DAG (Directed Acyclic Graph), the edges are the transactions, and the weights the number of times were confirmed.

Unlike the previous solutions presented in the above references, our proposed solution's goal: The design of efficient distributed authentication and access control management for internet of things using blockchain and not depending on the access control policy model implemented, Ensure a secure management access control system of IoT devices (registration, admission, misbehavior notification and revocation) in a totally decentralized manner to avoid single point of failure, A lightweight authentication scheme that eliminates the heavy computation resource to verify the digital certificate and enable authentications using simple lookup. As result we have a full control system management of the IoT network and a secure communication between the devices, furthermore our solution can be used for public government project or companies' private projects in order to secure their IoT networks from external unsafe network communications.

3   Bolckchain Based Efficient Authentication and Access Control System Management for IoT

In this paper, we propose a new blockchain-based authentication and access control system management mechanism for internet of things network. The design objective is to eliminate the single point of failure and reduce the communication and verification overheads, which exist in the centralized PKI while ensuring authentication. To achieve such an objective, the blockchain-based authentication mechanism for IoT has to ensure the following mandatory set of functionalities:

(1) Registering the public key of IoT devices.
(2) Validating the membership of IoT device's public key.
(3) Looking up/verifying the validity of IoT's public key.
(4) Revoking of IoT's public key from the network.

The detailed description of these functionalities' implementation is given in the balance of this section. Before that, we first provide an overview of our proposed system.

Due to IoT's limited characteristics features like the energy of the battery of IoT devices, we choose to implement the access control system with elliptic curve cryptography ECC [14] and Elliptic Curve Digital Signature ECDSA [15] algorithm for the digital signature to maintain the energy consumption instead pf using Public Cryptography RSA [16].

3.1   System Overview

Our goal is to enable large-scale deployment of IoT network while preserving its security. Traditional existing solution of IoT promote the use of PKI with a centralized certification authority to ensure integrity, authentication and non-repudiation. However, such approach introduces a single point of failure and imposes heavy cost in terms of computation and communication overhead, which negatively affects the network performances and the IoT devices. Our proposed system leverages the use of blockchain technology to tackle these issues. Intrinsically, blockchain provides distributed, secure and immutable records of any kind of data. When putting the authentication information, such as certificates, on blockchain, exchanging and verifying such information becomes unnecessary. In addition, the distribution nature of blockchain eliminates the need of a trusted third party to manage and secure data, which leads to avoiding the single point of failure scenario and averting serious cyber threats (i.e., DoS attacks), which are possible in conventional PKI-based systems.

Figure 1 shows a general architecture of our system where the blockchain network is overlaid on top of the existing IoT network. In our proposed system, information about IoT admission/revocation are posted to a permissioned blockchain, where we refer to the entities writing such information as "validators". Thus, we eliminate the single point of failure by delegating decisions about IoT admission/revocation to a set of validators. We assign the validation role to a set of smart object of the city such as road side units, smart traffic light panels, base transceiver station, smart light panels...etc any fixed smart objects that have processing and storage power. As they are deployed over the whole smart cities's network, easily reachable by IoT devices and are generally interconnected by the mean of specialized link or over the Internet. In this permissioned blockchain, both IoT devices and authorities can only read from or submit transactions to the blockchain. By executing a distributed consensus algorithm, the validators decide to accept or reject the received transactions from both IoT devices and authorities.

In practice, the role of the authorities, such as the department of vehicles, e-government, manufacturers and companies ...etc. is to certify that a particular IoT conforms to membership requirements. However, instead of collecting all certificates from the different authorities into one single place for decision, in our system all certificates are pushed to the blockchain network then used by the validators for decision making in a fully distributed manner. This is very important from a security perspective, as there is no single entity controlling the admission of IoT devices to the network. In addition, for the revocation process, the decision for evicting a IoT device is performed by the set of validators instead of a single authority. IoT devices that detects misbehaviour send an embedded notification within the transaction to the blockchain, then the final decision about revoking a suspected IoT device is taken by the set of validators following some predefined rules. The admission/revocation information recorded in the blockchain are used by IoT devices to authenticate each other with a minimum communication and computation overhead.

A IoT device no longer needs to append its certificate to each message and the receiver has only to make a simple lookup to check if the sender has an entry in the blockchain with a valid status.

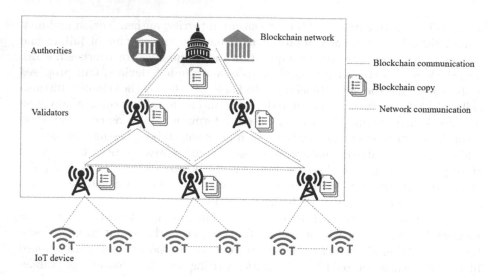

Fig. 1. General architecture of the system

3.2 IoT Device Registration

Before a IoT device IoT_i can join the network it needs first to generate a public-private key pair ($pkIoT_i$; $skIoT_i$), where the private key is kept secret and used to sign messages sent by IoT_i. The public key of IoT_i is made known to other IoT devices and is used by message recipients to verify message integrity, to authenticate the sender, and to check the membership status of IoT_i on the blockchain. To have a valid membership status on the blockchain, IoT_i needs to get enrollment certificates from corresponding authorities. Each authority a_j using its private key ska_j can issue a signed certificate to IoT_i if it is eligible. Finally, the obtained certificate is pushed to the blockchain network for validation through a registration transaction. The certificates are pushed by the according authorities and the transaction has the following format: $\langle$cert, registered, sig(sk_{a_j}, cert)$\rangle$, where cert is the generated certificate by the authority a_j, and sig is the signature of the certificate using sk_{a_j}. Mainly, the certificate contains the public key of the IoT device and the validity period.

3.3 IoT Device Admission

The blockchain network consists of a set of validators, $M = \{ m_1, m_2, m_3, .., m_k\}$, that execute a consensus algorithm to reach agreement about the state (authorization) of IoT devices. When the blockchain network receives a registration transaction from an authority to authorize a new IoT device, or reauthorize a revoked IoT device, the transaction will be accepted if it comes from an authenticated authority. When sufficient certificates for a particular IoT device IoT_i are received, one of the validators will generate a new admission transaction to add and mark the public key of the IoT device as valid in the blockchain.

The admission transaction has the following format: $\langle \text{pkIoT}_i, \text{valid}, \text{sig}(sk_{m_j}, pk_{IoT_i})\rangle$ of course the remaining validators will first check the correctness of the transaction before adding it to their local blockchain copy. The verification mainly consists of checking the validator's signature and that the concerned IoT device has sufficient certificates (registration transactions) on the blockchain.

3.4 IoT Device Authentication

Once a particular IoT device IoT_i is added and labelled in the blockchain as valid, it can join the network and start sending messages. Each IoT device that receives a message from IoT_i checks if the public key of IoT_i exists in the blockchain and is marked as valid. The receiver has to perform a simple lookup by searching the blockchain for a matching public key value. In contrast to a traditional PKI-based system, where the sender and the receiver have to include and verify a digital certificate, respectively, in our system a certificate is no longer included in the messages and the verification is replaced by a simple lookup function. The lookup function is much faster than the cryptographic signature verification of the certificate. This will considerably increase the performance of the system and improve the timeliness of incident announcements.

3.5 IoT Device Revocation

To enable a distributed revocation process, each IoT device IoT_j that detects misbehavior of IoT_i has to send a misbehavior transaction to notify the blockchain network. The misbehavior transaction has the following format: $\langle pk_{IoT_i}, \text{misbehavior}, \text{sig}(sk_{IoT_j}, Pk_{IoT_j})\rangle$, where pk_{IoT_i} is the public key of the suspected vehicle and sk_{IoT_j} is the private key of the IoT device that report the misbehavior. The validators will accept and add these transactions to the blockchain if they are originated from valid IoT device. These transactions will be later collectively considered to decide about whether revoking the membership of IoT_i is warranted. In order to revoke a suspected IoT device, a distributed revocation protocol will be executed by the blockchain validators. The revocation is generally based on rules set by a high authority and enforced by the validators. For instance, the validators can decide to revoke a particular IoT device IoT_i if more than n authentic misbehavior transactions for IoT_i are added to the blockchain in the past 24 h. If IoT_i is evicted from the network, one of the validators will create a revocation transaction and broadcast it to the blockchain network. The revocation transaction has the following format: $\langle pk_{IoT_i}, \text{revoked}, \text{sig}(sk_{m_j}, pk_{IoT_i})\rangle$, where pk_{IoT_i} is the public key of the IoT device to be evicted and sk_{m_j} is the private key of the validator. Once receiving the revocation transaction, the other validators will add it to the blockchain after checking the authenticity of its source. A summary of the different transactions used by our system is presented in Table 1.

Table 1. Summary of the used transactions

Transaction type	Sender	Transaction
Registration	Authorities	$\langle$cert, registered, sig(sk_{a_j}, cert)$\rangle$
Admission	Validators	$\langle$pkIoT$_i$, valid, sig(sk_{m_j}, pk_{IoT_i})$\rangle$
Misbehavior	IoT devices	$\langle pk_{IoT_i}$, misbehavior, sig(sk_{IoT_j}, Pk_{IoT_j})$\rangle$
Revocation	Validators	$\langle pk_{IoT_i}$, revoked, sig(sk_{m_j}, pk_{IoT_i})$\rangle$

4   Discussion

4.1   Storage Requirement and Optimization

1. **Multiple blockchains:** Instead of having only one blockchain that holds the different information related to IoT device registration, admission, misbehavior and revocation, each type of data can be stored in a distinct blockchain. In this case, IoT devices will use only the admission and revocation blockchains as they are sufficient to authenticate the source of any received message. Therefore, a considerable memory space can be saved.
2. **Cryptographic accumulator:** Another technique for optimizing the blockchain storage is by using cryptographic accumulator. As discussed in [12], the idea is to accumulate the set of valid IoT devices into one single digital object, where each IoT device IoTj will have a membership witness to prove that IoTj is already registered in the accumulator. In this case, only the accumulator will be saved on the blockchain, and vehicles have only to include their witness in their messages in order to allow the receiver to check the membership by applying a simple function. This will considerably decrease the size of the blockchain and can scale for very large network sizes without affecting the storage performance.

4.2   Performance Verification

By using a blockchain, the verification of IoT devices communication messages turns into a simple lookup to find whether the sender's public key exists with a valid status. In order to evaluate the verification time when using our scheme and compare it to the signature verification of digital certificate in conventional PKI, we have conducted the following experiment. To test the lookup function on a real scenario, we selected the Bitcoin blockchain as it is the largest existing one with millions of transaction entries. In Bitcoin, to speed up access and search operations, the levelDB database is used [3]. Bitcoin uses mainly two databases, the first one contains metadata about all known blocks and their location on disk. The second database contains a compact representation of all currently unspent transaction outputs (UTXO), in order to make it easier to validate a transaction for redeeming some bitcoins. It is worth noting that the database scheme can be customized to fit a specific requirement. In our experiment we calculated the response time when searching for a particular transaction in the blockchain database. By using levelDB C++, we can access directly to the database and then search for a particular transaction by its identifier (TXID). Several queries have been issued in the experiments and the response time has been averaged. A summary of the used database and the hardware setup for the experiment is given in Table 2. The result, by averaging 1000 queries shows that the average required time to look up for a transaction is about 0:012 ms. Whereas, when verifying a digital signature, by executing the program "Openssl speed ECDSA" which gives the verification time of the ECDSA, the result is about 0:1 ms for a key size of 256. The advantage of using blockchain in this case is very clear as the verification delay is nearly dropped by a factor of 10.

Table 2. Experiment setup

CPU	8 * Intel R Core(TM) i7-6700HQ 2.60 GHZ
CPU-cache	6144 KB
LevelDB	Version 1.1
Number of transactions	36328994

5 Conclusion

To sum up, using blockchain for securing authentication and access control management for internet of things is an efficient alternative to the traditional PKI-based systems. In this paper, we have presented a blockchain-based access control system management for IoT, which avoids the presence of a single point of failure and reduces both the communication and computation overhead. Our system take advantage of the distributed nature of the blockchain and the immutability of its records to provide a secure and lightweight authentication mechanism for inter IoT devices communication. Our system supports IoT devices registration, admission, misbehavior notification and revocation in a completely decentralized manner. Moreover, our system design eliminates the inherent heavy computation when verifying digital certificates and enables authentication using a simple lookup function. In summary, we believe that our proposed access system is a viable solution that offers better security and performance than the existing solutions.

References

1. Espiner, T.: Trustwave sold root certificate for surveillance (2012)
2. Fisher, D.: Final report on DigiNotar hack shows total compromise of CA servers
3. Swan, M.: Blockchain: Blueprint for a New Economy. O'Reilly Media Inc., Sebastopol (2015)

4. Conoscenti, M., Vetr, A., Martin, J.C.D.: Blockchain for the internet of things: a systematic literature review. In: The Third International Symposium on Internet of Things: Systems, Management and Security (IOTSMS 2016) (2016)
5. Wilson, D., Ateniese, G.: From pretty good to great: enhancing PGP using bitcoin and the blockchain. CoRR abs/1508.04868 (2015)
6. Zyskind, G., Nathan, O., Pentland, A.S.: Decentralizing privacy: using blockchain to protect personal data (2015)
7. Cha, S.-C., Chen, J.-F., Su, C., Yeh, K.-H.: A blockchain connected gateway for BLE-based devices in the internet of things. IEEE J. (2018). https://doi.org/10.1109/ACCESS.2018.2799942
8. Zhang, Y., Dukkipati, C., Cheng, L.C.: Decentralized, blockchain based access control framework for the heterogeneous internet of things. ACM (2018). https://doi.org/10.1145/3180457.3180458
9. Xu, R., Yu, C., Blasch, E., Chen, G.: A BLockchain-ENabled Decentralized Capability-Based Access Control for IoTs, BlendCAC (2018). https://arxiv.org/pdf/1804.09267.pdf
10. Ouaddah, A., Elkala, A.A., Ouahman, A.A.: Towards a novel privacy-preserving access control model based on blockchain technology in IoT. In: Europe and MENA Cooperation Advances in Information and Communication Technologies (2017)
11. Zhang, Y., Wen, J.: An IoT electric business model based on the protocol of bitcoin. In: Proceedings of the 2015 18th International Conference on Intelligence in Next Generation Networks, ICIN 2015, pp. 184–191. IEEE, France, February 2015
12. Crosby, M., Pattanayak, P., Verma, S., Kalyanaraman, V.: Blockchain technology: beyond bitcoin. Appl. Innov. **2**, 6–10 (2016)
13. Popov, S.: The tangle (2016). https://iota.org/IOTAWhitepaper.pdf
14. Miller, V.S.: Use of elliptic curves in cryptography. In: Williams, H.C. (ed.) CRYPTO 1985. LNCS, vol. 218, pp. 417–426. Springer, Heidelberg (1986). https://doi.org/10.1007/3-540-39799-X_31
15. Johnson, D., Menezes, A., Vanstone, S.: The elliptic curve digital signature algorithm (ECDSA). Int. J. Inf. Secur. **1**, 36–63 (2001)
16. Rivest, R.L., Shamir, A., Adleman, L.: A method for obtaining digital signatures and public-key cryptosystems. Commun. ACM **21**(2), 120–126 (1978)

Design of a New Patch Antenna Using EBG Structures and Superstarte Operating in the Ku-Band for 5G Cellular Networks

Sanae Dellaoui[✉], Adel Asselman, Saida Ahyoud,
Abdelmoumen Kaabal, Loubna Rmili, and Mustapha Elhalaoui

Optics and Photonics Team, Faculty of Sciences,
Abdelmalek Essaadi University, P.O. Box: 2121, Tetouan, Morocco
Sanae.dellaoui@gmail.com

Abstract. This paper describes a novel patch antenna operating in Ku-band at 17 GHz for the upcoming fifth generation (5G) cellular communication. A dielectric layer of an Electromagnetic Band Gap (EBG) superstrate is applied above the antenna and four metallic EBGs structures are added for further directivity improvement. AL-shape slot generates the resonance and enhances the antenna performance. The overall size of the antenna is 20 * 20 mm. The antenna is linearly polarized in the band 17 GHz with an impedance bandwidth from 16.59 GHz to 18.19 GHz for $|S_{11}| < -10$ dB. The proposed antenna using EBGs has a directivity of greater than 9 dBi over frequency band. This proposed antenna is designed with CST Microwave Studio. The simulated results show that the directivity of the antenna is significantly improved. Due to the remarkable performance of the proposed antenna, it can be suitable to be used in 5G network communication.

Keywords: Electromagnetic Band Gap (EBG) · Fifth generation (5G) ·
Patch antenna

1 Introduction

In recent years, have been significant developments in the research on 5th Generation (5G) system networks to be launched in 2020. They must support the growing demand for unprecedented numbers of antennas and extreme base station and device densities. Predictably, 5G will provide ultrafast broadband as an 4G, in addition to integrating low-latency and ultra-reliable features that will enable a wide range of new services [1].

High directivity antenna and the broadband are required to increase the rate of data transmitted per second, and provide as much as possible the same quality of service everywhere responding to the rise of smart devices.

To increase the directivity, this article proposes a new patch antenna using four EBGs Structures etched on the substrate near to the patch. And adding the EBG superstrate dielectric above the ground plane by a half wavelength ($\lambda_0/2$) and of a quarter dielectric wavelength thicknesses ($\lambda_g/4$) [2–4].

É. Renault et al. (Eds.): MSPN 2019, LNCS 11557, pp. 61–68, 2019.
https://doi.org/10.1007/978-3-030-22885-9_6

Electromagnetic band-gap (EBG) structures are periodic and are widely used, notably for antenna applications [5, 6], which may be realized by drilling or etching on the metal or dielectric substrates, to improve the performance of antennas, especially to improve the gain/radiation patterns, and to decrease losses in transmissions. EBG structures are the very promising candidates to exterminate the problems created by surface waves while at the same time improving the performance [7, 8]. By using the EBG substrates for patch antennas, the surface wave effects are significantly reduced and are able to provide relatively broadband frequency performance.

A patch antenna operating at 17 GHz for the upcoming 5G applications is presented. The EBG superstrate and a novel EBGs structures are designed to improve the directivity with a good radiation behavior [9]. The proposed antenna is constructed using a classical patch rectangular with an L-shape slot and other shaped slots on the top corners of the patch. The simulated results show that the proposed antenna can achieve the reflection coefficient less than −10 dB over 16.6–18.22 GHz, and increase the directivity more than 9 dBi with a large bandwidth which increases the data transmission.

2 Proposed Antenna

The configuration of the proposed antenna is demonstrated in Fig. 1. An L-shape slot is etched on the patch; it generates the resonance and enhances the antenna performance. The dimensions of the patch are: width W = 5 mm, length L = 7 mm. Antenna is printed on a FR4 substrate (relative permittivity ε_0 = 4.4, loss tangent tanδ = 0.025 and thickness h = 0.8 mm) and it is alimented by a 50 Ω microstrip line feed. And the dimensions of the L-shape are: a = 3.1 mm, b = 1.8 mm and c = 0.9 mm. The ground plane is placed on the bottom side of the substrate. The total size of the antenna is 20 mm × 20 mm.

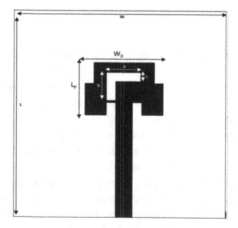

Fig. 1. Proposed microstrip patch antenna

The proposed antenna is designed by CST Microwave Studio Electromagnetic Solver. And it has a resonant frequency of 17 GHz, Fig. 2(a) shows the reflection coefficient (<−35 dB) of the antenna resonating at 17 GHz with the bandwidth from 16.56 GHz to 18.19 GHz (1.63 GHz). And Fig. 2(b) shows us the 3D radiation pattern of the antenna; the proposed antenna gets 7.02 dB at 17 GHz.

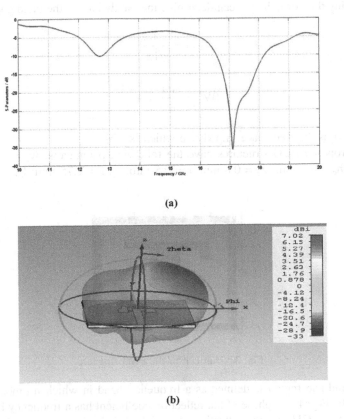

(a)

(b)

Fig. 2. The simulated characteristics of the proposed antenna, (a) the reflection coefficient and (b) the 3D radiation pattern

3   EBG Structure

We propose a novel compact EBG structure; shown in Fig. 3. It consists of a patch, a dielectric substrate, a via to connect the patch and a metallic ground plane.

The parameters of the EBG structure are labeled as patch width w_e, length L_e, and via radius r. The inductor L dues to the current along adjacent vias, and the capacitor C results from the gap effect between the adjacent metal patches. The values of the inductor L and the capacitor C of the LC circuit are determined by the following formula

$$L = \mu_0 \mu_r h \tag{1}$$

$$C = \left(\frac{\frac{W \varepsilon_0 (1 + \varepsilon_r)}{\pi} \cosh^{-1}(w + g)}{g} \right) \tag{2}$$

By using this formula, we can determine the bandwidth of the band gap frequency

$$\omega = \frac{1}{\sqrt{LC}} \tag{3}$$

$$BW = \frac{\Delta \omega}{\omega} = \frac{\frac{1}{\eta} \sqrt{L}}{\sqrt{C}} \tag{4}$$

Where η is the free space impedance which is 120π.

The proposed EBG structures have the following parameters: $w_e = 4.7$ mm; $l_e = 4.7$ mm; $h_e = 0.3$ mm; $g_e = 0.8$ mm; $r = 0.5$ mm; $we1 = 2.75$ mm; $l_{e1} = 0.75$ mm.

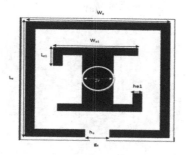

Fig. 3. Unit cell of the EBG structure

The band gap region is defined as a frequency band in which no mode is propagated. In the Fig. 4, the phase of the reflection coefficient has a frequency band gap of 10.5 GHz to 18 GHz for the reflection phase which is in the range of +90° ±45°.

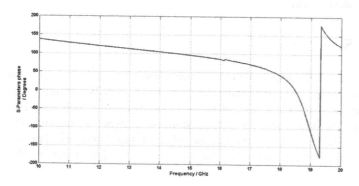

Fig. 4. Reflection phase of the EBG structure

An EBG superstrate dielectric layer the FR4 of a thickness $\lambda_g/4$ is mounted over a radiating patch antenna at a distance $\lambda_0/2$, (see Fig. 5); and is used to improve the directivity. Multiple reflections that happen between the patches and the EBG superstrate provide a spatial filtering for focusing the main beam radiation of the antenna that allows enhancement for the antenna directivity.

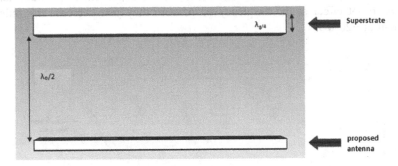

Fig. 5. Proposed antenna with EBG superstrate dielectric

4 Directivity Improvement Using EBG

4.1 Proposed Antenna Using EBGs

The proposed antenna (Fig. 6) contains of rectangular microstrip patch antenna with L-shape slot, four EBGs metal structures etched on the substrate FR4 and separated by distance g = 0.3 mm. And a dielectric superstrate applied above the antenna by 8.53 mm with thickness 2.1 mm.

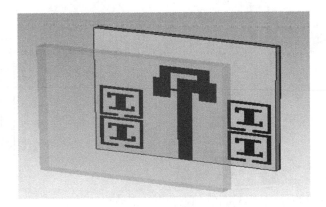

Fig. 6. Proposed antenna with EBGs

4.2   Simulation and Results

All simulations and the optimization process are performed using a software simulator CST, which is based on Finite Integration Technique (FIT). The reflection coefficient of the proposed antenna acts as a disruption to the transmission of data ($S_{11} < -10$ dB) then 90% of power excited is transmitted. The Fig. 7 shows the reflection coefficient of the antenna with and without the EBGs structures and the superstrate. We found that the EBGs have not effect at the frequency adaptation; they just decrease the reflection coefficient at -26 dB.

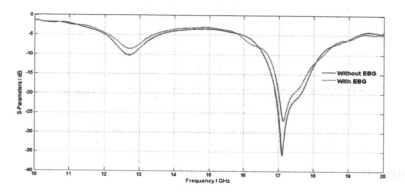

Fig. 7. The simulated S_{11} with and without the EBGs

The 3D radiation pattern for the proposed antenna is shown in Fig. 8; the directivity increase more than 9 dB. The radiation efficiency is rather good that is more than 76% at 17 GHz frequency band. And it notices that it is a directional antenna with the small back lobes, and allows us to visualize where the antenna transmits or receives power.

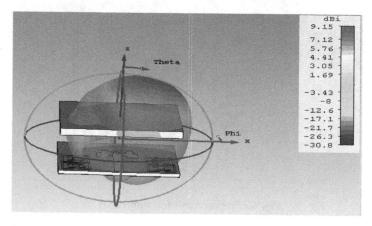

Fig. 8. The 3D radiation pattern for the proposed antenna with EBGs at 17 GHz

Figure 9 presents the directivity of the antenna without and with the EBG structures and the EBG cover as the frequency varies. One can see from Fig. 9 that the directivity reaches its maximum at a frequency of 17 GHz with the EBGs. For a frequency below 17 GHz, the EBG forbids electromagnetic waves to propagate through the EBG superstrate, and thus decreases the directivity. For a frequency above 17 GHz, the electromagnetic field can propagate through the superstrate, but has a component parallel to the upper surface, and this decreases the directivity. Table 1 demonstrates the increase in peak directivity after loading with EBGs.

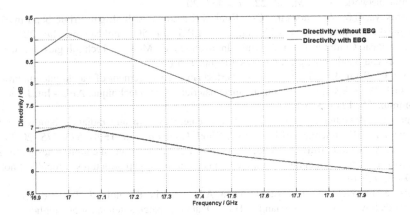

Fig. 9. Directivity versus frequency.

Table 1. Performance of antenna configurations with and without EBGs

	Without EBGS	With EBGS
BW (GHz)	1.68	1.63
S_{11} (dB)	−35	−26
Directivity (dB)	7.02	9.15

5   Conclusion

In this paper, a new patch antenna and a novel configuration of EBG structures have been applied to increase the directivity and to have a good bandwidth (1.63 GHz) for the band at 17 GHz (16.6–18.22 GHz). High directivity characteristics have been achieved by employing four EBGs structures and an EBG dielectric superstrate. The proposed antenna is a good candidate for 5G applications.

References

1. Andrews, J.G., et al.: What Will 5G Be? IEEE J. Sel. Areas Commun. **32**(6), 1065–1082 (2014)
2. Qiu, M., He, S.: High-directivity patch antenna with both photonic bandgap substrate and photonic bandgap cover. Microw. Opt. Technol. Lett. **30**(1), 41–44 (2001)
3. Kaabal, A., et al.: Design of EBG antenna with multi-sources excitation for high directivity applications. Proc. Manuf. **22**, 598–604 (2018)
4. Dellaoui, S., et al.: Patch array antenna with high gain using EBG superstrate for future 5G cellular networks. Proc. Manuf. **22**, 463–467 (2018)
5. Karthikeya, G.S., Abegaonkar, M.P., Koul, S.K.: Low cost high gain triple band mmWave Sierpinski antenna loaded with uniplanar EBG for 5G applications. In: 2017 IEEE International Conference on Antenna Innovations & Modern Technologies for Ground, Aircraft and Satellite Applications (iAIM), pp. 1–5 (2017)
6. Arora, C., Pattnaik, S.S., Baral, R.N.: Performance enhancement of patch antenna array for 5.8 GHz Wi-MAX applications using metamaterial inspired technique. AEU - Int. J. Electron. Commun. **79**, 124–131 (2017)
7. Leger, L., Monediere, T., Jecko, B.: Enhancement of gain and radiation bandwidth for a planar 1-D EBG antenna. IEEE Microw. Wirel. Compon. Lett. **15**(9), 573–575 (2005)
8. Kaabal, A., Halaoui, M.E., Ahyoud, S., Asselman, A.: A low mutual coupling design for array microstrip antennas integrated with electromagnetic band-gap structures. Proc. Technol. **22**, 549–555 (2016)
9. Souza e Silva Neto, A., Torres de Oliveira, A.L., de Brito Espinola, S., Freire de Melo, J.R., Lucas da Silva, J., Chaves Fernandes, H.C.: Dual band patch antenna for 5G applications with EBG structure in the ground plane and substrate. In: Rocha, Á., Correia, A.M., Adeli, H., Reis, L.P., Costanzo, S. (eds.) WorldCIST 2017. AISC, vol. 570, pp. 1044–1049. Springer, Cham (2017). https://doi.org/10.1007/978-3-319-56538-5_107

A Data-Filtering Approach
for Large-Scale Integrated RFID
and Sensor Networks

Mourad Ouadou[1]([✉]), Hajar Sahbani[1], Ouadoudi Zytoune[1,2],
and Mohamed Ouadou[1]

[1] LRIT Laboratory, Faculty of Science, Mohammed V University in Rabat,
Rabat, Morocco
mourad.ouadou@gmail.com
[2] Systems Engineering Laboratory, Ibn Tofail University, 14060 Kenitra, Morocco

Abstract. Radio-Frequency identification, referred as RFID, is a technology for storing and retrieving data remotely using radio-labeled tags.
Tags are small objects, and can be pasted or incorporated into objects
and products or even implanted in living organisms. In the last years,
several researches have focused on how to take benefit from this technology to build performing rechargeable sensor networks. The fusion of
both technologies can extend widely the network's lifetime and improve
it performances since radio communications are only performed between
readers and not between sensor tags. However, the RFID sensor networks present some drawbacks due to the random deployment especially
for large scale systems, which can disturb the system's performances and
cause issues such as data duplication, and medium access control (MAC)
collisions. In this paper, we deal especially with the redundancy problem by proposing an algorithm that avoids a priori the transmission of
duplicated data before sending it into the network. Our approach can
be considered as proactive since it predicts duplication by planning a
first network discovery phase. Our scheme showed good performances in
terms of latency, packet delivery, and computational cost.

Keywords: RFID · Sensors · Reader/tag · Collision · Filtering

1 Introduction

Nowadays, Wireless Sensor Networks (WSNs) are increasingly used in many
applications [1–3], and gaining more scientific interest to improve the features of
such networks [4,5]. These networks are deployed to monitor the physical environment such temperature and humidity. As nodes are small components that
suffer from very limited energy resources, several research works have focused
on the problem of network's lifetime prolongation [6–8]. However, the contributions proposed in the literature, which tend to optimize the network's lifetime by
proposing new routing protocols for example, have recently showed their limits.

© Springer Nature Switzerland AG 2019
E. Renault et al. (Eds.): MSPN 2019, LNCS 11557, pp. 69–81, 2019.
https://doi.org/10.1007/978-3-030-22885-9_7

The trend is now for searching new solutions taking benefit from many energy harvesting technologies [9]. Among these technologies, we can find techniques of recovering energy from ambient environment as Radio Frequency waves [10,11]. In this area, the Radio Frequency Identifications (RFID) has emerged as an alternative solution of typical battery-limited sensors [12,13]. This technology is used since 1970 in order to track objects and animals [14]. It uses electromagnetic fields to automatically identify and track labels attached to objects. The tags contain information stored electronically [15]. There are two types of tags: Passive and Active [16]. Passive tags collect energy from reader that interrogates it using radio waves. Active tags have a local power source such as a battery and can operate hundreds of meters from the RFID reader. The integration of RFID technology with the sensor networks is a fairly recent idea. Indeed, conventional RFID systems that only harvest simple data such as an identification as a single numerical value. The idea here is to combine RFID systems with sensors embedded on tags. Such integration takes benefit from the synergy between the two technologies by converging the sensing capability of WSNs with the RFID identification capabilities for an integration into the internet of things (IoT) context [17]. This conducts to several applications which require a strong synergy between the detection and the marking, in particular in the industrial and agricultural fields.

However, in RFID systems, several issues are reported and many challenges need to be addressed. Among these issues, we mention the problems of medium access control (MAC) layer collisions [18] and data redundancy [19] and also security. In fact, the deployment of RFID systems, that include tags and readers, is usually not optimal. The tags can be located in the reading area of two or more readers. These two problems may decrease significantly the performances of the system [20].

This work is motivated by a concern of reducing of the impact of RFID system issues over the integrated network. We propose in this paper a solution based on a proactive approach that deals with the data duplication problem. The pro activity of our approach is very important since it allows the elimination of redundant data before it transmission into the network.

The remain of the paper is organized as follow; we start with presenting the problematic faced by the RFID systems related to the random deployment, in Sect. 3 we present our solution of the data duplication problem to the problem. In Sect. 4 we present simulation results where we validate our solution. Finally, Sect. 5 gives a conclusion and presents some perspectives to future works.

2   Problem Presentation

In this section, we introduce some issues related essentially to the random deployment of RFID tags.

2.1   Deployment Problem

One of the most relevant problems in any RFID system is the deployment problem [21]. This problem can be defined as a problem of energy supply. The solutions for this problem tend to optimize the network in order that all sensor tags receive a minimum of energy to transmit data to the readers. However this solution has to take into consideration the overlap between the reading fields of readers as illustrated in Fig. 1.

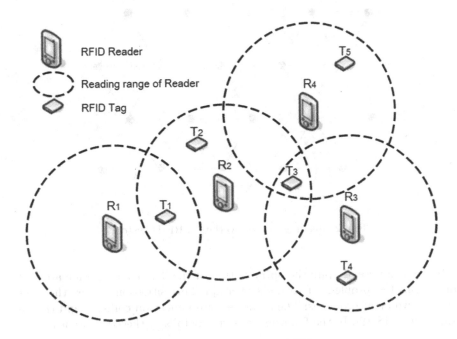

Fig. 1. Reading range overlap in RFID system.

Definition 1. *A RFId tag i is powered by reader if the average recharge power it receives P_r is higher than a minimum power P_s necessary to perform send data. We also say that the entire network is powered if all the tags are powered.*

This problem is similar to the coverage problem in traditional WSNs, where sensors are deployed to sufficiently monitor a region of interest. However, an essential difference between the two problems is the direction of signal transmission: Tags are charged from the RF signals transmitted by the deployed readers while the sensor nodes are deployed to detect the signal transmitted by the targets in a typical coverage problem. Since the wireless recharge model of tags is fundamentally different from the sensor detection model, existing solutions to the coverage problem in traditional WSNs can't be applied to the energy powered problem.

For this purpose, we refer to the point provisioning solution presented in [22] to define the conditions where it is considered that a tag is energy provisioned by a reader. So we consider the situation where a minimal number of readers are deployed over the area. Figure 2 shows the adopted model based on triangle deployment.

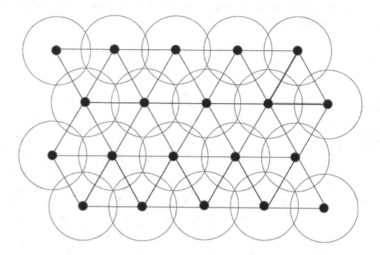

Fig. 2. Reading ranges overlap in RFID system.

As we can note, despite the optimization of the deployment, some areas still suffer from the problem of reader's overlap. This situation causes the occurrence of two main problems: The reader's communication collision and the data redundancy [18,19]. In the following, we give details of these two issues.

2.2   Reader's Communication Collision

In a multi-channel network, readers could use different channels to read tags, but that does not prevent collisions. To better illustrate this problem, we consider Fig. 3 where the dashed lines represent the communication links between readers, the small circles show the reader's radius of action, the dashed circles show the interference radius of the adjacent channels, and the large circles illustrate the radius of the reader interference. The readers R1 and R2 can communicate in a wireless manner and they are in the communication range of each other. In a multi-channel RFID network, if two readers use the same frequency to read labels, regardless of the distance between them, the tags in the overlapping area of their fields will not be read. But if two players use different playback channels, even if they are active at the same time, the tags in the overlay area of their fields will be read successfully if and only the distance between the readers is greater than 3.3 dRT [23].

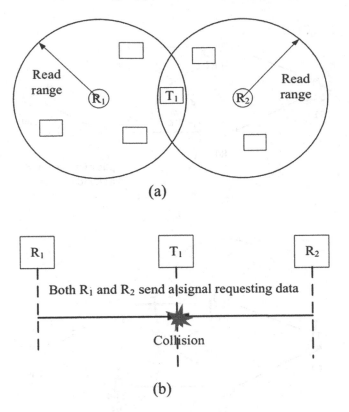

Fig. 3. Reading ranges overlap in RFID system.

2.3   Data Redundancy Problem

As previously explained, the majority of architectures proposed for the integration of RFID with sensor networks consider the tags as semi-active. In this situation, tags are equipped with small and low-capacity batteries in order to perform local tasks, such as capturing and processing data. So the most energy consuming task related to sending and receiving data, is not supported by the sensor's battery. This explains the passivity of the tags during data transmission. However, this passivity has lead to a situation where tags ignore the topology of network, so the transmission of data is performed blindly.

So when a reader is located on the reading area of two tags, there is no way the tag can detect that the generated data will go to two or more readers since it's passive at this moment. This is the cause why data duplication is triggered without being detected by the tags.

In this paper, we first consider that only readers form the topology, and tags are considered passives. We also consider that the topology formed is a mesh, where readers exchange routing tables. To better control the problem, and following a policy of divide and rule, we partition the problem of data redundancy

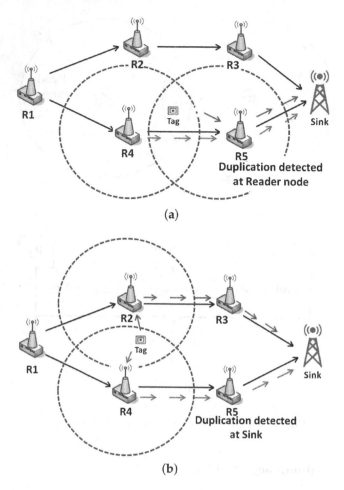

Fig. 4. Data duplication problem (a) intra-path data duplication between Reader 4 and Reader 5; (b) extra-path data duplication between Reader 2 and Reader 4.

as two sub-problems: intra and extra path problems. For this purpose, we consider that mesh topology is adopted to organize the communication between readers also considered as routers.

As we can notice in Fig. 4a, the intra-path duplication of data can be easily detected and removed at one hop. Meanwhile, extra path duplication shown in Fig. 4b is difficult to detect before reaching the sink. That explains why the main effort of this paper is to try to resolve the extra path duplication problem by prediction.

3 Proposed Solution

In this section, we present a solution for the extra path problem caused by the overlapping readers. Our solution is based on three phases to prepare the network: Preliminary phase (PP), network discovery phase (NDP).

3.1 The Preliminary Phase

In this first phase, the network has to choose which readers will start the NDP phase. For this purpose, the sink will send a message to all readers including the number of hops (incremented at each hop) and a sequence number. The main goal is to identify for each potential route, the node with maximum number of hops to reach the sink. If a reader considers itself as the node with maximum hops to sink, it will be elect to start the second phase. In Fig. 5, we can see an example of the message broadcast over the network.

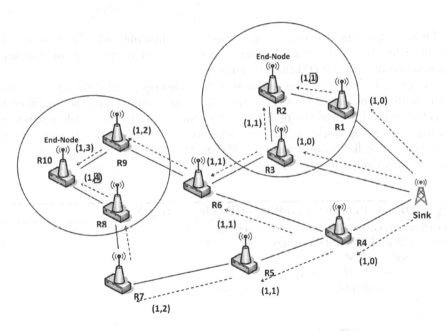

Fig. 5. Message broadcast over the network.

3.2 Network Discovery Phase

In this phase, the goal is to detect which reader nodes generate duplicated data. To do that, the nodes elected at the previous phase will send a message (Discovery Message) including a list of the tags located in their reading area. The final goal at end will be to obtain a list of all tags associated to readers. However, in order to deal only with extra path duplication, the detected intra-path duplication, detected at this phase will be removed. At the end we will only obtain redundancy caused by the extra path problem.

The Discovery Message (DM) includes the list of tag for reach reader. This list will be updated at each hop. Also for each tag, we include the number of hops and a filtered status. The structure of the DM is shown in Fig. 6.

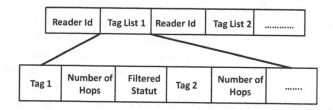

Fig. 6. Structure of discovery message.

During this phase, two algorithms must be implemented. The first one is executed by the all the reader nodes and the second is executed by the sink when it receives all the DM from all routes.

In the first algorithm, the reader starts by checking and deleting the intra-path duplication. The process is simple, if a tag coming from the neighbor is detected in the PM, and the reader has the same tag in it list, it delete it before sending the message forward. Each reader that receives the PM will perform this step, add it tag list, and forward the PM to the sink via the next reader. The process is explained in Algorithm 1.

Algorithm 1. Filtering Algorithm at Reader During NDP

Require: Discovery Message (DM) received
Ensure: Send Filtered DM to next hop
1: On receiving DM
2: **if** $\exists$ $Owntag \in DM$ **then**
3:     Filter Duplication
4: **end if**
5: $DM \leftarrow DM \oplus t_i$
6: Increment number of hops
7: Send DM to next reader

When all the DMs arrive to the sink, the second algorithm can be executed. It has first to detect the duplication. Since all intra-path duplication has been removed, the redundancy detected must necessarily be an extra path. When duplication is detected for the same tag, knowing that each tag is associated with it reader, the algorithm will check which tag id has the minimum number of tags. The tag with minimum number of hops will be stored in a message called request message, which will be later sent to each reader. Finally the main goal is to predict which generate the duplication, filter the duplication with maximum number of hops, and ask for the readers with minimum number of hops to send the list of tags and eventually the related data. At the end of this phase, a request message (RM) is sent to each reader with a list of tags that he can send into the network. The rest will be filtered locally. This process is explained in Algorithm 2.

Algorithm 2. Filtering Algorithm at Sink during NDP

Require: All Discovery Messages Received
Ensure: Send Request Messages
1: **if** DM_i received **then**
2:     $S \leftarrow S \oplus DM_i$ {Add the ith Discovery message (DM) to sink list (S).}
3: **end if**
4: **for all** Tag Ids in S **do**
5:     **if** $\exists\ S_i$ duplicated with S_j **then**
6:         Filter tag with minimum number of hops
7:     **end if**
8: **end for**
9: Send Request Message $RM_{id_{reader}}$ from S to each Reader.

---

4   Simulation and Results

In this section, we evaluate the performances of our approach by calculating the amount of transmitted data into the network. The main goal was to improve the capacities of the RFID systems by reducing the number of packets transmitted, which conduct to the reduction of delay and computational cost. The simulations were performed using the Network Simulator 2 (NS-2). In the performed simulations, we consider a case of a random deployment of tags over a restricted area of 200×200 m. We consider that tags are semi-actives. Thus, the communications will only be performed between readers. Table 1 show more simulations details.

In order to evaluate the performances of the system, we focus on three main metrics that will reflect the capacity of predicting the data duplication. These parameters are cited below:

– Number of packets transmitted
– Number of filtered packets into the network
– Average delay

To obtain significant result, we compare our approach with to other methods in literature based in tree topology [24] called In-network phased filtering mechanism -INPFM and the second one based on clustering called clustering called In-network RFID data filtering IRFD [25]. Note that in the figures, we call our method: Proactive Data-Filtering-Scheme PDFS.

Table 1. Simulation parameters

Simulation parameters	Values
Deployment area	200 m × 200 m
Maximum number of tags	300
Minimum number of readers	40
Reading range	10 m
Transmission range	30 m
Reading period	15 s
Duplication rates	10%; 40%

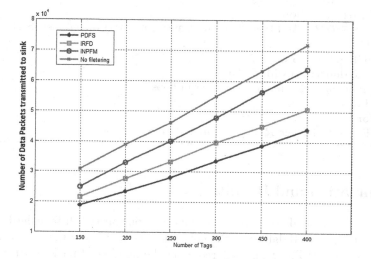

Fig. 7. Number of transmitted packets.

Let's start with the first result. As we can see in Fig. 7, the number of transmitted packets is considerably reduced when using our approach, in comparison with IRFD and INPFM.

The second result concerns the number of filtered packets filtered into the network shown in Fig. 8. As we can see, this number is reduced by our approach. This is not because our method filters less packets than other approaches, but it's due by the fact that in our scheme, data is filtered before being sent into the network. This reduce considerably the computational cost and delay in the system.

Thus, the final result concerns the delay. The fact that computational cost is reduced, and less data is sent into the network, reduce considerably the average delay into the network as we can notice in Fig. 9.

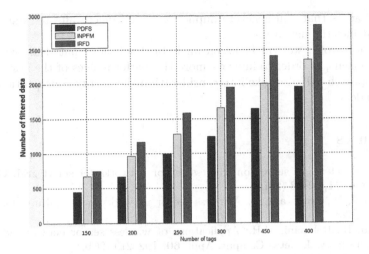

Fig. 8. Number of filtered packets into the network.

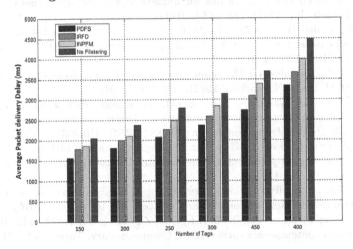

Fig. 9. Number of filtered packets into the network.

5   Conclusion and Perspectives

In conclusion, the integration of RFID system with wireless sensor networks technology has a major advantage in terms of reducing the transmission costs that the sensors must support. In these systems, readers are responsible for the transmission of data, when sensors (integrated to tags) simply read the data and stores.

However, such type of sensor networks has to deal with problems related to RFID systems. In this paper we presented the major problems for these systems: MAC layer collisions and data duplication. In this context, we detailed our solution for the second problem. Our scheme was based on a predictive approach that detects readers that will generate duplication, and delete affected data before sending it into the network.

In future work, we will focus on an hybrid solution that deals with both RFID problems, in order to improve more the performances of the system. Our future approach will also take into consideration the energy consumption of the RFID readers.

References

1. Fadel, E., et al.: A survey on wireless sensor networks for smart grid. Comput. Commun. **71**, 22–33 (2015)
2. Shinghal, D., Srivastava, N.: Wireless sensor networks in agriculture: for potato farming (2017)
3. Rashid, B., Rehmani, M.H.: Applications of wireless sensor networks for urban areas: a survey. J. Netw. Comput. Appl. **60**, 192–219 (2016)
4. Han, G., Liu, L., Jiang, J., Shu, L., Hancke, G.: Analysis of energy-efficient connected target coverage algorithms for industrial wireless sensor networks. IEEE Trans. Industr. Inf. **13**(1), 135–143 (2017)
5. Kurt, S., Yildiz, H.U., Yigit, M., Tavli, B., Gungor, V.C.: Packet size optimization in wireless sensor networks for smart grid applications. IEEE Trans. Industr. Electron. **64**(3), 2392–2401 (2017)
6. Chang, J.H., Tassiulas, L.: Maximum lifetime routing in wireless sensor networks. IEEE/ACM Trans. Networking **12**(4), 609–619 (2004)
7. Yao, Y., Cao, Q., Vasilakos, A.V.: EDAL: an energy-efficient, delay-aware, and lifetime-balancing data collection protocol for heterogeneous wireless sensor networks. IEEE/ACM Trans. Networking (TON) **23**(3), 810–823 (2015)
8. Dong, M., Ota, K., Liu, A., Guo, M.: Joint optimization of lifetime and transport delay under reliability constraint wireless sensor networks. IEEE Trans. Parallel Distrib. Syst. **1**, 1–1 (2016)
9. Shaikh, F.K., Zeadally, S.: Energy harvesting in wireless sensor networks: a comprehensive review. Renew. Sustain. Energy Rev. **55**, 1041–1054 (2016)
10. Lu, X., Wang, P., Niyato, D., Kim, D.I., Han, Z.: Wireless networks with RF energy harvesting: a contemporary survey. IEEE Commun. Surv. Tutorials **17**(2), 757–789 (2015)
11. Naderi, M.Y., Chowdhury, K.R., Basagni, S.: Wireless sensor networks with RF energy harvesting: energy models and analysis. In: 2015 IEEE Wireless Communications and Networking Conference (WCNC), pp. 1494–1499. IEEE, March 2015
12. Farris, I., Militano, L., Iera, A., Molinaro, A., Spinella, S.C.: Tag-based cooperative data gathering and energy recharging in wide area RFID sensor networks. Ad Hoc Netw. **36**, 214–228 (2016)
13. Mejjaouli, S., Babiceanu, R.F.: RFID-wireless sensor networks integration: decision models and optimization of logistics systems operations. J. Manuf. Syst. **35**, 234–245 (2015)
14. Kim, S.H., Kim, D.H., Park, H.D.: Animal situation tracking service using RFID, GPS, and sensors. In: 2010 Second International Conference on Computer and Network Technology (ICCNT), pp. 153–156. IEEE, April 2010
15. Rofougaran, A.R., Rofougaran, M., Shameli, A.: U.S. Patent No. 7,679,514. Washington, DC: U.S. Patent and Trademark Office (2010)

16. Bouet, M., Dos Santos, A.L.: RFID tags: positioning principles and localization techniques. In: Wireless Days, WD 2008. 1st IFIP, pp. 1–5. IEEE, November 2008
17. Cuomo, F., Della Luna, S., Cipollone, E., Todorova, P., Suihko, T.: Topology formation in IEEE 802.15. 4: cluster-tree characterization. In: Sixth Annual IEEE International Conference on Pervasive Computing and Communications, PerCom 2008, pp. 276–281. IEEE, March 2008
18. Liu, Q., Xu, J., Yang, L., Hu, J., Song, T.: An energy-aware and time-efficient adaptive multi-tree anti-collision protocol for RFID systems. In: 2018 IEEE International Conference on RFID Technology and Application (RFID-TA), pp. 1–6. IEEE, September 2018
19. Bashir, A.K., Lim, S.J., Hussain, C.S., Park, M.S.: Energy efficient in-network RFID data filtering scheme in wireless sensor networks. Sensors 11(7), 7004–7021 (2011)
20. Yoon, W.J., Chung, S.H., Lee, S.J.: Implementation and performance evaluation of an active RFID system for fast tag collection. Comput. Commun. 31(17), 4107–4116 (2008)
21. Grover, A., Berghel, H.: A survey of RFID deployment and security issues. J. Inf. Process. Syst. 7(4), 561–580 (2011)
22. He, S., Chen, J., Jiang, F., Yau, D.K., Xing, G., Sun, Y.: Energy provisioning in wireless rechargeable sensor networks. IEEE Trans. Mob. Comput. 12(10), 1931–1942 (2013)
23. Amadou, I., Mitton, N.: HAMAC: high adaptive MAC protocol for dense RFID reader-to-reader networks. In: International Conference on Ad Hoc Networks (AdHocNets), September 2015
24. Choi, W., Park, M.S.: In-network phased filtering mechanism for a large-scale RFID inventory application. In: Proceedings of the 4th International Conference on IT and Applications (ICITA), pp. 401–405, January 2007
25. Bashir, A.K., Park, M.-S., Lee, S.-I., Park, J., Lee, W., Shah, S.C.: In-network RFID data filtering scheme in RFID-WSN for RFID applications. In: Lee, J., Lee, M.C., Liu, H., Ryu, J.-H. (eds.) ICIRA 2013. LNCS (LNAI), vol. 8103, pp. 454–465. Springer, Heidelberg (2013). https://doi.org/10.1007/978-3-642-40849-6_46

High Gain Metallic Electromagnetic Band Gap Antenna for WLAN Applications

Loubna Rmili[✉], Adel Asselman, Abdelmoumen Kaabal,
Sanae Dellaoui, and Mustapha El Halaoui

Optics and Photonics Team, Faculty of Sciences, Abdelmalek Essaadi, P.O.
BOX: 2121, Tetouan, Morocco
loubnarmili@gmail.com

Abstract. In this paper we presented a Metallic electromagnetic band gap antenna operated on the frequency band 5 GHz which it can be suitable for wireless Local Area Network (WLAN). The proposed antenna contains vertical and horizontal M-EBG printed on a FR4 substrate fed by a 50 Ω feed line. The results exhibit that the proposed antenna shows better performances with M-EBG structures than without M-EBG structures. The antenna design parameters have been optimized by High Frequency Structural Simulator (HFSS), the simulated results shows that the gain of the proposed antenna with metallic electromagnetic band gap had improved and reaches more than 11 dB, the main purpose of this work is to validate the importance and the influence of Metallic electromagnetic band gap.

Keywords: Metallic Electromagnetic Band Gap M-EBG · HFSS · WLAN

1 Introduction

The research that has been done over the past decade has resulted to propose new structures for the antennas design and has always led to improvement.

Sectorial antennas [1] are typically used at base stations in cellular communication systems [2]. They have a directional beam in one plane and a broader beam in the other. In addition, these antennas can be vertically or horizontally polarized depending on the current application [3].

Electromagnetic Band Gap (EBG) structures used in several applications such as wireless local networks area (WLAN) [4] and satellite communication. The strong development of wireless telecommunications networks [5, 6] requires base station antennas with sectorial radiation pattern. A strong gain is necessary to cover ever larger cells. Studies carried out on metallic Electromagnetic Band gap (M-EBG) materials [7–9] which leads to design those antennas. These materials have allowed researches to replace very binding by simple structures and easy to achieve, and addition they brought innovation in several fields of electromagnetism and telecommunications [10].

High gain antenna is required to increase the performance of those antennas, and to increase it, this paper proposes an antenna covered by horizontal and vertical Metallic Electromagnetic Band Gap. The structure proposed is can be able to generate the norm IEEE 802.11a WLAN applications (Wireless Local Area Network) which it can

É. Renault et al. (Eds.): MSPN 2019, LNCS 11557, pp. 82–87, 2019.
https://doi.org/10.1007/978-3-030-22885-9_8

evidently operate at the frequency 5 GHz. The Metallic Electromagnetic Band Gap shows a good radiation behavior, the simulated results show that the proposed antenna could achieve the return loss less than −10 dB, and increase the gain more than 11 dB with a directive behavior.

2 Proposed Antenna

The design geometry of the proposed antenna is shown in Fig. 1. It contains such as horizontal and vertical Metallic Electromagnetic Band Gap, printed on a FR4 substrate with dielectric constant 4.4 and thickness h = 1.6 mm. the dimension of the patch are: width = 40 mm, length = 184 mm calculated with the Eqs. (1) and (3) [11], the patch is excited by a SMA coaxial whose internal conductor diameter is equal to 0.0635 mm and the external conductor diameter is equal to 2.1 mm.

$$W = \frac{c}{2fr\sqrt{\frac{\varepsilon r+1}{2}}} \tag{1}$$

The effective permittivity εeff is given by:

$$\varepsilon eff = \frac{\varepsilon r + 1}{2} + \frac{\varepsilon r - 1}{2}\left(1 + 12\frac{h}{w}\right) \tag{2}$$

The parameter L of the patch has determined by the following formula [11]:

$$L = \frac{c}{2fr\sqrt{\varepsilon eff}} - 2\Delta L \tag{3}$$

Where εeff is the effective permittivity of the proposed antenna, the additional line length ΔL is given by the equation below:

$$\Delta L = \frac{0.421h(\varepsilon eff + 0.3)(\frac{h}{w} + 0.26)}{(\varepsilon eff - 0.258)(\frac{w}{h} + 0.8)} \tag{4}$$

The parameter of the EBG structure is calculated with the Eq. (5) and the dimension of the M-EBG are calculated to have WLAN-band at 5 GHz.

$$a = \frac{\lambda g}{4} = \frac{c}{4f0\sqrt{\varepsilon e}} \tag{5}$$

The height of the cavity is computed by the Eq. (6):

$$Hcavity = \frac{\lambda 0}{2} \tag{6}$$

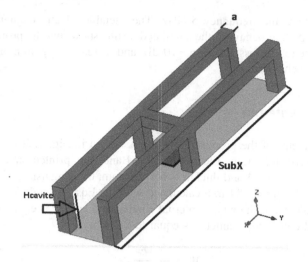

Fig. 1. The proposed antenna

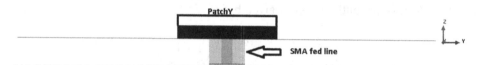

Fig. 2. The side view of the proposed antenna

The table below shows the parameters of the proposed antenna.

Table 1. Parameters of the proposed antenna

Description	Parameter	Value (mm)
Length of patch	Patch X	15
Width of patch	Patch Y	12
Length of the substrate	Sub X	184
Width of the substrate	Sub Y	40
Height of the cavity	Hcavite	26
Thickness of the metal layer	a	9

3   Simulation Results

3.1   Return Loss S_{11}

The S_{11} parameter of proposed antenna has simulated using Ansoft HFSS as shown in Fig. 3. the reflection coefficient of the suggested antenna has proved satisfactory results for both structures with and without M-EBG, therefore, after observing the return loss coefficient of the proposed antenna with and without M-EBG, it obviously reveals that the antenna resonating at the frequency 5 GHz measured at −10 dB. And the existing of M-EBG does not influence the resonant frequency of the antenna.

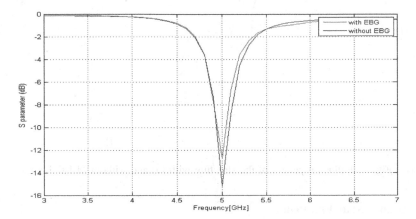

Fig. 3. Return loss of the structure with and without M-EBG

3.2 Radiation Pattern

The 3D radiation pattern at the frequency 5 GHz, with and without the M-EBG are shown in Fig. 4. Also, Fig. 5 present the radiation pattern (gain) at 5 GHz, it is clearly observed that the best radiation performance is achieved by the M-EBG antenna structure. An antenna gain up to 11.4 dB is achieved at the resonant frequency 5 GHz while the antenna without M-EBG structure obtained a gain about 5.26 dB. Moreover, the antenna had become more directive while using M-EBG structure.

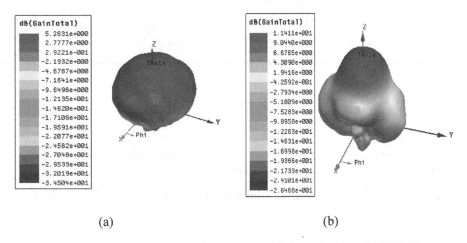

(a)   (b)

Fig. 4. 3D radiation pattern of the structure with (a) and without M-EBG (b).

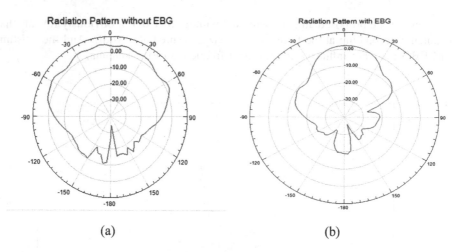

(a)   (b)

Fig. 5. Radiation pattern of the structure with (a) and without M-EBG (b).

3.3 Gain Versus Frequency

The Fig. 6 illustrious the gain according to frequency for the structure with M-EBG and without M-EBG. We acknowledge that the M-EBG curve structure has better performances than without M-EBG structure, and it reaches its maximum for the antenna with M-EBG structure. The Table 2 demonstrates the enhancement of values after loading M-EBG structure.

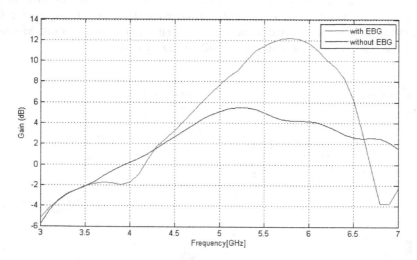

Fig. 6. Gain versus frequency

Table 2. Performance of antenna configuration with and without M-EBG

Frequency (GHz)	Without M-EBG	With M-EBG
S11 (dB)	−15.2	−12.77
Gain (dB)	5.26	11.4
Directivity (dB)	6.82	12.64

4 Conclusion

In this paper, an antenna with horizontal and vertical metallic electromagnetic band gap for the WLAN applications is presented; the design steps of the antenna have been presented and simulated using High Frequency Structural Simulator (HFSS). The simulation results shows remarkable performance with M-EBG instead of without M-EBG, increasing gain have been achieved which it proves the significant influence of M-EBG.

References

1. Hajj, M., Thevenot, M., Monediere, T., Jecko, B.: A novel dual-band sectoral Metallic Electromagnetic Band Gap (M-EBG) antenna for Hiperlan2 application. In: 2009 IEEE International Workshop on Antenna Technology, Santa Monica, CA, USA, pp. 1–4 (2009)
2. Neto, A., de Macedo Dantas, M.L., dos Santos Silva, J., Fernandes, H.C.C.: Antenna for Fifth Generation (5G) Using a EBG Structure. In: Rocha, A., Correia, A.M., Costanzo, S., Reis, L.P. (eds.) New Contributions in Information Systems and Technologies. AISC, vol. 354, pp. 33–38. Springer, Cham (2015). https://doi.org/10.1007/978-3-319-16528-8_4
3. Kaabal, A., El Halaoui, M., Ahyoud, S., Asselman, A.: Dual band-notched WIMAX/WLAN of a compact ultrawideband antenna with spectral and time domains analysis for breast cancer detection. Progress Electromag. Res. C 65, 163–173 (2016)
4. Kuo, Y.-L., Wong, K.-L.: Printed double-T monopole antenna for 2.4/5.2 GHz dual-band WLAN operations. IEEE Trans. Antennas Propag. 51(9), 2187–2192 (2003)
5. Dang, L., Lei, Z.Y., Xie, Y.J., Ning, G.L., Fan, J.: A compact microstrip slot triple-band antenna for WLAN/WiMAX applications. IEEE Antennas Wirel. Propag. Lett. 9, 1178–1181 (2010)
6. Sultan, K.S., Abdullah, H.H., Abdallah, E.A., Hashish, E.A.: Low-SAR, miniaturized printed antenna for mobile, ISM, and WLAN services. IEEE Antennas Wirel. Propag. Lett. 12, 1106–1109 (2013)
7. Chuprin, A.D., Parker, E.A., Batchelor, J.C.: Resonant frequencies of open and closed loop frequency selective surface arrays. Electron. Lett. 36(19), 1601 (2000)
8. Kushwaha, N., Kumar, R.: Study of different shape electromagnetic band gap (EBG) structures for single and dual band applications. J. Microwaves, Optoelectron. Electromagnet. Appl. 13(1), 16–30 (2014)
9. Shaban, H.F., Elmikaty, H.A., Shaalan, A.A.: Study the effects of electromagnetic band-gap (EBG) substrate on two patches microstrip antenna. Prog. Electromag. Res. B 10, 20 (2008)
10. Salonen, P., Yang, F., Rahmat-Samii, Y., Kivikoski, M.: WEBGA - wearable electromagnetic band-gap antenna. In: IEEE Antennas and Propagation Society Symposium, 2004, Monterey, CA, USA, vol. 1, pp. 451–454 (2004)
11. Balanis, C.A.: Antenna Theory: Analysis and Design, 3rd edn. Wiley, Hoboken (2005)

Toward Design of Advanced System-on-Chip Architecture for Mobile Computing Devices

Mohammed S. BenSaleh, Syed Manzoor Qasim[✉],
and Abdulfattah M. Obeid

Communications and Information Technology Research Institute,
King Abdulaziz City for Science and Technology (KACST), Riyadh 11442,
Saudi Arabia
mqasim@kacst.edu.sa

Abstract. In this paper, we present the design of an advanced system-on-chip architecture for mobile computing devices. The presented architecture facilitates connectivity to an ARM compatible host processor, high-speed intellectual property (IP) cores and slower peripherals using industry standard advanced microcontroller bus architecture. The system consist of standard set of peripherals, such as clock generator, real time clock, a watchdog timer, an interrupt controller, programmable I/O, I^2C Host, SPI master, UARTs, trusted platform module, NAND flash controller and USB controllers. Third party 2D/3D graphics engine, audio/video encoder-decoder, wireless network controller IPs are also integrated to provide a complete platform architecture for the development of mobile computing devices.

Keywords: Mobile computing device · System-on-Chip · SoC ·
System architecture

1 Introduction

Mobile computing devices such as tablets and netbook PCs, which require access to advanced system-on-chip (SoC) technology currently dominate the consumer electronics industry. SoC is a rapidly growing segment of the semiconductor industry and is already dominating the market [1]. Some of the major global players in SoC are Apple, Samsung, Intel, NVidia, Texas Instruments, Qualcomm, Broadcom, Freescale Semiconductor, Marvell Technology Group, Mediatek and STMicroelectronics.

SoC is a complex heterogeneous chip, which is designed and fabricated for specific application. It is a particular form of an application-specific integrated circuit (ASIC) [2–4]. SoC always includes at least one processor and runs embedded software on top of it. ASIC, as compared to SoC, may not necessarily include a processor hence it is considered to be a subset of SoC. A block diagram of typical mobile SoC is shown in Fig. 1.

As can be seen, it is an integration of application processor, modem processor, hardware accelerators for audio/video processing, on-chip interconnect and memory subsystem. Mobile computing device SoCs demand higher computing performance,

© Springer Nature Switzerland AG 2019
É. Renault et al. (Eds.): MSPN 2019, LNCS 11557, pp. 88–95, 2019.
https://doi.org/10.1007/978-3-030-22885-9_9

lower power consumption and small form factor with fully integrated system functionality and flexibility [5–7].

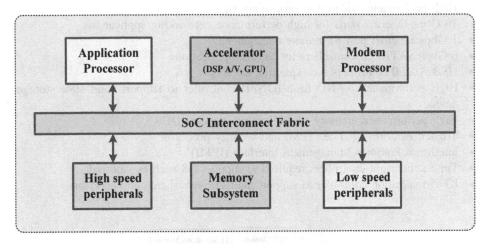

Fig. 1. Top-level diagram of mobile computing device SoCs

In this paper, we present system architecture, which can be used as the building block for developing advanced SoC used in mobile computing devices. The proposed architecture facilitates connectivity to an ARM compatible processor along with high-speed IPs and slower peripherals using industry standard advanced microcontroller bus architecture (AMBA).

The rest of the paper is organized into five sections. The system architecture is presented in Sect. 2. Section 3 discusses the proposed bridge-based architecture. The detailed description of each of these bridges are also provided in this section. Intellectual property (IP) based SoC design is discussed in Sect. 4. The verification methodology and emulation are further discussed in Sect. 5. The concluding remarks are presented in Sect. 6.

2 System Architecture

The proposed architecture is a high performance, low power design for ultra-mobile, digital home and cloud computing applications. The design provides all major functionalities required for mobile computing devices. The proposed architecture is based on the logical integration of multi-core processors with other IPs. It consists of several advanced subsystems used in various computing, networking, storage and connectivity solutions as shown in Fig. 2. The main features of the proposed design are summarized below:

- 8 Gb PCIe 3.0 interface to host processor
- High performance GPU for 2D and 3D graphics supporting OpenGL-ES 2.0/3.0 API

- Video codec capable of decoding high-definition (HD) video streams for 3D TVs and encoding single video stream for video conferencing applications respectively.
- Integrated audio processor for encoding and decoding audio streams
- High performance video post processing engine
- 10 Gbps Ethernet ports for high performance networking applications
- 1 Gbps Ethernet port for remote management
- 6 Gbps SATA 3.0 controllers for storage applications
- USB 3.0/2.0 controllers for expansion devices
- High performance NAND flash (ONFI) controller to support solid state storage devices
- High performance memory controller that supports DDR3
- Trusted Platform Module (TPM) and security processor
- Intelligent Platform Management Interface (IPMI)
- Timers, interrupt controllers required to support OS such as Android
- IO virtualization controller to support platform virtualization/hypervisors.

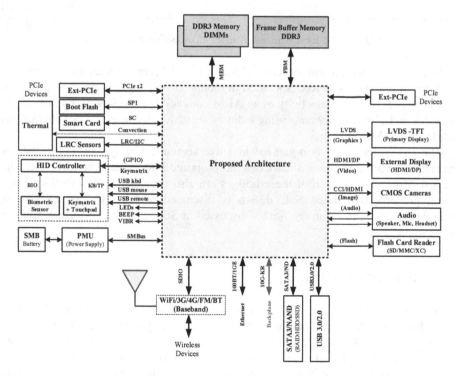

Fig. 2. Proposed system architecture

3 Architectural Details

The proposed architecture as shown in Fig. 3 essentially consist of five mega blocks/bridges, which describe the overall functionality required for mobile computing device SoCs. The details of these functional blocks are discussed below.

- North Bridge: It interconnects processor, memory and I/O interfaces
- South Bridge: It provides system management functionality including Timers, BIOS flash interface and connectivity to slow peripherals
- West Bridge: It provides multimedia and graphics functionality
- East Bridge: It provides network and storage connectivity
- Central Bridge: It implements a PCI express interface to host processor, a DDR memory controller and other processor specific functionality

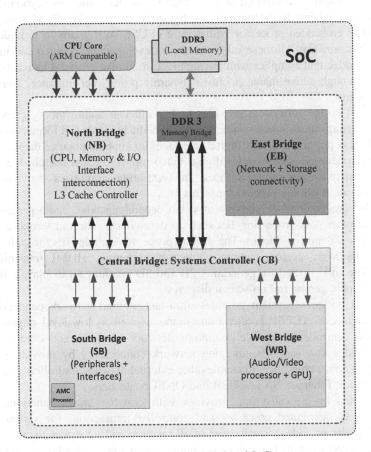

Fig. 3. Functional blocks of SoC

A north bridge typically handles communication between the host processor (CPU), direct memory access (DMA) controller, DDR controller, L3 cache controller, PCIe host, GPU, auxiliary processor (AMC) and the central bridge.

The south bridge implements the low bandwidth I/O in a system. It is also responsible for providing access to the non-volatile BIOS memory used to store system configuration data. The south bridge is categorized into the following subsystems: AMC, APB, APC and TPM. The AMC subsystem is composed of auxiliary processor with various I/O subsystems to provide advanced configuration and power interface (ACPI) master controller functionality.

APB subsystem is composed of basic industry standard architecture (ISA) devices, such as Boot BIOS, GPIO and various serial interfaces for subsystems control. It also includes the SPI BIOS controller, which provides subsystems control mechanism for interfacing to SPI Flash memory that we will be used to hold boot BIOS for the system.

APC subsystem is composed of user interface devices, such as keyboard, mouse and various serial interfaces for sensor subsystems control. The TPM subsystem is composed of embedded processor with secure eFUSE subsystems to provide trusted platform functionality. All these subsystems are developed as specified and integrated into south bridge that complies with the architecture. It also provides increased system reliability through active management of dynamic power, performance, thermal and battery features.

The west bridge subsystem provides highly efficient audio, video, graphics and image processing capabilities to support various media contents and formats used in the market. It also provides various digital interfaces to support popular display devices and sound systems. It also provides digital video inputs to support embedded camera sensors or external video capture devices. The west bridge comprises of an audio/video (AV) processor, a display processor and a GPU.

The AV processor block consists of video decoder/encoder, audio processor unit (APU) and other post-processing IPs such as deinterlacer, chroma format converter, deblocking and denoising blocks. The display processor includes IPs for scaling, alpha blending, hardware cursor, gamma correction, dithering, HDMI transmitter and receiver. The GPU is used for generating 2D and 3D graphics for display. It is mostly used for graphic games and on-screen displays.

The east bridge subsystem provides ultra-fast secured network connectivity by utilizing high level TCP/IP acceleration engine as well as low-level physical communications controllers to enable ubiquitous network interfaces and storage devices. The east bridge also supports emerging network connectivity by providing flexible peripheral interface controllers to enable other external network controllers and devices such as Gigabit Ethernet, SATA, USB and ONFI controllers.

The central bridge subsystem provides with crossbar bridge functionality that coordinates all distributed processor and controller transactions for various shared resources. It also provides virtualization of all memory and IO spaces to create unified systems architecture with heterogeneous hardware to support backwards compatible software application.

The central bridge also contains an IO memory management unit (IOMMU) that is responsible for managing direct device accesses to memory via DMA. The IOMMU controller provides IO space virtualization such that legacy devices and application software could be virtually integrated into new advanced processor architectures. This allows virtualization of all memory and IO spaces to create truly effective virtual machines. The IOMMU must support all the devices concurrently accessing memory.

4 IP-Based SoC Design

Digital IP cores are used as plug-in module in complex multiprocessor system-on-chip (MPSoC) design in order to reduce the total time-to-market [8, 9]. IP cores implement predefined logic functions such as digital signal processing (DSP), bus interfaces and peripheral interfaces as shown in Fig. 1. Designing an IP block generally requires greater effort and higher cost. However, due to its reusable architecture, once an IP is designed and verified, its reuse in future designs saves significant time and effort in the long run. Designers can either outsource these reusable blocks from third-party IP vendors or design them in-house. To provide various levels of flexibility for reuse and optimization, IP cores are classified as hard IP, soft IP and firm IP [10, 11].

Hard IP are available in the form of pre-implemented blocks such as processor cores, gigabit interfaces, multipliers, adders, etc. in GDSII format. These blocks are available in different varieties, optimized for power, area and speed depending on the requirements. Soft IP on the other hand are library of high-level functions, which are typically represented using register-transfer level (RTL) hardware description language (HDL) such as Verilog or VHDL.

Firm IP are provided as netlist representation of the required function, optimized for a target technology (FPGA or ASIC). Single or multiple instances of these IP can be used in the design as required. Most of the IP vendors provide a portfolio of digital and mixed-signal IP cores which are silicon-proven. The IPs are integrated in SoC using some of the most commonly used bus standards such as AMBA from ARM, CoreConnect from IBM, Wishbone from OpenCores, Avalon from Altera, STBus from STMicroelectronics, etc. [12].

Synopsys provides the DesignWare IP Cores (DWC), which provides designers with a comprehensive portfolio of synthesizable IP and hardened PHYs for ASIC, SoC and FPGA designs. These DWC provide system designers with silicon-proven, digital and mixed-signal IP for some of the world's most recognized computer, consumer electronics and communication products.

The DWC family includes industry leading connectivity IP such as PCI Express, PCI Express PHY, USB 2.0, USB On-the-Go (OTG), USB 2.0 PHY, USB 3.0, USB 3.0 PHY, SATA, SATA PHY, Ethernet and ARC embedded processor. Some of these Synopsys DWCs are used in the design and integration phase of this chip. The on-chip interconnect logic IP is developed in-house. The verification IPs (VIPs) available from Mentor Graphics is used in the verification phase of the project. Vivante 2D/3D GPU IPs are used for providing 2D/3D graphics capability to the system.

5 Verification Methodology and Emulation

The verification of a complex SoC is a challenge. Universal verification methodology (UVM) provides a consolidated solution to the verification challenge faced by designers. In this work, UVM environment is created around the proposed chip. The UVM environment provides System Verilog tasks, classes for drivers and monitors, which are called by stand-alone tests to generate sequences of transactions on the interfaces. Synopsys VCS/Mentor Questasim is used as simulator for verification. The device under test (DUT) is connected to PCIe agent on one side and multiple device agent interfaces on the other side. The host PCIe agent is responsible for configuring, initializing and enabling the processing units. The device agents on the other hand are responsible for receiving/providing the data to the chip.

For emulation, Veloce Quattro emulator is used due to its fast compiles, modeling accuracy, productive debug, and time-to visibility features [13]. It covers the SoC validation requirements of peripherals interfaces, testing with live data from outside world. In addition, it tests the performance of software and hardware under development [14]. The top-level view of the emulation environment used in this work is illustrated in Fig. 4.

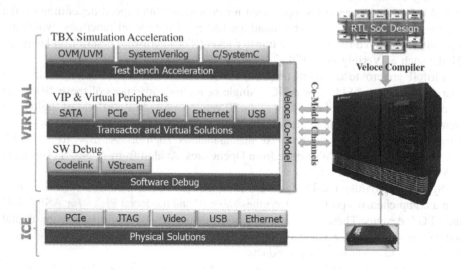

Fig. 4. Top-level view of emulation environment

6 Conclusion

In this paper, we presented a system architecture for use in portable mobile computing device SoCs. The proposed architecture is modular and consists of several mega blocks to achieve the required functionality of SoC desired in mobile computing devices. The presented architecture is compatible with ARM v7 based processor core. It also provides PCIe interface to connect to the host processor. As a future work, the designed architecture will be integrated with multi-core processors to achieve fully integrated SoC for portable mobile computing devices such as tablets and netbook PCs.

References

1. International Technology Roadmap for Semiconductors: ITRS, 2013. http://public.itrs.net
2. Classen, T.A.C.M.: An industry perspective on current and future state of the art in system-on-chip technology. Proc. IEEE **94**(6), 1121–1137 (2006)
3. Saleh, R., et al.: System-on-chip: Reuse and integration. Proc. IEEE **94**(6), 1050–1069 (2006)
4. Sinha, R., Roop, P., Basu, S.: Correct-by-Construction Approaches for SoC Design. Springer, New York (2014). https://doi.org/10.1007/978-1-4614-7864-5
5. Suzuki, T., Saito, K.: ASIC technology for the implementation of System-on-a-chip. Hitachi Rev. **47**(4), 100–106 (1998)
6. Kawasaki, I., Kikuchi, A., Tachiuchi, T.: SuperH RISC Engine Chip Set for Handheld PC. Hitachi Rev. **47**(4), 115–120 (1998)
7. Stamenkovic, Z.: SoC design for wireless communication. J. Circuit Syst. Comp. **20**(8), 1505–1527 (2011)
8. Chauhan, P., Clarke, E.M., Lu, Y., Wang, D.: Verifying IP-core based system-on-chip designs. In: Proceedings of 12th Annual IEEE International ASIC/SoC Conference, pp. 27–31 (1999)
9. Coussy, P., Baganne, A., Martin, E.: A design methodology for IP integration. In: Proceedings of IEEE International Symposium on Circuits and Systems (ISCAS), pp. 711–714 (2002)
10. Keating, M., Bricaud, P.: Reuse Methodology Manual for System-on-a-Chip Designs. Kluwer Academic Publishers, Boston (2002)
11. Nekoogar, F., Nekoogar, F.: From ASICs to SOCs: A Practical Approach. Pearson Education, New Jersey (2003)
12. Mitic, M., Stojcev, M.: An overview of on-chip busses. Facta Univ. Ser. Electron. Energ. **19** (3), 405–428 (2006)
13. Veloce Emulation Platform. https://www.mentor.com/products/fv/emulation-systems
14. BenSaleh, M.S., Qasim, S.M., AlJuffri, A.A., Obeid, A.M.: Design of an advanced system-on-chip architecture for internet-enabled smart mobile devices. In: Proceedings of 30th IEEE International Conference on Microelectronics, pp. 1–4 (2018)

A Multiresolution-Based Fusion Strategy for Improving Speech Emotion Recognition Efficiency

Sara Sekkate[1(✉)], Mohammed Khalil[1], Abdellah Adib[1], and Sofia Ben Jebara[2]

[1] Team Networks, Telecoms & Multimedia, LIM@II-FSTM,
B.P. 146, 20650 Mohammedia, Morocco
sarasekkate@gmail.com, medkhalil87@gmail.com, adib@fstm.ac.ma
[2] COSIM Laboratory, Higher School of Communications of Tunis,
Carthage University, Route de Raoued Km 3.5, Cité El Ghazala,
2083 Ariana, Tunisia
sofia.benjebara@supcom.tn

Abstract. This paper presents a multiresolution-based feature extraction for speech emotion recognition in unconstrained environments. In the proposed approach, Mel Frequency Cepstral Coefficients (MFCC) are derived from Discrete Wavelet Transform (DWT) sub-band coefficients. The extracted features are further combined with conventional MFCCs and pitch-based features to form the final feature vector. Linear Discriminant Analysis (LDA) is used to reduce the dimension of the resulting features set prior to Naive Bayes classification. To assess the performance of the proposed approach in unconstrained environments, noisy speech data are generated by adding real world noises to clean speech signals from the Berlin German Emotional Database (EMO-DB) The proposal is also tested through speaker-dependent and speaker-independent experiments. The overall performance results show improvement in speech emotion detection over baselines.

Keywords: Speech Emotion Recognition (SER) · Wavelet analysis · MFCC

1 Introduction

Speech signals not only carry the message that is conveyed but also information that is much wider including the speaker's emotional state. The process of automatically identifying the emotion of the speaker from a given utterance is referred to as Speech Emotion Recognition (SER). At present, SER is a widely used research topic due to its numerous applications especially within the broad area of Human-Computer Interaction (HCI) [1]. Examples of such applications are the detection of Parkinson and Alzheimer diseases [2] or call centers [3], where tracking customer's emotional state can be useful for detecting deception or frustration.

© Springer Nature Switzerland AG 2019
E. Renault et al. (Eds.): MSPN 2019, LNCS 11557, pp. 96–109, 2019.
https://doi.org/10.1007/978-3-030-22885-9_10

Despite years of research, the majority of the works on SER are carried out in clean environments. To enhance recognition performance in noisy surroundings, various researches interfere in different stages of the recognition process. As a first step, noise removal or speech enhancement techniques have been applied to improve the signal prior to feature extraction. In [4], denoising speech was performed through speech sample reconstruction. The effectiveness of the proposed method was tested using five emotions from the EMO-DB database [5] in the presence of Additive White Gaussian Noise (AWGN) with a Signal-to-Noise-Ratio (SNR) of 20dB. In [6], noise compensation over the speech representation based on histogram equalization was applied on speech data from Polish emotional speech database [7]. In [8], a speech enhancement method based on the adaptive thresholding in wavelet domain was used for noise cancellation. The proposed framework was shown to improve SER under different recorded noises in addition to white Gaussian noise. In [9], spectral subtraction and masking-based speech enhancement techniques were applied to deal with AWGN in a self-built Chinese database.

The next important consideration for the SER in noisy environments is the extraction of the suitable features, which state the emotion of the speaker even in challenging environments. There are two fundamentally different approaches to this problem. The first one consists on using or finding more noise-robust features such as Log Frequency Power Ratio (LFPR) [10], Rate-Scale (RS) [11], Teager-Energy based Mel-Frequency Cepstral Coefficients (TEMFCCs) [12] or Power Normalized Cepstral Coefficients (PNCC) [13]. The second approach is combinatorial in nature and make use of different features to form large features sets. Examples of such approach could be found in [14] where 286 features were extracted to deal with babble noise; in [15] where sub-band spectral centroid Weighted Wavelet Packet Cepstral Coefficients (W-WPCC) were fused with WPCC, prosodic and voice quality features or in [16] which combine, among others, formants, MFCC and VOC19 features.

Finding the most appropriate features is arguably one of the daunting tasks in SER. This paper investigates SER subjected to different types of noise. The use of compensation techniques to cope with noise contamination assumes the availability of certain a priori knowledge of noise. Hence, we propose a feature fusion method and show that a usage of a relatively low-dimensional feature set can be conceivable for application to SER even in unconstrained conditions. To achieve this, we employ a combination based on conventional features and wavelet analysis. Besides, in order to approach real-world scenarios, the effectiveness of the proposed method is tested in the presence of different real-world noises

The paper is organized as follows. In Sect. 2, we detail the proposed methodology and include a brief description of different features that are involved in the present study. The experimental set-up and the validation results are discussed in Sect. 3. Finally, the paper is concluded in Sect. 4.

2   Proposed Methodology

In this section, we introduce our proposed method for SER. It consists mainly of three phases as shown in Fig. 1. First, we generate the feature set from speech signals using the proposed extraction procedure. The dimensionality of the resulting feature set is further reduced with Linear Discriminant Analysis (LDA). Classification is finally performed using Naive Bayes. Each part is detailed in the following.

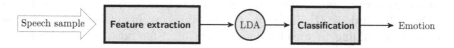

Fig. 1. Illustration of the proposed SER architecture.

2.1   Feature Set Construction

We discuss here the use of multiresolution-based features for recognizing the emotions. In addition to the derived features, MFCCs are used for extracting the vocal tract information. Pitch-based features are also explored for recognizing emotions from speech. Extraction of the above mentioned features is discussed in brief. Figure 2 shows the different blocks of the proposed feature extraction algorithm.

MFCCs are short-term spectral-based features that were first introduced by Davis and Mermelstein [17] for speech recognition. Because of their design that imitates the non-linear characteristics of the human auditory system, their use has been extended to speaker and SER [18,19]. MFCCs extraction can be summarized as follows:

- Pre-emphasis filtering: employed as a preprocessing step to provide more information by boosting the speech signal energy at higher frequencies. The pre-emphasis filter is a special kind of Finite Impulse Response (FIR) and its transfer function is described as

$$H(z) = 1 - \alpha z^{-1} \tag{1}$$

  where the parameter α controls the slope of the filter and is usually chosen between 0.4 and 1 [20]. In this paper, the value of α is set to 0.97.
- Framing: each speech signal is then divided into frames that are N samples long and shifted by M $(M < N)$ samples from the previous frames.
- Windowing: is applied to signal frames to reduce the spectral leakage effect at the beginning and end of each frame. If the windowing function is assigned as $w(n)$ $(0 < n < N - 1)$, then the output is found to be

$$y(n) = x(n)w(n) \tag{2}$$

where $x(n)$ stands for the input signal. In this work, we applied the most commonly used window function which is the Hamming window and is defined as $w(n) = 0.54 - 0.46 \cos (2\pi n/N - 1)$.

- Fast Fourier Transform (FFT): to convert the windowed frames from time to frequency domain.
- Mel-frequency warping: the resulting frequency spectrum is then warped onto Mel-scale by using Mel filter banks with a triangular bandpass frequency response. The use of these filter banks is motivated by the desire of imitating the human ear's perception of frequency.
- Discrete Cosine Transform (DCT): is performed to convert the log Mel spectrum back to time domain.

The number of the resulting MFCCs are usually chosen between 12 and 20 [21]. In this paper, the MFCC feature vector consists of the first 13 static coefficients in which the zeroth one is replaced with the log of the total frame energy. Liftering is also applied to the final features so as to de-emphasize higher MFCCs. In order to further decrease the dimensionality of the extracted feature vectors, the following statistics were computed over the set of MFCCs: Mean, variance and kurtosis.

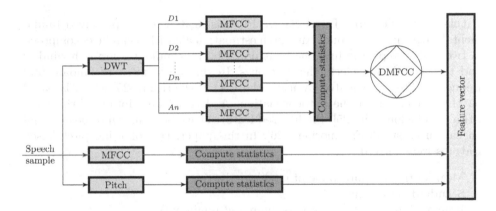

Fig. 2. The proposed feature extraction process

Multiresolution-Based Feature Extraction. Wavelet analysis has been proven as an effectual signal processing technique for a variety of digital signal processing problems [22,23]. DWT analyzes the signal in both time and frequency domain. This feature makes it suitable for studying non-stationary signals. In DWT, the input signal is passed through low-pass and high-pass filters. The output of which are decimated by two and these are termed approximation and details coefficients, respectively. The approximate signal at each level is further decomposed using the same low-pass and high-pass filters to get the approximation and detail components for the next stage. The process is repeated as many times as it is desirable resulting in κ levels of decomposition.

This procedure is known as multi-resolution decomposition of a signal. Low-pass and high-pass filters are linked to two sets of functions namely scaling function and wavelet function. Practically, DWT is performed by an algorithm known as Mallat's algorithm or sub-band coding algorithm. According to [24], a discrete signal $x(n)$ can be decomposed as

$$x(n) = \sum_k a_{j_0,k}\phi_{j_0,k}(n) + \sum_{j=j_0}\sum_k d_{j,k}\psi_{j,k}(n) \tag{3}$$

where $\phi_{j_0,k}(n) = 2^{j_0/2}\phi(2^{j_0}n - k)$ is the scaling function at a scale of 2^{j_0} shifted by k, $\psi_{j,k}(n) = 2^{j/2}\psi(2^j n - k)$ is the mother wavelet at a scale of 2^j shifted by k, $a_{j_0,k}$ is the approximation coefficients at a scale of 2^{j_0} and $d_{j,k}$ is the detail coefficients at a scale of 2^j. In the present work, the number of decomposition levels was chosen to be 4 using Daubechies fourth-order wavelet (db4). Thus, the signal is decomposed into four details and one final approximation coefficient. From each subband, MFCC features were extracted and four statistical characteristics were used to represent the time–frequency distribution of speech signals: mean, variance, skewness and kurtosis. The feature vector of the obtained coefficients is denoted by DMFCC.

Pitch-Based Feature Extraction. Pitch is related to the perceived fundamental frequency of a sound. Any pitch estimation algorithm can be decomposed in two major steps: the first one finds potential F0 candidates for each window and the second one selects the best ones. In this work, pitch or fundamental frequency (F0) is estimated by using the RAPT algorithm [25] which is based on the calculation of the autocorrelation. A detailed description of the algorithm can be found in [25]. Pitch-based features have been shown to be essential on capturing speaker's emotions [26]. In this paper, the following pitch-based features were derived:

- Mean of the absolute value of pitch's derivative;
- Standard deviation;
- Range (Difference between maximum and minimum);
- Ratio between maximum and mean.

2.2   Linear Discriminant Analysis (LDA)

LDA [27] aims at finding a linear combination of the predictor variables while maintaining the class-discriminatory information. The idea is to find a projection of the data where the variance between classes is large compared to the variance within classes. Its aim objective is to find a projection matrix W_{lda} that maximizes the so-called Fisher criterion

$$W_{lda} = \arg\max_W \frac{|W^T S_b W|}{|W^T S_w W|} \tag{4}$$

where S_b and S_w are the scatter between-class and within-class matrices, respectively each defined as

$$S_b = \frac{1}{g} \sum_{i=1}^{g} (\mu_i - \mu)(\mu_j - \mu)^T \tag{5}$$

$$Sw = \frac{1}{g} \sum_{i=1}^{g} \frac{1}{\beta_i} \sum_{i \in C_i} (v_j - \mu_i)(v_j - \mu_i)^T \tag{6}$$

where g is the number of classes, μ_i and μ the class mean and overall mean, respectively. v_j are samples from class C_i and β_i is the number of samples in class C_i.

2.3   Naive Bayes Classification

Emotion classification involves two steps: learning and feature or pattern matching. In the learning step, each emotion is modeled using a set of speech samples in the training phase, which are translated into a set of feature vectors that is generated and saved in a database. In the second step, when it comes to recognize emotions from a unknown speech sample, features are extracted and pattern matching techniques are used to map them to one of the known emotion models. Common classifiers in SER include Neural Networks (NNs) [28], Support Vector Machines (SVMs) [29], Hidden Markov Models (HMMs) [30] and Naive Bayes (NB) [31] which is used in this paper.

NB [32] is a statistical classifier based on Bayes theorem for making the predictions. Bayes theorem says that we can compute the probability of our hypothesis H given some evidence X by instead looking at the probability of the evidence given the hypothesis, as well as the unconditional probabilities of the hypothesis and the evidence. In other words, let X be the input speech and H be some hypothesis that X belongs to class C. The probability that H holds on X is the posterior probability defined as

$$P(H|X) = \frac{p(X|H)p(H)}{p(X)} \tag{7}$$

where $p(H)$ and $p(X)$ are the prior probabilities of H and X respectively, and $P(X|H)$ is the posterior probability of X conditioned on H.

3   Experiments

The proposed method is evaluated with the German Emotional Speech Database (EMO-DB) [5]. It consists of ten speakers (five males and five females), who read ten German sentences each time expressing an emotion. The total number of utterances is 535 divided among seven emotional states: fear, disgust, happiness, boredom, sadness, anger, in addition to neutral state. Recordings were made with 16-bit precision and at a sampling rate of 16 kHz.

3.1   Experimental Setup

Experiments have been carried out in a way to study the speaker independency of the emotion recognition system. Accordingly, two data sets (Set 1 and Set 2) were derived from the EMO-DB. Set 1: Speaker-dependent SER. Here, since the sizes of the available data for each emotion are different, the evaluation was set up through an iterative random split validation procedure. The experimental data was split into two sets randomly, the training set took 70% of the data, and the testing set took the remaining 30% of the data. Considering the Set 2: Speaker-independent SER, we applied leave-one-subject-out (LOSO) cross validation, where each time, training is performed leaving one speaker out of the training set and the performance is tested on the speaker left out.

For both sets, the same front-end was used: MFCCs were extracted with a frame size of 25 ms and a frame shift of 10 ms. The parameters are summarized in Table 1.

Table 1. Parameters and setup used in all experiments

Parameters	Experimental setup
Sampling rate	16 kHz
Frame length	25 ms
Frame shift	10 ms
Number of MFCC filters	22
Database	EMO-DB
No. speakers	10
Language	German
Classifier	Naive Bayes
Types of noise	Restaurant, train, exhibition, street, car, babble and airport
SNR levels in dB	0, 5, 10, 15, 20, 25 and 30

3.2   Emotion Recognition in Clean Environment

We first assess the performance of the proposed approach in clean environment i.e. no noise was added to the data. We investigate the performance of MFCC, pitch and DMFCC, separately and using different combinations. Each of the extracted feature vectors are projected with LDA. Emotion recognition accuracy of the considered features is shown in Figs. 3 and 4 for both speaker-independent and speaker-dependent modes. Obviously, the recognition rates show considerable improvement after combining features. The highest accuracy is achieved with the feature set of MFCC + DMFCC + Pitch. On average, the recognition rate is 20% and 28% higher than that achieved using each feature alone for speaker-independent SER and speaker-dependent SER, respectively, demonstrating that the proposed feature set enables better separability in terms of SER. Tables 2 and 3 show the confusion matrices averaging the results of ten

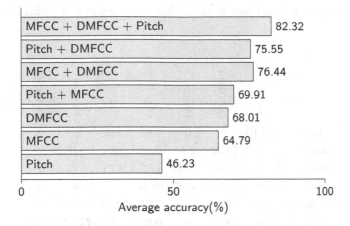

Fig. 3. Average accuracy for speaker-independent SER in clean environment

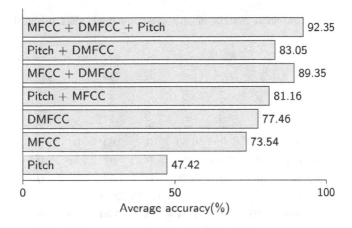

Fig. 4. Average accuracy for speaker-dependent SER in clean environment

and five separate experiments for speaker-independent and speaker-dependent SER, respectively and using the proposed feature extraction scheme. The values in the main diagonal give the recognition accuracy of each emotion. They reveal that among the seven emotions, anger and sadness are easily recognized in speaker-independent and speaker-dependent mode respectively, with an accuracy over than 90%. On the other side, it seems that disgust and neutral show the lowest recognition rates in speaker-independent mode, while in the independent one, it reveals that fear and happiness are more difficult to be recognized.

Table 2. Average confusion matrix of speaker-independent SER using the proposed approach (%)

	Anger	Boredom	Disgust	Fear	Happiness	Neutral	Sadness
Anger	92.10	0	0	1.60	5.69	0	0
Boredom	0	78.39	2.5	0.27	3	10.01	0
Disgust	0	10	74.25	1.25	3.75	3.25	0
Fear	0	0	3.98	80.10	12	0	0
Happiness	3.41	0	2.25	5.71	79.54	0	0
Neutral	0	19.03	0	0.91	0	74.22	1.43
Sadness	0	2.86	0	0	0	0	79.89

Table 3. Average confusion matrix of speaker-dependent SER using the proposed approach (%)

	Anger	Boredom	Disgust	Fear	Happiness	Neutral	Sadness
Anger	96.84	0	0.53	0	2.63	0	0
Boredom	0	97.14	0	0	0	2.86	0
Disgust	0	0	96.92	0	1.54	0	0
Fear	0	0	0	84.26	12.58	2.11	0
Happiness	5.05	0	1.11	8.43	83.30	2.11	0
Neutral	0	6.16	0	0	0	87.84	1.8
Sadness	0	0	0	0	0	0	98.89

3.3 Comparison of the Recognition Performance with that of State-of-the-Art

A direct comparison of the performance with that of state-of-the-art works is not viable due to the lack of consistency in the way the systems are developed in each literature work. However, in this section, our aim is to make a generic comparison with some of the available works based on features combination. Many features have been tested and assessed in the literature considering their performance. Example of such works include [33], where Conventional MFCCs and Linear Predictive Cepstral Coefficients (LPCCs) were fused with formants and classified using Gaussian Mixture Model (GMM) and Artificial Neural Networks (ANN). Another example is [34], where LPCCs and MFCCs were fused with WLPCC and WMFCC, which are features derived from LPCC and MFCC, respectively. The features dimension was reduced using vector quantization method and the obtained feature vector was used as input to a Radial Basis Function Neural Network (RBFNN) classifier. In [35], a 225-dimensional feature vector was generated by fusing features consisting of pitch, energy, ZCR, Linear Predictive Coding (LPC) and MFCC and fed to SVMs for classification. Alternative procedures for speaker-independent SER using feature fusion are found in [36] and [37]. In the proposed works, Wavelet Packet Coefficients (WPC) and DWT performed on decomposed speech data obtained via Empirical Mode Decomposition (EMD) were used to produce the final feature vectors. The wavelet-based features were then passed to SVMs and K-Nearest Neighbors (KNN) classifiers, respectively.

Table 4. Brief review on feature combination using EMO-DB

Speaker-dependent			
Work	Feature	Classifier	Accuracy
[34]	LPCC + WLPCC + MFCC + WMFCC	RBFNN	91.82%
[35]	Pitch + Energy + ZCR + LPC + MFCC	SVM	89.8%
[38]	Rythm + Temporal	ANN	80.60%
[33]	Formants + MFCC Formants + LPCC	GMM and ANN	63%68%
[13]	PNCC	ML	75.85%
[14]	Formants + Pitch + Energy + spectral + MFCC + PLP + LPC	NB	82.26%
	Our proposal	NB	**92.35%**
Speaker-independent			
[36]	WPC	SVM	79.5%
[37]	EMD-DWT	KNN	80.55%
	Our proposal	NB	**82.32%**

Table 4 compares the obtained averaged recognition rates to those obtained with other methods that have been tested on the same emotional speech database using feature fusion and gives an overview of the results. From the reported results, we can notice that extracting larger feature sets does not necessarily helps on achieving a better performance. Here, we have used a feature set that combines MFCC, DMFCC and pitch-based features and achieved a better performance than that obtained using a combination of three features at least, with an average improvement of 4%.

3.4 Emotion Recognition in the Presence of Noise

In this section, we offer a comprehensive study on the proposed prominence features obtained using our method in realistic conditions, where speech data is usually corrupted by background noises. In this regard, seven types of real-world noises were added to the speech data at various Signal-to-Noise-Ratio

(SNR) levels (from 0 to 30dB with 5dB step). The considered background noises are based on the ones constructed for the AURORA noisy speech evaluation [39] and include: Airport, train, babble, street, car, exhibition and restaurant noise. Street and babble (Mixture of a lot of speakers voices) noises are non-stationary and the remaining ones are stationary. In all the experiments, the models are trained using only the original clean speech data and tested on the noise-corrupted versions of the testing set. The comparative results are reported in Table 5 for both speaker-dependent and speaker-independent modalities.

Table 5. Average accuracies (%) of SER in the presence of different background noises

Speaker-independent	SNR						
	0dB	5dB	10dB	15dB	20dB	25dB	30dB
Train	55.28	65.18	72.25	75.91	77.66	78.03	79.79
Exhibition	58.89	65.29	69.10	70.29	74.13	74.58	78.40
Street	54.60	66.51	72.25	76.09	79	79.65	81.73
Car	51.72	62.73	67.13	72.34	76.52	78.12	80.19
Restaurant	56.74	64.47	71.33	75.29	75.99	78.05	79.59
Babble	50.63	63.67	68.70	74.17	76.48	77.80	79.83
Airport	44.71	62.39	73.62	76.47	78.85	80.44	81.14
Average accuracy	53.22	64.32	70.63	74.36	76.95	78.10	80.10
Speaker-dependent							
Train	62.61	73.91	81.29	85.37	85.95	87.20	89.37
Exhibition	65.41	72.19	74.88	78.99	82.95	86.64	88.71
Street	64.04	72.50	79.24	82.64	85.64	87.55	89.18
Car	55.82	71.50	76.07	81.01	83.99	86.06	87.72
Restaurant	62.02	72.99	77.64	82.02	86.25	88.82	90.87
Babble	59.39	71.10	75.69	82.94	85.84	87.04	89.39
Airport	52.39	73.65	81.81	84.54	85.90	87.70	88.41
Average accuracy	60.24	72.55	78.09	82.50	85.22	87.29	89.09

In comparison with the obtained results in [13] where the use of PNCCs was investigated for robust speaker-dependent SER. The reported accuracies for babble noise were about 55% at 5dB and 62% at 10dB with a maximum accuracy of 70% at 20dB. However, with our proposal, we reached an average accuracy of 71.10% at 5dB, 75.69% at 10dB and 85.84% at 20dB for the same type of noise. Table 6 compares the obtained results for speaker-dependent task on EMO-DB with that of literature works in the presence of noise.

It is clearly seen that the proposed feature set achieve a lower performance in comparison to that of obtained in [14]. This may be due to the use of a larger feature set which include 286 features combining formants, energy, pitch,

Table 6. Reported results in literature works in the presence of noise

Work	Noise	SNR				
		0dB	5dB	10dB	15dB	20dB
[14]	Babble	62.90%	74.58%	78.13%	-	-
[13]	Babble	43%	55%	62%	68%	70%
Our proposal	Babble	59.39%	71.10%	75.69%	82.94%	85.84%

spectral, MFCCs, Perceptual Linear Prediction (PLP) as well as LPC coefficients. However, using such a larger set achieved a recognition rate of 82.26% in clean environment while we reached 92.35% with our proposal. This means that using increasing size of the feature set does not necessarily mean that a better performance will be achieved.

4 Conclusion

In this paper, a feature-level approach was proposed for SER. The multiresolution-based proposal is a combination of pitch-based features, short-term MFCCs and MFCCs derived from sub-band DWT coefficients. Finally, several comparative experiments were conducted to validate the efficacy of the proposed features. The results show that the proposed feature set seems to be quite promising for both speaker-dependent an speaker-independent SER when tested on Berlin database. Therefore, it should be further evaluated in a larger database in a future research. Additional experiments investigated the efficiency of the proposed approach in the presence of noise. The results show an improvement compared to state-of-the-art works and seems to perform well even in unconstrained environments. We conclude that the challenging task in SER is to find a feature set that maximizes the trade-off between the feature vector size and the achieved performance in both of noisy and clean environments.

References

1. Cowie, R., et al.: Emotion recognition in human-computer interaction. IEEE Signal Process. Mag. **18**(1), 32–80 (2001)
2. López-de Ipiña, K., et al.: On automatic diagnosis of Alzheimer's disease based on spontaneous speech analysis and emotional temperature. Cogn. Comput. **7**(1), 44–55 (2015)
3. Petrushin, V.: Emotion in speech: recognition and application to call centers. In: Proceedings of Artificial Neural Networks in Engineering (2000)
4. Xiaoqing, J., Kewen, X., Yongliang, L., Jianchuan, B.: Noisy speech emotion recognition using sample reconstruction and multiple-kernel learning. J. China Univ. Posts Telecommun. **24**(2), 1–17 (2017)
5. Burkhardt, F., Paeschke, A., Rolfes, M., Sendlmeier, W.F., Weiss, B.: A database of German emotional speech. In: INTERSPEECH, ISCA, pp. 1517–1520 (2005)

6. Juszkiewicz, Ł.: Improving noise robustness of speech emotion recognition system. In: Zavoral, F., Jung, J.J., Badica, C. (eds.) Intelligent Distributed Computing VII. Studies in Computational Intelligence, vol. 511, pp. 223–232. Springer International Publishing, Cham (2014). https://doi.org/10.1007/978-3-319-01571-2_27

7. Staroniewicz, P., Majewski, W.: Polish emotional speech database – recording and preliminary validation. In: Esposito, A., Vích, R. (eds.) Cross-Modal Analysis of Speech, Gestures, Gaze and Facial Expressions. LNCS (LNAI), vol. 5641, pp. 42–49. Springer, Heidelberg (2009). https://doi.org/10.1007/978-3-642-03320-9_5

8. Tawari, A., Trivedi, M.M.: Speech emotion analysis in noisy real-world environment. In: 2010 20th International Conference on Pattern Recognition, pp. 4605–4608, August 2010

9. Huang, C., Chen, G., Yu, H., Bao, Y., Zhao, L.: Speech emotion recognition under white noise. Arch. Acoust. **38**(4), 457–463 (2013)

10. Hyun, K., Kim, E., Kwak, Y.: Robust speech emotion recognition using log frequency power ratio. In: 2006 SICE-ICASE International Joint Conference, pp. 2586–2589, October 2006

11. Yeh, L.Y., Chi, T.S.: Spectro-temporal modulations for robust speech emotion recognition. In: INTERSPEECH (2010)

12. Georgogiannis, A., Digalakis, V.: Speech emotion recognition using non-linear teager energy based features in noisy environments. In: 2012 Proceedings of the 20th European Signal Processing Conference (EUSIPCO), pp. 2045–2049, August 2012

13. Bashirpour, M., Geravanchizadeh, M.: Speech emotion recognition based on power normalized cepstral coefficients in noisy conditions. Iran. J. Electr. Electron. Eng. **12**, 197–205 (2016)

14. Karimi, S., Sedaaghi, M.H.: Robust emotional speech classification in the presence of babble noise. Int. J. Speech Technol. **16**(2), 215–227 (2013)

15. Huang, Y., Tian, K., Wu, A., Zhang, G.: Feature fusion methods research based on deep belief networks for speech emotion recognition under noise condition. J. Ambient Intell. Humaniz. Comput. **10**(5), 1787–1798 (2017)

16. Schuller, B., Arsic, D., Wallhoff, F., Rigoll, G.: Emotion recognition in the noise applying large acoustic feature sets. In: Speech Prosody (2006)

17. Davis, S., Mermelstein, P.: Comparison of parametric representations for monosyllabic word recognition in continuously spoken sentences. IEEE Trans. Acoust. Speech Signal Process. **28**(4), 357–366 (1980)

18. Lalitha, S., Geyasruti, D., Narayanan, R., Shravani, M.: Emotion detection using MFCC and cepstrum features. Procedia Comput. Sci. **70**, 29–35 (2015). Proceedings of the 4th International Conference on Eco-friendly Computing and Communication Systems

19. Chelali, F.Z., Djeradi, A.: Text dependant speaker recognition using MFCC, LPC and DWT. Int. J. Speech Technol. **20**(3), 725–740 (2017)

20. Picone, J.W.: Signal modeling techniques in speech recognition. Proc. IEEE **81**(9), 1215–1247 (1993)

21. Kopparapu, S.K., Laxminarayana, M.: Choice of Mel filter bank in computing MFCC of a resampled speech. In: 10th International Conference on Information Science, Signal Processing and their Applications (ISSPA), pp. 121–124, May 2010

22. Subasi, A., Gursoy, M.I.: EEG signal classification using PCA, ICA, LDA and support vector machines. Expert Syst. Appl. **37**(12), 8659–8666 (2010)

23. Sekkate, S., Khalil, M., Adib, A.: A feature level fusion scheme for robust speaker identification. In: Tabii, Y., Lazaar, M., Al Achhab, M., Enneya, N. (eds.) BDCA 2018. CCIS, vol. 872, pp. 289–300. Springer, Cham (2018). https://doi.org/10.1007/978-3-319-96292-4_23

24. Mallat, S.: A Wavelet Tour of Signal Processing, 2nd edn. Academic Press, San diego (1998)
25. Talkin, D.: A robust algorithm for pitch tracking (RAPT). In: Klein, W.B., Palival, K.K. (eds.) Speech Coding and Synthesis. Elsevier, Amsterdam (1995)
26. Chebbi, S., Jebara, S.B.: On the use of pitch-based features for fear emotion detection from speech. In: 2018 4th International Conference on Advanced Technologies for Signal and Image Processing (ATSIP), pp. 1–6, March 2018
27. Fisher, R.A.: The use of multiple measurements in taxonomic problems. Ann. Eugenics **7**(2), 179–188 (1936)
28. Darekar, R.V., Dhande, A.P.: Emotion recognition from marathi speech database using adaptive artificial neural network. Biologically Inspired Cogn. Archit. **23**, 35–42 (2018)
29. Aouani, H., Ayed, Y.B.: Emotion recognition in speech using MFCC with SVM, DSVM and auto-encoder. In: 2018 4th International Conference on Advanced Technologies for Signal and Image Processing (ATSIP), pp. 1–5, March 2018
30. Gómez-Lopera, J., Martínez-Aroza, J., Román-Roldán, R., Román-Gálvez, R., Blanco-Navarro, D.: The evaluation problem in discrete semi-hidden Markov models. Math. Comput. Simul. **137**, 350–365 (2017). MAMERN VI-2015: 6th International Conference on Approximation Methods and Numerical Modeling in Environment and Natural Resources
31. Bhakre, S.K., Bang, A.: Emotion recognition on the basis of audio signal using naive Bayes classifier. In: 2016 International Conference on Advances in Computing, Communications and Informatics (ICACCI), pp. 2363–2367, September 2016
32. Duda, R., Hart, P.: Pattern Classifications and Scene Analysis. Wiley, New York (1973)
33. Rao, K.S., Koolagudi, S.G.: Robust emotion recognition using pitch synchronous and sub-syllabic spectral features. In: Rao, K.S., Koolagudi, S.G. (eds.) Robust Emotion Recognition using Spectral and Prosodic Features, pp. 17–46. Springer, New York (2013). https://doi.org/10.1007/978-1-4614-6360-3_2
34. Palo, H.K., Mohanty, M.N.: Wavelet based feature combination for recognition of emotions. Ain Shams Eng. J. **9**(4), 1799–1806 (2018)
35. Seehapoch, T., Wongthanavasu, S.: Speech emotion recognition using support vector machines. In: 2013 5th International Conference on Knowledge and Smart Technology (KST), pp. 86–91, January 2013
36. Wang, K., An, N., Li, L.: Speech emotion recognition based on wavelet packet coefficient model. In: The 9th International Symposium on Chinese Spoken Language Processing, pp. 478–482, September 2014
37. Shahnaz, C., et al.: Emotion recognition based on EMD-wavelet analysis of speech signals. In: 2015 IEEE International Conference on Digital Signal Processing (DSP), pp. 307–310, July 2015
38. Bhargava, M., Polzehl, T.: Improving automatic emotion recognition from speech using rhythm and temporal feature. In: ICECIT, pp. 2229–3116, March 2013
39. Pearce, D., Hirsch, H.G., Gmbh, E.E.D.: The aurora experimental framework for the performance evaluation of speech recognition systems under noisy conditions. In: ISCA ITRW ASR 2000, pp. 29–32 (2000)

ECG Beat Classification Based on Stationary Wavelet Transform

Lahcen El Bouny[(✉)], Mohammed Khalil, and Abdellah Adib

Networks, Telecoms & Multimedia Team, LIM@II-FSTM,
B.P. 146, 20650 Mohammedia, Morocco
lahcenbouny@gmail.com, medkhalil87@gmail.com, adib@fstm.ac.ma

Abstract. ECG processing is a non-invasive technique that is frequently used for diagnosis of various cardiac diseases. One of the crucial steps of an ECG diagnosis system is the heartbeat classification. In this work, we propose a new method for QRS complex classification based on Stationary Wavelet Transform (SWT), and two classifiers, which are Support Vector Machine (SVM) and K-Nearest Neighbors (KNN). In our scheme, SWT was used to extract the discriminatory features from the useful frequency sub-bands for each QRS complex class. The extracted features were used as inputs of SVM and KNN in order to classify five types of heartbeats, which are Normal (N), Premature Ventricular Contraction (PVC), Atrium Premature Contraction (APC), Left Bundle Branch Block (LBBB), and Right Bundle Branch Block (RBBB). The experimental results obtained on MIT-BIH Arrythmia database (MITDB), show that the proposed system yields acceptable performances with an overall classification accuracy of 98.56% and 98.74% for KNN and SVM classifiers respectively, using the 10-cross validation technique.

Keywords: ECG · QRS classification · Feature extraction · SWT · SVM · KNN

1 Introduction

1.1 ECG Overview

The heart is the principle muscle of the human cardiovascular system that contracts and pumps blood throughout the body. For this reason, studying the functional and structural state of this component is very important. In this regard, ECG signal is a medical diagnosis tool that is widely used for that purpose. In the standard electrocardiography systems, ECG signal is recorded by placing a number of electrodes on some specific locations on the person's body. In normal recordings, ECG signal consists of five principal waves P, Q, R, S and T [7]. Among these waves, the QRS complex contains the most useful information about the heart's electrical activity. For an automatic ECG diagnosis system, ECG beat classification is a preliminary step that must be done accurately.

© Springer Nature Switzerland AG 2019
E. Renault et al. (Eds.): MSPN 2019, LNCS 11557, pp. 110–123, 2019.
https://doi.org/10.1007/978-3-030-22885-9_11

The ultimate goal of this step is to achieve a robust discrimination between normal and pathological beats for an ECG record, using various machine learning algorithms. Figure 1 shows the different stages of an automatic ECG processing system. It includes three main steps, which are: (1) ECG pre-processing, including ECG waves detection, (2) Feature extraction and (3) ECG beat classification.

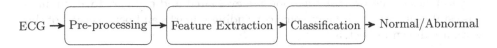

Fig. 1. General scheme of an ECG beat classification system

1.2 Related Works

Several approaches have been reported in the literature in order to give an accurate classification between normal and abnormal beats. One of the common steps of the most of existing techniques is the feature extraction process. The major aim of this step is to define a discriminatory feature vector for each ECG beat. These features can be extracted in time domain, frequency domain and time-frequency domain including wavelet transform [16], as well as with the help of some statistical measures [11]. Prior to the feature extraction step, most of state-of-the-art methods suggest an ECG waves detection stage, aiming specially to detect the QRS complex locations. Numerous QRS detectors have been developed during the last three decades including derivatives approaches such as Pan and Tompkins [20], digital filters [1], Wavelet transforms [4,5,12,15], Hilbert Transform [2], Empirical Mode Decomposition [9], Moving Average Filters [5], Neural Networks [10], Genetic Algorithms [21] and many other works.

Once the QRS beats are detected, the extracted features for each QRS wave can be used as inputs for a classification algorithm. In this context, a large number of algorithms have been used in the literature, including Artificial Neural Networks (ANN) [18], Multi-Layer Perceptron (MLP) [22], Support Vectors Machine (SVM) with different kernels [17], K-Nearest Neighbors (KNN) [11] and Probabilist Neural Networks (PNN) [16]. In recent works, Deep Learning approaches have attracted much attention like Convolutional Neural Networks (CNN) and Recurrent Neural Networks (RNN) [8]. An extensive review on the different ECG beat classification algorithms can be found in [8,13].

Although several algorithms have been proposed in the literature, ECG beat classification still remains an open challenging task. In this work, we propose a novel ECG classification system based on Stationary Wavelet Transform (SWT) and two classifiers (SVM and KNN). In the proposed approach, QRS complex time positions (i.e. R peak times) are determined manually from the standard database MIT-BIH Arrhythmia database (MITDB) [14]. Further, some morphological and statistical informative features were extracted from the useful SWT frequency sub-bands for a QRS wave. Finally, SVM and KNN algorithms will be used to discriminate between five ECG beats (One normal and four abnormals). To evaluate the effectiveness of the presented work, we have used MITDB with the aid of 10-cross validation technique, and the obtained results are compared with some of the state-of-the-art methods.

The remainder of this paper is organized as follows: Sect. 2 describes the dataset used in this work as well as an overview about the Wavelet Transforms. The detailed steps of our approach are given in Sect. 3. In Sect. 4, the performance of the proposed method are evaluated and compared with numerous established works. Finally, some concluding remarks and perspectives of this work are drawn in Sect. 5.

2   Materials and Methods

This section describes briefly the different tools and algorithms used in our proposed ECG heartbeats classification methodology.

2.1   MIT-BIH Arrhythmia Database (MITDB)

MITDB is considered as the standard database to evaluate the performance of an ECG processing algorithm. It contains 48 ECG records from different patients (Male and Female), sampled at 360 Hz with 30 min duration, taken in the majority of cases with the modified Limb II (ML-II). MITDB contains different ECG morphologies, which makes it more suitable to evaluate the performance of an ECG classification system. In this work, we are focused on five ECG waveforms that constitute the predominant classes of the MITDB, which are Normal beats (N), Premature Ventricular Contraction (PVC), Atrial Premature Beats (APC), Left Bundle Branch Blocks (LBBB) and Right Bundle Branch Blocks (RBBB). Figure 2 shows the different ECG waveforms used in this work.

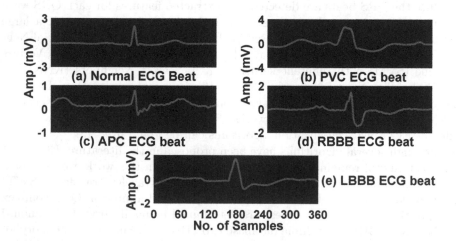

Fig. 2. Illustration of the principal ECG beats from MITDB for a period of 360 samples

2.2   Wavelet Transform

In recent decades, time-frequency/scale approaches like wavelet transform (WT) have shown many applications in different signal processing fields. Discrete Wavelet Transform (DWT) is one popular of the time-scale techniques that is used in various ECG processing tasks like ECG denoising, feature extraction and ECG classification [16]. At each level j, DWT decomposes an ECG signal $x[n]$ by passing it successively through a low pass filter $h[n]$ and high pass filter $g[n]$. The output low frequency components of $h[n]$ are termed approximation coefficients $A_j[n]$, and the output high frequency components of $g[n]$ are called detail coefficients $D_j[n]$. The DWT process at the first level is given as follows

$$A_1[k] = \sum_n x[n]h[n - 2k] \tag{1}$$

$$D_1[k] = \sum_n x[n]g[n - 2k] \tag{2}$$

The same process is then repeated many times to the approximation coefficient $A_j[n]$ until the desired level is attained.

Nevertheless, DWT suffers from the lack of the shift invariance property, resulting from the down-sampling step by factor of 2 at each decomposition level. To deal with this problem, the Stationary Wavelet Transform (SWT) is proposed [19]. In similar way to DWT, SWT decomposes $x[n]$ into $A_j[n]$ and $D_j[n]$ coefficients. However, SWT does not incorporates the down sampling process to the wavelet coefficients. Indeed, SWT up-samples the filter coefficients $h_j[n]$ and $g_j[n]$ at each level j. Consequently, $A_j[n]$ and $D_j[n]$ have the same length as the original signal $x[n]$. In this study, we evaluate the performances of our proposed ECG classification approach when using DWT and SWT respectively. The proposed algorithm was described in the following section.

3   Proposed Methodology

The schematic diagram of our proposed approach is illustrated in Fig. 3. It consists of three main steps, which are (1) ECG pre-processing, (2) Feature extraction on the wavelet domain and (3) ECG beat classification. These steps will be explained in the following sub-sections.

3.1   ECG Pre-processing

This stage consists of two main steps:

(1) **ECG beat segmentation**: In this study, the R peak times are extracted manually from the annotation files '*.atr' from MITDB. Each annotation file contains the R peaks time occurrence and important informations about the normality or the abnormality of the QRS features. The latter are annotated independently by two or more expert cardiologists. Subsequently, we define the QRS segment by taking a time window of length L of 250 samples, i.e. 80 samples before the R peak and 169 samples after the peak.

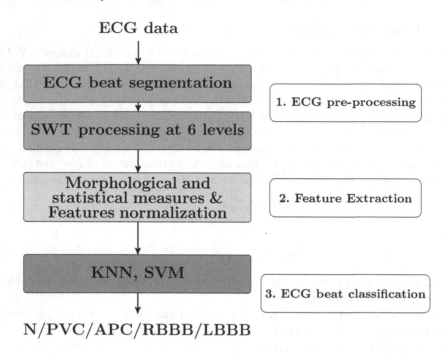

Fig. 3. Illustrative diagram of the proposed ECG beat classification system

(2) **SWT processing**: Each QRS wave of 250 samples[1] was decomposed with SWT using the Daubechies 'db4' wavelet mother[2] until level 6, resulting on six detail coefficients $D_{1,...,6}[n]$ and the approximation coefficient $A_6[n]$. The frequency content of the different SWT sub-bands for an ECG signal sampled at 360 Hz from MITDB are given in Table 1.

Based on the ECG processing literature, the main energy of the ECG signal is mainly centered at the frequency range of [3–40 Hz][23]. Consequently, in this work, we retain only the detail coefficients at levels 3, 4, 5, 6, and we discard the remaining coefficients. Indeed, the details $D_1[n]$ and $D_2[n]$ are dominated by the high frequency noises (e.g. EMG: muscle activity), while the approximation $A_6[n]$ is affected by the low frequency artifacts (e.g. Baseline wandering).

3.2   Feature Extraction

After the pre-processing process, the following morphological and statistical features were extracted from the retained SWT sub-bands $D_j[n]$:

---

[1] Since SWT requires that the signal length should be multiple of 2^{Level}, the QRS wave was zeros padded with 6 zeros samples (i.e. 256 samples).

[2] In this work, we have used 'db4' wavelet due to its great similarity with the QRS complex.

Table 1. Frequency content of the SWT sub-bands at 6 level for an ECG signal from MITDB (Fs = 360 Hz)

SWT sub-band	Frequency range [Hz]
$D_1[n]$	90–180
$D_2[n]$	45–90
$D_3[n]$	22.5–45
$D_4[n]$	11.25–22.5
$D_5[n]$	5.625–11.25
$D_6[n]$	2.81–5.625
$A_6[n]$	0–2.81

Morphological features:

1/ The minimum value of each sub-band $min_j = min(D_j[n])$;

2/ The maximum value of each sub-band $max_j = max(D_j[n])$;

Statistical features:

3/ The mean absolute value of the coefficients in each sub-band computed as follows

$$m_j = \frac{1}{L} \sum_{i=1}^{L} |D_j[i]| \tag{3}$$

4/ The standard deviation of the coefficients in each sub-band

$$\sigma_j = \sqrt{\frac{1}{L} \sum_{i=1}^{i=L} (D_j[i] - m_j)^2} \tag{4}$$

5/ The energy of the coefficients in each sub-band:

$$E_j = \sum_{i=1}^{i=L} D_j^2[i] \tag{5}$$

6/ The third order moment (Skewness) defined as follows

$$S_j = \frac{\frac{1}{L} \sum_{i=1}^{i=L} (D_j[i] - m_j)^3}{\left(\frac{1}{L} \sum_{i=1}^{i=L} (D_j[i] - m_j)^2\right)^3} \tag{6}$$

7/ The fourth order moment (Kurtosis) computed by Eq. (7)

$$K_j = \frac{\frac{1}{L} \sum_{i=1}^{i=L} (D_j[i] - m_j)^4}{\left(\frac{1}{L} \sum_{i=1}^{i=L} (D_j[i] - m_j)^2\right)^2} \cdot \tag{7}$$

Based on the above measures, each QRS beat was represented with $4*7 = 28$ features, constructing a feature vector X_I. For all QRS beats, let define a feature matrix X_{IJ}. Where I represents the Ith row, i.e. the Ith QRS complex features, and J represents the Jth column, i.e. the Jth extracted feature ($J = 1, \ldots, 28$). However, the representative features are different for all QRS beats taken from different ECG Signals, so their normalization is very important before passing to the classification process. In this work, the X_{IJ} observations were subjected to the following normalization rule [25]

$$\tilde{X}_{IJ} = tansig\left[\frac{X_{IJ} - \mu_J}{\delta_{X_J}}\right] \tag{8}$$

where X_{IJ} is the Jth attribute of the Ith feature vector X_I, X_J is the Jth column vector, μ_J and δ_{X_J} are the mean and the standard deviation of X_J respectively, and $tansig[.]$ is the symmetric sigmoid transfer function computed by Eq. (9). The objective of this function is to make all values of X_{IJ} in the range $[-1\ 1]$.

$$tansig[n] = \frac{2}{(1 + exp[-2 * n])} - 1 \tag{9}$$

For final classification, the normalized features are then fed to the machine learning algorithms described below.

3.3 Heartbeats Classification

A large variety of classification algorithms have been developed in the literature. In this work, we have used two popular of them namely SVM and KNN described in the following paragraphs.

KNN is a simple non-parametric learning algorithm that is employed in several purposes of ECG classification. Considered as a lazy learning algorithm, KNN is based on finding the Knearest training samples for each new test sample. That is, KNN aims to classify a new unclassified sample based on its distance to the classified training set. KNN based classification can be summarized in the following steps:

1. Compute the similarity between the new test sample and all samples of the training set using a distance function;
2. Find the K-Nearest Neighbors to the new sample in the training set;
3. Use the majority voting decision rule to predict the class of the new sample.

For K-NN classifier, the distance metric as well as the value of K are needed to be defined. In this paper, we have tested different K values with two standard distance functions, which are the Euclidean and City block distances (also known as Manhattan distance or L1 norm) defined in Eqs. (10) and (11) respectively.

$$D_{X,Y} = \sqrt{\sum_{i=1}^{n}(X_i - Y_i)^2} \tag{10}$$

$$D_{X,Y} = \sum_{i=1}^{J=n} |X_i - Y_i| \qquad (11)$$

where X_i and Y_i are values of ith attribute of the feature vectors X and Y respectively, and n is the number of the extracted features ($n = 28$ in this work).

SVM is a well-known learning algorithm that is based on the statistical learning theory introduced by Vapnik et al. [3,24]. SVM has been used successfully in many real-world problems of data classification and regression. The goal of the SVM classifier is to create an optimal separate hyperplane between the different patterns. In fact, SVM aims to maximize the margin between the hyperplanes corresponding to the different classes. This task is done by resolving a number of quadratic programming and optimization problems. For more details, the readers are invited to refer to [6]. However, real data are not linearly separable. To handle with this problem, the original input patterns to be classified are mapped to higher dimensional feature space using a kernel trick. In this study, we have tested two different kernels namely Radial Basis Function (RBF) and Polynomial kernel of power p, expressed respectively by the following equations

$$K_{RBF}(X_i, X_j) = exp(\frac{-||X_i - X_j||^2}{2\sigma^2}) \qquad (12)$$

$$K_{Pol}(X_i, X_j) = (X_i X_j' + 1)^p \qquad (13)$$

where σ the scaling factor of RBF kernel and p the order of polynomial kernel. In this work σ and p are chosen to be 2.5 and 3 respectively.

In its basic learning scheme, SVM is a binary classifier. However, in the multi-classes classification problems like our study, it exists different SVM classification strategies including the One vs rest (one-vs-all) and the Pairwise (one-vs-one, all-vs-all) approaches. In this paper, we have used the One-vs-all (OVA) approach due to its implementation simplicity and its great efficiency.

4 Results

In this section, we describe the experimental protocol of this study. Also, the performance of the proposed algorithm was evaluated and compared with state-of-the-art techniques.

4.1 Experimental Setup

In this work, we have tested the proposed classification algorithm on MITDB to classify five classes (Normal 'N', Premature Ventricular Contraction 'PVC', Atrial Premature Beats 'APC', Left Bundle Branch Blocks 'LBBB' and Right Bundle Branch Blocks 'RBBB'). In order to create a data set that contains all QRS beat types, we have used different ECG records. Table 2 reports the composition of dataset used in this work.

Table 2. The composition of the dataset used in this study

QRS beat type	ECG records	Number of beats
N	100, 101, 103, 105, 112, 113, 114, 115, 117 121, 122, 123, 202, 205, 219, 230, 234	3150 (70.87%)
PVC	106, 116, 119, 200, 201, 210, 213, 214, 215 217, 221, 223, 228, 233	395 (8.88%)
APC	209, 220, 222, 223, 232	300 (6.75%)
RBBB	118, 124, 212, 231, 232	300 (6.75%)
LBBB	109, 111, 207, 214	300 (6.75%)
Total	42 records	4445 (100%)

4.2 Performances Evaluation Metrics

To evaluate the performance of our approach, k-cross validation scheme was applied for training and testing the classifiers. In this technique, the entire dataset is sub-sampled randomly into k subsets (Folds) having approximately the same distribution of the different classes. At each time, the $k-1$ subsets were used to train the classifier, while the remaining one subset was used to test the classifier and to evaluate the performance metrics. The process is then repeated k times, and the final results are given by averaging the performances of k folds. The 10-cross validation ($k = 10$), corresponding to a proportion of 90% of dataset for training and 10% for testing phases, was used in this work. Generally, performance of classifiers is evaluated using four statistical metrics: The sensitivity Se, the Specifity Sp, the Positive Predictivity P+ and the Accuracy Acc.

Let denotes an ECG beat class by C and the other remaining classes by $\bar{C}$. The statistical measures are given respectively as the following equations

$$Se(\%) = \frac{TP}{TP + FN} * 100 \tag{14}$$

$$Sp(\%) = \frac{TN}{TN + FP} * 100 \tag{15}$$

$$P+(\%) = \frac{TP}{TP + FP} * 100 \tag{16}$$

$$Acc(\%) = \frac{TP + TN}{TP + TN + FP + FN} * 100 \tag{17}$$

where TP (True Positive): the number of ECG beats from class C correctly classified by the algorithm, TN (True Negative): the total number of ECG beats from classes $\bar{C}$ correctly classified by the algorithm, FP (False Positive): the number of ECG beats from class C incorrectly classified by the algorithm and FN (False Negative): the total number of ECG beats from classes $\bar{C}$ incorrectly classified by the algorithm. For example, when $C = $ 'N', then $\bar{C} = $ 'PVC', 'APC',

'RBBB' and 'LBBB'. The overall accuracy of the system can be also obtained using the following equation

$$Acc(\%) = \frac{TP_N + TP_{PVC} + TP_{APC} + TP_{RBBB} + TP_{LBBB}}{All\quad ECG\quad beats} * 100 \qquad (18)$$

4.3 Results and Comparison with Existing Techniques

Table 3 shows the average results obtained by the proposed method when using the KNN algorithm combined with DWT and SWT for different K values (K = 1,3,5,7), and for the two considered distances. In this table, the statistical parameters Se, Sp, P+ and Acc are calculated for each ECG beat class and further averaged. As can be seen in Table 3, the highest performances are achieved when using the KNN algorithm with the city block distance and 1 nearest Neighbor (1-NN), resulting on an average accuracy of 99.21% and 99.41% for DWT and SWT respectively. In Table 4, the average classification performances obtained by DWT and SWT coupled with SVM with different kernels are depicted. This table reveals that the RBF kernel gives the best classification accuracy for DWT (Acc = 99.38%), while the polynomial kernel achieves the best results when applying SWT for extracting the discriminative features (Acc = 99.49%).

Table 3. Average performances of the proposed DWT-SWT/KNN algorithm

Proposed method	Classifier	Se (%)	Sp (%)	P+ (%)	Acc (%)
DWT-KNN	KNN-Euclidean(K = 1)	94.64	99.28	95.21	99.14
	KNN-Euclidean(K = 3)	93.55	99.07	94.51	98.94
	KNN-Euclidean(K = 5)	93.24	98.96	94.42	98.89
	KNN-Euclidean(K = 7)	91.86	98.70	93.71	98.68
	KNN-CityBlock(K = 1)	95.02	99.38	95.41	**99.21**
	KNN-CityBlock(K = 3)	94.55	99.26	94.96	99.10
	KNN-CityBlock(K = 5)	93.38	99.05	94.07	98.90
	KNN-CityBlock(K = 7)	93.36	98.96	94.52	98.90
SWT-KNN	KNN-Euclidean(K = 1)	95.64	99.39	96.53	99.33
	KNN-Euclidean(K = 3)	94.88	99.20	96.20	99.19
	KNN-Euclidean(K = 5)	94.59	99.13	96.12	99.15
	KNN-Euclidean(K = 7)	93.54	98.93	95.25	98.95
	KNN-CityBlock(K = 1)	96.33	99.51	96.79	**99.41**
	KNN-CityBlock(K = 3)	95.68	99.35	96.43	99.30
	KNN-CityBlock(K = 5)	95.18	99.24	96.27	99.22
	KNN-CityBlock(K = 7)	94.37	99.12	95.62	99.09

The best average parameters have been marked with boldface text

Table 4. Average performances of the proposed DWT-SWT/SVM algorithm

Proposed method	Classifier	Se (%)	Sp (%)	P+ (%)	Acc (%)
DWT-SVM	SVM-RBF($\sigma = 2.5$)	96.47	99.52	96.54	**99.38**
	SVM-Polynomial(p = 3)	94.92	99.26	95.61	99.17
SWT-SVM	SVM-RBF($\sigma = 2.5$)	96.96	99.60	96.97	99.47
	SVM-Polynomial(p = 3)	97.27	99.54	97.43	**99.49**

The confusions matrix for all 10 folds corresponding to the best combinations (i.e. SWT-KNN and SWT-SVM) are shown in Tables 5 and 6 respectively. Meanwhile, the sensitivity Se(%), the specifity(%), the positive predictivity (%), the classification accuracy Acc (%) for each ECG beat as well as the overall classification accuracy of the proposed method are reported in Table 7.

Table 5. Confusion matrix for ECG beats classification using SWT-KNN

Annotated	Recognized				
	Normal	PVC	APC	RBBB	LBBB
Normal	3144	2	3	1	0
PVC	4	380	0	2	9
APC	8	0	283	8	1
RBBB	2	0	18	280	0
LBBB	2	4	0	0	294

Table 6. Confusion matrix for ECG beats classification using SWT-SVM

Annotated	Recognized				
	Normal	PVC	APC	RBBB	LBBB
Normal	3138	3	7	2	0
PVC	5	377	3	0	10
APC	9	1	287	3	0
RBBB	1	0	5	294	0
LBBB	2	5	0	0	293

Table 7 shows that the proposed method can yields acceptable performances for all types of ECG beats for both SWT-KNN and SWT-SVM. As depicted in Table 7, the proposed classification systems achieve an overall accuracy of 98.56% and 98.74% for SWT-KNN and SWT-SVM respectively. This leads that the proposed algorithm based on SWT and discriminative features can be used

Table 7. Performance analysis of the proposed algorithm for all ECG beats

ECG beat class	SWT-KNN				SWT-SVM			
	Se(%)	Sp(%)	P+(%)	Acc(%)	Se(%)	Sp(%)	P+(%)	Acc(%)
Normal	99.80	98.72	99.49	99.50	99.61	98.65	99.46	99.34
PVC	96.20	99.85	98.44	99.52	95.44	99.77	97.66	99.38
APC	94.33	99.49	93.09	99.14	95.66	99.63	95.03	99.36
RBBB	93.33	99.73	96.21	99.29	98.00	99.87	98.32	99.75
LBBB	98.00	99.75	96.71	99.63	97.66	99.75	96.69	99.61
Average	96.33	99.51	96.79	99.41	97.27	99.54	97.43	99.49
	Overall accuracy rate = 98.56%				Overall accuracy rate = 98.74%			

as an efficient tool for the problem of ECG beat classification. To confirm this viewpoint, the proposed system was compared with the literature. The comparison results between our approach and some existing ECG classification techniques in term of the classification accuracy Acc(%) are resumed in Table 8. As reported in this table, the proposed ECG classification system can reaches higher or comparable performances with respect to the state-of-the-art. Unfortunately, a fair comparison between all existing ECG classification techniques is very difficult because of the presence of many difficulties including: the large variety of explored classifiers, the number of ECG beats used in each study, as well as the number of classes, the ECG datasets used in each work, the steps of pre-processing stage (e.g. ECG filtering, ECG waves detection) and more.

Table 8. Quantitative comparison of proposed method with other established methods

Methods	Classes	Features set	Classifier	Acc(%)
Martis et al. [17]	5	ECG+PCA	LS-SVM	98.11
Martis et al. [16]	5	DWT+ICA	PNN	99.28
Sahoo et al. [22]	4	DWT+Temporal+Morphological	SVM	98.39
			NN	97.67
Proposed method	5	SWT+Morphological and Statistical measures	KNN	98.56
			SVM	98.74

NN: Neural Network, PNN: Probabilist Neural Network, LS-SVM: Least Square SVM, PCA: Principal Component Analysis, ICA: Independent Component Analysis

5   Conclusion and Perspectives

In this work, we have proposed a novel approach for ECG beat classification purpose. The proposed algorithm is based on two wavelet transform (DWT and SWT) and tested with two classifiers (SVM and KNN). In our method, morphological and statistical features are extracted from the useful DWT/SWT frequency sub-bands corresponding to each ECG beat. The extracted features are input to the SVM and KNN algorithms for final ECG beat classification.

When testing the proposed method on different ECG beats from MITDB, the obtained results show that our approach can be considered as an efficient method for ECG classification purpose, with an overall accuracy of 98.56% and 98.74% for KNN and SVM classifiers respectively. Also, the obtained performances are comparable with some established works in the literature. In a future work, our aim is to improve the proposed methodology by using some dimensionality reduction methods for features reduction such as Principal Component Analysis (PCA), Linear Discriminant Analysis (LDA) and Independent Component Analysis (ICA).

Acknowledgments. This research was supported by the center for Scientific and Technical Research of Morocco (CNRST) (grant number: 18UH2C2017).

References

1. Afonso, V., Tompkins, W., Nquyen, T., Luo, S.: ECG beat detection using filter banks. IEEE Trans. Biomed. Eng. **46**(2), 192–201 (1999)
2. Benitez, S., Gaydecki, P., Zaidi, A., Fitzpatrick, A.: The use of the Hilbert transform in ECG signal analysis. Comput. Biol. Med. **31**, 399–406 (2001)
3. Boser, B.E., Guyon, I.M., Vapnik, V.N.: A training algorithm for optimal margin classifiers. In: Proceedings of the Fifth Annual Workshop on Computational Learning Theory, COLT 1992, pp. 144–152. ACM, New York (1992). https://doi.org/10.1145/130385.130401
4. Bouaziz, F., Boutana, D., Benidir, M.: Multiresolution wavelet-based QRS complex detection algorithm suited to several abnormal morphologies. IET. Signal Process. **8**(7), 774–782 (2014). https://doi.org/10.1049/iet-spr.2013.0391
5. Chen, S., Chen, H., Chan, H.: A real-time QRS method based on moving-averaging incorporating with wavelet denoising. Comput. Methods Prog. Biomed. **82**(3), 187–195 (2006)
6. Christianini, N., Taylor, J.S.: An Introduction to Support Vector Machines and Other Kernel based Learning Methods. Cambridge University Press, Cambridge (2000)
7. Clifford, G.D., Azuaje, F., McSharry, P.E.: Advanced methods and tools for ECG data analysis. Engineering in Medicine and Biology Series, Artech House, Inc. (2006). ISBN 1580539661
8. Faust, O., Hagiwara, Y., Jen Hong, T., Shu Lih, O., Acharya, U.R.: Deep learning for healthcare applications based on physiological signals: a review. Comput. Methods Prog. Biomed. **161**, 1–13 (2018). https://doi.org/10.1016/j.cmpb.2018.04.005
9. Hadj Slimane, Z.E., Nait-Ali, A.: QRS complex detection using Empirical Mode Decomposition. Digit. Signal Process. **20**(4), 1221–1228 (2010)
10. Hu, Y.H., Tompkins, W., Urrusti, J., Afonso, V.: Applications of artificial neural networks for ECG signal detection and classification. J. Electrocardiol. **26**, 66–73 (1993)
11. Kutlu, Y., Kuntalp, D.: Feature extraction for ECG heartbeats using higher order statistics of WPD coefficients. Comput. Methods Prog. Biomed. **105**, 257–267 (2012). https://doi.org/10.1016/j.cmpb.2011.10.002
12. Li, C., Zheng, C., Tai, C.: Detection of ECG characteristic points by wavelet transforms. IEEE Trans. Biomed. Eng. **42**(1), 21–28 (1995)

13. Luz, E.J.d.S., Schwartz, W.R., Camara-Chavez, G., Menotti, D.: ECG-based heartbeat classification for arrhythmia detection: a survey. Comput. Methods Prog. Biomed. **127**, 144–164 (2016). https://doi.org/10.1016/j.cmpb.2015.12.008

14. Mark, R., Moody, G.: MIT-BIH-Arrhythmia Database. http://www.physionet.org/physiobank/database/mitdb

15. Martinez, J., Almeida, R., Olmos, S., Rocha, A., Laguna, P.: A wavelet based ECG delineator: evaluation on standard database. IEEE Trans. Biomed. Eng. **51**(4), 570–581 (2004)

16. Martis, R., Acharya, U., Lim, C.: ECG beat classification using PCA, LDA, ICA and discrete wavelet transform. Biomed. Signal Process. Control **8**(5), 437–448 (2013)

17. Martis, R., Acharya, U., Mandana, K., Ray, A., Chakraborty, C.: Application of principal component analysis to ECG signals for automated diagnosis of cardiac health. Expert Syst. Appl. **39**, 11792–11800 (2012). https://doi.org/10.1016/j.eswa.2012.04.072

18. Moavenian, M., Khorrami, H.: A qualitative comparison of artificial neural networks and support vector machines in ECG arrhythmias classification. Expert Syst. Appl. **37**, 3088–3093 (2010). https://doi.org/10.1016/j.eswa.2009.09.021

19. Nason, G., Silverman, B.: The stationary wavelet transform and some statistical applications. In: Antoniadis, A., Oppenheim, G. (eds.) Wavelets and Statistics. LNS, vol. 103, pp. 281–299. Springer, New York (1995). https://doi.org/10.1007/978-1-4612-2544-7_17

20. Pan, J., Tompkins, W.: A real time QRS detection algorithm. IEEE Trans. Biomed. Eng. **3**(32), 230–236 (1985)

21. Poli, R., Cagnoni, S., Valli, G.: Genetic design of optimum linear and nonlinear QRS detectors. IEEE Trans. Biomed. Eng. **42**, 1137–1141 (1995)

22. Sahoo, S., Kanungo, B., Behera, S., Sabut, S.: Multiresolution wavelet transform based feature extraction and ECG classification to detect cardiac abnormalities. Measurement **24**, 63–71 (2017). https://doi.org/10.1016/j.measurement.2017.05.022

23. Thakor, N., Webster, J., Thompkins, W.: Estimation of the QRS complex power spectra for design of a QRS filter. IEEE Trans. Biomed. Eng. **31**(11), 702–706 (1984)

24. Vapnik, V.: Statistical Learning Theory. Willey, New York (1998)

25. Zidelmala, Z., Amirou, A., Ould Abdeslam, D., Merckle, J.: ECG beat classifcation using a cost sensitive classifier. Comput. Methods Prog. Biomed. **111**, 570–577 (2013). https://doi.org/10.1016/j.cmpb.2013.05.011

Cross-Subject EEG Signal Classification with Deep Neural Networks Applied to Motor Imagery

Mouad Riyad[✉], Mohammed Khalil, and Abdellah Adib

Networks, Telecoms and Multimedia Team, LIM@II-FSTM, B.P. 146,
20650 Mohammedia, Morocco
riyadmouad1@gmail.com, medkhalil87@gmail.com, adib@fstm.ac.ma

Abstract. The Brain-Computer Interface (BCI) is a system able to serve as a mean of communication between machine and human where the brainwaves are the control signals acquired by electroencephalography (EEG). One of the most used brainwaves is the sensorimotor rhythm (SMR) which appears for real or imagined motor movement. In general, EEG signals need feature extraction methods and classification algorithms to interpret the raw signals. Deep learning approaches; however, permit the processing of the raw data without any transformation. In this paper, we present a deep learning neural network architecture to classify SMR signals due to its success for some previous works and to visualize the learned features. The architecture is composed of three parts. The first part contains a temporal convolution operation followed by a spatial convolution one. The second part contains recurrent layers. Finally, we use a dense layer to assign the signal to its class. The model is trained with Adam optimizer algorithm. Also, we use various regularization techniques such as dropout to prevent learning problem like overfitting. To evaluate the performance of the proposed architecture, the well known Dataset IIa of the BCI Competition IV is used. As a result, we get equivalent results to those ones of EEGNet.

Keywords: EEG · BCI · Convolutional neural network · Recurrent neural network · Hybrid network

1 Introduction

Brain-Computer Interface (BCI) is a system that links the brain with the computer using brain activity as a control signal [16]. Such a system processes the brain activities with the signal processing methods, machine learning algorithms and tries to match the observations with neuroscience knowledge. This link can be used for a medical purpose like neurological disease detection [14,23], or non-medical purposes like in entertainment and gaming [15,17].

Brain activity can be recorded with many technologies that can detect electrical, magnetic or chemical brain activities. The electrical activity is often used

© Springer Nature Switzerland AG 2019
E. Renault et al. (Eds.): MSPN 2019, LNCS 11557, pp. 124–139, 2019.
https://doi.org/10.1007/978-3-030-22885-9_12

with electroencephalography (EEG) where sensors placed in the head scalp sense any electrical activity produced by neurons. Many other technologies are used in the litterarture but EEG still the most used one due to its simplicity against others that require complex sensors, and brings a noteworthy temporal resolution. The EEG uses a convention called 10–20 to record the signals. That is is designed to cover the main areas of the brain like the motor cortex that is in charge of the body's movement. For example, when a person performs a movement with its hand, the EEG records what is called a sensorimotor rhythm (SMR) which is a rhythm produced in a specific area of the motor cortex, with a frequency included in the band [8 Hz, 13 Hz] called mu waves. The most impressive fact is that those waves just appear with imagining the movement [19]. This kind of signal will constitute the target of this paper.

The BCI follows, in general, the same pattern recognition step like other fields [16]: The first step is to record the data, using the EEG or other techniques. Secondly, the raw data is preprocessed to remove the artifact like the heartbeat (Electrocardiogram), eyes blink (Electrooculogram) or muscular movement (Electromyogram) [25]. Thirdly, the data is transformed into meaningful information by extracting the most important features with signal processing methods. Fourthly, the features are classified with machine learning into the appropriate class. Finally, the user will get feedback. However, those steps require for many cases to be adjusted to some neurophysiology phenomena like using a filter to get some specific frequency band or the need of a human expert to take some decision during the preprocessing. In this work, only the third step and the fourth one are aimed. In the literature, several methods have been proposed [27]. For feature extraction, Hjorth parameters were created for the EEG signal [7]. Also, a wide range of methods from signal processing were used like Parametric modeling or Wavelet Transform has been used. For the classification, several works used linear classifier like the linear discriminant analysis. Further, probabilistic methods like hidden Markov models were widely used as the main classifier [13].

The traditional approach can raise compatibility issues between the targeted signals, features extraction techniques, and classification methods. On the other hand, deep learning advocates an end-to-end approach where a neural network can process raw data without any preprocessing [5]. This paradigm has permitted to solve many challenging problems in many fields like computer-vision and natural language processing with spectacular performances. Its most imposing characteristics is that it learns how to decompose the data into multiples levels of abstract to extract most relevant feature automatically. Also, it permits the visualizing the learned features to understand the functioning of some neural phenomena. Many works tried the deep learning for BCI, the most relevant results were the ones [21] where several convolutional neural networks (ConvNets) outperformed the state-of-the-art Filter Bank Common Space Pattern (FBCSP) for SMR decoding and proposed the visualization the filters to understand the learning process [12,21]. The work contains many architecture, a shallow convolutional composed with two convolutional layers was proposed, the first convolutional layer is performed to extract the temporal information, then a second convolution layer to get the spatial knowledge than a dense layer to aggregate the extracted data. Also, a deeper network with five aggregation convolutional layers was introduced. In [11], the authors studied the model of the previous work and created a new model that outperforms the FBCSP and the Riemann geometry method which is another state of the art method. Their model is composed of three convolutions. Firstly, a convolution layer is applied to extract the temporal information. Secondly, a convolution in the spatial axis with Depthwise convolution to reduce the number of parameters. Thirdly, a convolution is used to extract more temporal information. We note that this work justified that the size of the convolutions are linked with the sampling frequency of the signal which is not the cases in many works. Also, this model was used with many EEG signals and got high accuracy which proved that BCI and deep learning are compatible. In another work, [28] used a different configuration of the Recurrent Neural Network (RNN) composed with long short time memory (LSTM) cell with different depth and found out that there is no improvement with more than three layers. All the previous works used many methods that are specifics to deep learning. Due to many problems, the models included Exponential Linear Unit (ELU) which is the main activation function for Convnet [3]. Also, the dropout and batch normalization were used to regularize and optimize the network [1]. All those dispositions are a protection against the overfitting and gradient vanishing which disturb the Convnet learning. Furthermore, the pooling is used to reduce the size of the data. For that, we propose to use deep learning for the BCI system.

In this paper, we propose a new Hybrid network composed of a Convnet and an RNN, capable of outperforming the FBCSP, and getting a similar performance of existant deep learning methods. The choice came from the inspiration of many works on other BCI problems where hybrid networks gave high performances [24]. Also, the proposed method will get the best from Convnet which is capable of understanding the spatial feature, and RNN which is designed for sequence-like data. Hence, we develop a hybrid neural network composed of a stacked Convnet followed by a RNN, unlike some parallel hybrid network. We use a convolution to extract temporal information parallel to a depthwise convolution to filtrate spatially the data. There are many possibilities to tweak this part so we choose schemes of [11] which is more accurate and justified. Then, we connect the previous ConvNet with two layers of Gated Recurrent Unit (GRU) cells with 128 units each in the opposite of the LSTM cell that can be complex to train. Finally, we aggregate the output with a dense layer for classification. We use ELU as activation function for the ConvNet which performs better than rectifier linear unit. The batch normalization and the dropout are present on every layer to prevent from overfitting and optimize the result. On the other side, we visualize the learned filter of the ConvNet part as in [11] where neurophysiologically interpretable features extracted and analyzed. The main goal of visualization is to learn how the networks act with the data and which information are the most discriminant.

We organize the paper as follows: In Sect. 2 we provide an introduction to the SMR waves and to Deep Learning neural networks. Then, we introduce the dataset and the experimental protocol, and the proposed method in Sect. 3. The result is discussed in Sect. 4. And finally, the conclusion is in Sect. 5.

2   Background

2.1   EEG and SMR

The EEG records the electrical activity of the brain with electrodes placed in the scalp according to a convention 10–20. It is the most used option in the BCI due to its low complication. For example, it offers a better time resolution in the opposite of the Magnetoencephalography (MEG), or it does not need surgery like the Electrocorticography (ECoG) that requires to put a matrix of sensors in the surface of the brain with irreversible damage [9]. It is very useful to detect neurological or phycological issues.

Some tasks produce a specific signals like in Fig. 1 where it represents SMR signals. It is a rhythm that is occurred in the motor cortex in a frequency band mu [8 Hz, 13 Hz] and beta [13 Hz, 30 Hz] [20]. The rhythms are triggered by motor action like the movement of a hand or legs. The most significant fact about those rhythms is that they are occurred by just imagining the movement. This is what is called Motor Imagery (MI). Such a signal is characterized with a low signal-to-noise ratio which make its detection a complicated challenge [19].

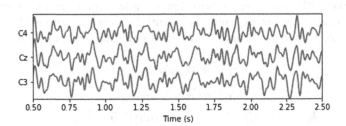

Fig. 1. Sample of the EEG from the dataset IIa of the BCI competition

2.2   ConvNet

The Convnets are a type of deep neural networks that are inspired from visual cortex which can process a data with grid shape, raw in most the cases like images or video [5].

In those networks, there are multiple layers of learnable kernels (also called filter), that can detect most relevant features from the input and assign to each layer a level of abstraction (hierarchical learning). In each layer, the kernels are mostly small compared with the input and are used in the same layer for each neuron which reduces the number of parameters and computational power and improves the efficiency of the networks.

Practically, it is composed of a convolution layer where a discrete convolution is applied to extract the meaningful features [5]. Due to the huge number of the parameters, the data is mostly downsampled to reduce the number of parameters. Also, a non-linearity function is applied with Rectifier Linear Unit of its derivate [3]. In general, a penalization is used to remove any non-relevant information, to prevents overfitting which is very common [1].

2.3   RNN

RNNs are a type of neural networks that are capable of processing sequence like data $(x_1,...,x_n)$ [5]. This is possible because the RNN take as input the previous data where x_{t-1}, the information produced previously to t is always used to understand. The past data is stored in what is called the hidden state and noted h_t.

In theory, the RNN can handle long term dependency. But due to its nature, the RNN suffer from vanishing gradient or exploding where the gradient becomes small or bigger than 1 canceling its effect of long term dependency [18]. To overcome this problem, the solution is then to use a gated mechanism to prevent any issue. Hence, the LSTM was proposed [8]; It works like a memory when it is added to a network, it has the ability to forget some gathered information to stay stable. Its mathematical propriety allows the gradient to be immune to the previous problem.

Then, the GRU was invented with low complex equations in the opposite of LSTM with few parameters which is essential in deep learning [2]. Also, It is capable to get better performance for the small datasets. Its equations are as follows:

$$z_t = \sigma(W_z.[h_{t-1}, x_t]) \tag{1}$$

$$r_t = \sigma(W_r.[h_{t-1}, x_t]) \tag{2}$$

$$h_t = (1 - z_t) * h_{t-1} + z_t * \tanh(W.[r_t * h_{t-1}, x_t]) \tag{3}$$

where W_r is the weights of the reset gate, W_z is the weights of the update gate, W is the weights of the cell, x_t the current input and σ is the sigmoid function. In the Eq. 1, z_t represents the update gate which is responsible to determine the amount of data that need to be used in the future, which eliminate the risk of the gradient vanishing. In the Eq. 2, r_t is the reset gate decide the past data to forgot in the present. The output h_t is the most important which is strongly related to z_t. If z_t is close to 1, a great amount of past data will be kept, and the current data will be lowly represented. And if z_t is close to 0, a small amount of past data will be kept, and the current data will be mostly represented.

With this strategy, the GRU and LSTM gave a high hope to deal with the sequence like data. We will use GRU due to its simplicity.

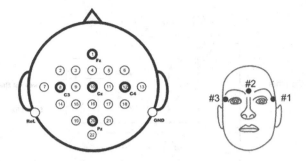

Fig. 2. Sensors position in the scalp which is important for denoising or for classification [26]

3   Method

3.1   Dataset and Experimental Protocol

For a fair comparison, we use the same public dataset and experimental protocol with codes provided by the authors [11, 21]:

The EEG data that is used in coming from the BCI competition IV dataset IIa [26]. It is a cue-based BCI paradigm where 9 subjects were asked to perform motor imagery of four movements 72 times after a cue: Left hand, Right hand, feet, and tongue. The subjects are generally asked to stay in an armchair in front of a screen, the goal of this step is to prevent any movement that can affect the quality of the recording. A beep prevents the subject to prepare himself then a cue is produced to start the motor imagery until a signal is given to them to stop the motor imagery. The data is recorded with a 22 Ag/gCl electrodes placed as in Fig. 2, 3 other electrodes are placed in the face to record the EOG for denoising purpose, sampled at 250 Hz and filtered to get the frequency band (0.5–100)Hz. The data is collected in 2 session where one is dedicated to the training set and the second one for the test set with a total of 288 trial for each one. The signals were resampled at 128 Hz and used the same preprocessing protocol with the software shared by its authors. Only the segment post-cue [0.5–2.5]s is used.

The data will be shaped into a matrix $M_{C,T}$ with a dimension of (22,256) where 22 is the number of channels, and 256 represent a segment of 2 s sampled at 128 Hz.

We choose the cross-subject protocol which imposes the following partitioning [11]: We discard the original training set of the target subject then we randomly choose training sets of five others to be the new training set, the remaining 3 training sets will be used to validate the model. Then, we remain the test set for the target. And, we remind that the training set will not be used which harden the testing. So, we will have a 1440 trial in the training set, 864 in the validation set, and 288 in the test set. This operation is repeated ten times by subject which leads to a 90 fold cross-validation. The mean and the variance are calculated for all folds and we use the one way ANOVA to compare the methods.

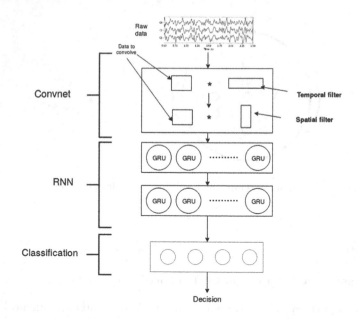

Fig. 3. Representation of the general architecture of the proposed model

3.2 Architecture of the Neural Network

We introduce a novel hybrid neural network based a ConvNet and a RNN. The ConvNet works on filtering the spatial and temporal information, then the RNN processes the sequence data. Then a dense layer is used for classification. The Fig. 3 represents the different blocks of the network, and Table 1 deals with detail of the architecture.

There are many approaches to create the ConvNet, but we choose to use the first block on EEGNet due to its relevancy and well-justified concept [11], we use the 8-2 version: First, it performs 8 2D convolutions kernels with a size of (1, 32) and it is justified with the fact that this size can capture all information above 4 Hz for a signal sampled at 128 Hz, (if the signals were high-passed at 2 Hz, the size would be of size (1, 64)). Then, a depthwise convolution is used on the spatial axis (C, 1), shown that splitting the convolutions into two is better than merging them. Also, authors explain that the use of the depthwise convolution permits to learn specific spatial kernels from each temporal kernel controlled by the parameter called depth that is set the value 2 in our case [11]. Initially, this method was proposed in computer vision; and it is inspired by the state of the art method FBCSP which filters the data with a filterbank then use the common space pattern to spatially filters the data. To optimize the layer and prevents from learning inconvenient, Batch Normalization is used to prevent from saturation of some activation by reducing the internal covariate shift, this is why the Batch Normalization is used before activation and between the 2 convolutions. Then, the ELU activation is applied. The number of parameters is

Table 1. Detail of the architecture of the proposed method

Block	Layer	#filters	#params	output	Activation
1	Input			(22,256)	
	Reshape			(1,22,256)	
	Conv2D	8@(1,32)	256	(8,22,256)	Linear
	BN		32	(8,22,256)	
	DepthwiseConv2D	2*8@(22,1)	352	(16,1,256)	Linear
	BN		64	(16,1,256)	
	Activation			(16,1,256)	ELU
	AveragePool2D	(1,4)		(16,1,64)	
	Dropout			(16,1,64)	
	Permute			(64,16,1)	
	Reshape			(64,16)	
2	Bidirectional GRU	100	70200	(64,200)	Tanh
	BN		256	(64,200)	
	Bidirectional GRU	100	180600	(200)	Tanh
	BN		800	(200)	
	Flatten				
3	Dense	4	804	4	
	Activation			4	Softmax

reduced with an average pooling layer which resamples the signal from 128 Hz to 32 Hz. Naturally, a dropout is used to prevent from overfitting with a rate of 0.2. As in [11], the spatial filter is regularized with a maximum norm of 1 on its weights. The output of this Layer has a shape of (16, 1, 64).

The novelty is unlike EEGNet, we will use a RNN to process the data, this is inspired by many previous works, that part is composed of 2 stacked layers GRU with 100 hidden states. The goal of this layer is to process the output of the previous layer as multivariate signal sampled at 32 Hz, composed with 64 timesteps and 16 features. And to emphasize the recurrent character of the network, we use a bidirectional RNN instead of a vanilla RNN, this will permit the network to train data in two directions (the positive time direction and negative time direction). A single layer of GRU was tested but wasn't efficient as it was expected which justified by some previous work [28]. We apply a Batch Normalization after each layer and use recurrent dropout and dropout with a rate of 0.3 as in the previous layer.

The last block is composed of a classification unit using softmax due to a 4-class problem. Only one dense layer is used to reduce the complexity of the system. A regularization with maximum norm constraint is used with a value of

0.25 [11]. To simplify the architecture, the bias is not used except for the last block and we save the weight of the model when the validation accuracy is at its maximum and used to compare.

3.3 Hyperparameter and Training Setup

All the models (the proposed and the EEGNet) are computed in the same machine with a NVIDIA K80 GPU, With CUDA 9.1, Tensorflow 1.12.0 in Keras API. The hyperparameters are the corner stone of the learning of the training because a wrong choice can gives low result. some workss does not give a justification of the choices as reported in [12]; in the following, we give some explanation about our choices in the Table 2.

Table 2. Detail of the hyperparameter

Hyperparameter	Value	Justification
Batch size	64	As in [11]
Learning rate	1×10^{-4}	This value seems to be more efficient based on a manual tuning
Optimizer	Adam	This optimizer is more efficient and faster. It is a generalization of many others [10]
Loss function	Categorical cross entropy	In a case of multi-class classification, this loss function is the appropriate
Epoch	250	We want a fast training and to discard any chance to get an overfitting
Initialization	Glorot	This method is the most used and relevent for BCI cases [4]
Dropout	0.3	It was occurred during our test that this value is enough and does not slow the training unlike higher values
Decay	No decay	In return, we increase the batch size. [22]
Bias	Only in dense layer	As in the work of lawhern [11]

4 Results

4.1 Classification

Because this work is inspired EEGNet, we will evaluate our approach by comparing with EEGNet. So we train the EEGNet 8-2 as in the original paper and we find a similar result. In the Fig. 4, and with ANOVA, we found that the proposed method is equivalent to EEGNet 8-2 with close result [11] according to the p-value shown in Table 3. Also, we remind that EEGNet 8-2 was compared with the state of the art method FBCSP and outperforms it [11]. During the training part, we observe that there is a high risk of overfitting and mislearning (the network does not learn anything with accuracy at 25%), high for EEGNet 8-2 and a little less for our method. So, we manually tune the learning rate, batch size, and the number of the epoch. We decrease the learning rate to 1×10^{-4} to get a correct fitting where higher values provoke an early overfitting and poor result, and lower values lead to and underfitting. Also, higher batch sizes can speed up the learning but lead to instability which explain the size of 64. Moreover, we observed that if some model learning does not improve significantly after 200, so we fix it at 250. the Table 3 shows that the proposed method has higher number of parameter than EEGNet. But due to the hardware and the difference in number of epochs, the training time is not significantly different.

Furthermore, we note that a hybrid networks learning is fast that a vanilla RNN, which mean that the ConvNet part acts like a compression layer where the input of (22,256) is reduced to (16,64).

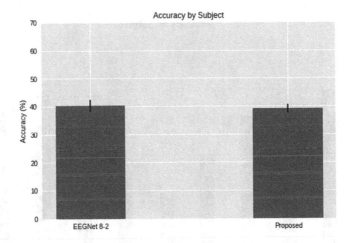

Fig. 4. Results of the classification showing that the two models are equivalent

Table 3. Detail of same statistics

	Mean	Variance	Number of parameters	P-value
Proposed	39.29	1.66	253364	0.69
EEGNet	40.21	2.15	1796	

To detail our results, we study the result of each subject. In Fig. 5. we can group them into three groups: high accuracy, where subject 1 and 8 got the maximum accuracy about 54%; medium accuracy, where subject 3, 9 get an average score between 48 % and 50%; and finally the low accuracy with scores below 40% for the others.

We can explain the low accuracy for all methods (proposed method, EEG-Net, and FBCSP) with the fact that the SMR signals are known to be hard to train because of the low signal-to-noise ratio (SNR) and the ConvNets are trained with just a minimum of preprocessing [21]. Also, each subject has its own specification, like it is shown in Fig. 5 that can ease the learning or fail it. This is why the conception of a universal classifier is a real challenge. For this reason, a calibration step most be required. In our case of a neural network, it is possible to retrain the model with a small learning rate with subject-specific data as proposed in [21]. Moreover, those accuracies in cross-subject are low likely because the BCI has small dataset compared with Computer-vision ones, which can be overcome with the use of Generative Adversary Network (GAN) and other techniques of data augmentation [6].

With all those arguments, the use of the deep neural network for BCI must be subject of more studies to overcome the problem that we highlight.

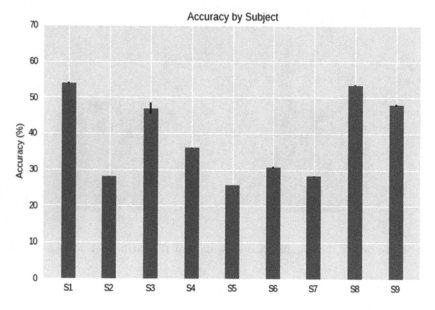

Fig. 5. Result of the proposed method by subject

4.2   Features Visualization

For the visualization of the temporal filter as Fig. 6, we draw the weights of the temporal convolutional filter as a signal of a duration of 0,25 s sampled at 128 Hz

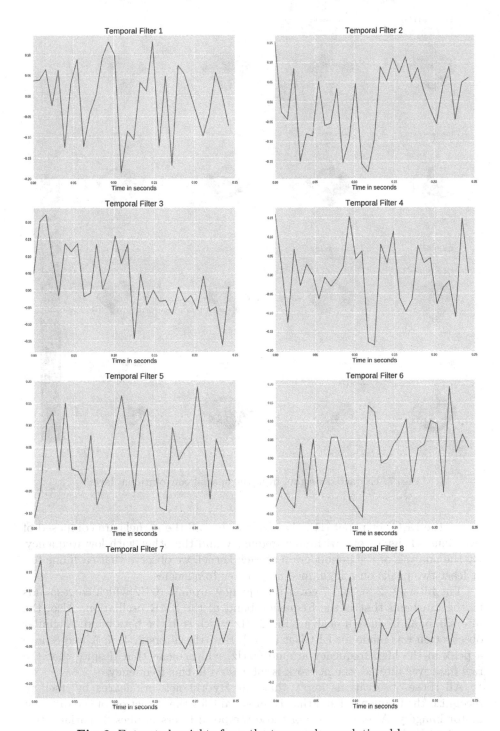

Fig. 6. Extracted weights from the temporal convolutional layer

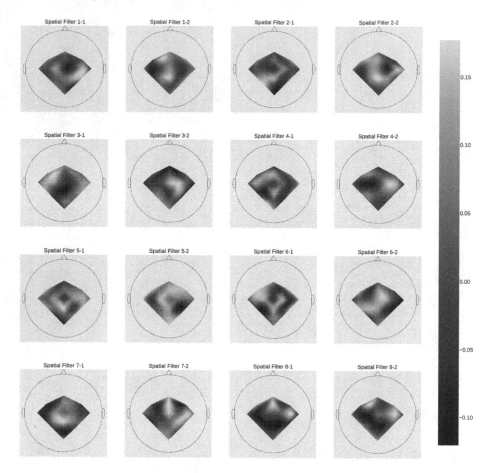

Fig. 7. Extracted weights from the spatial convolutional layer

like in the EEGNet paper [11]. We observe that all the kernels are composed of two sinusoid signals one with high frequency and the other with low frequency. By the analysis of the periodogram of each kernel, we observe that each one has at least two peaks on a high, medium, or low frequencies.

The filters 1, 2, 5, and 7 cover a frequency around 10 Hz which corresponds to the mu band that is the frequency band of the SMR oscillation. Also, the filters 3, 5, and 7 have a peak around 25 Hz which is in the beta band. A similar observation was made for EEGNet in [11]. But, the filters 2, 4, 6, 7, and 8 have a peak in the high frequency around 60 Hz, which mean that despite that the raw data was filtered, the network is interested in this frequency.

All those observations imply that our Hybrid network learns by itself to recognize the frequency band that is important for the detection of the different motor imagery. Also, each one of those temporal filters implies 2 spatial filters linked with the parameter D in 1. The spatial filters are shown in Fig. 7. We occur that there is a decorrelation around the electrode Cz in filter 1–1, 1–2, and 4–2. Moreover, the is a correlation around the electrode C3 in 5–2, 6–1, 3–1. For C4, it is the filter 4–2, 7–2, 8–1, and 8–2 where there is a correlation. This means that each temporal filter will be a bandpass filter for the motor imagery signal (mu and beta) then spatially filters the signal to locate the origin of the excitation as reported in [11]. Moreover, there is a resemblance between some of our filters and the FBCSP filters in the paper of [11].

5   Conclusion

We introduced a novel architecture based on the state-of-the art ConvNet for BCI capable of overcoming the FBCSP in the multiclasses motor imagery problem. The proposed model is based on several models that have proven their efficiency. First, the model perform Temporal and Spatial filtering with convolutional layers that work as the logic of the FBCSP, followed by a RNN composed with 2 stacked layers of GRU cells capable of aggregating the data that is feed with which has sequence structure, then a regression for multiclasses classification. The model was designed to resist to overfitting and gradient vanishing by using the regularisation, Batch Normalization, and GRU cells As RNN layer. We succeed to prove that our model has similar performance as EEGNet. Also, we shown that the low accuracy is strongly related to the nature of the SMR oscillation and the leak of data which was not an obstacle to our model to outperform FBCSP. Furthermore, we visualize the temporal filters and conclude that the network learns by itself to get only the information that corresponds to the frequency band of μ and β which is usually manually made in the feature extraction and preprocessing for the standard algorithm. Moreover, we deduce that the model can locate the area of the excitation to know which motor imagery is performed.

Future work will focus on the development of new strategy to solve the problem linked with the noisy nature of the SMR signals and dataset size.

References

1. Baldi, P., Sadowski, P.J.: Understanding dropout. In: Burges, C.J.C., Bottou, L., Welling, M., Ghahramani, Z., Weinberger, K.Q. (eds.) Advances in Neural Information Processing Systems 26, vol. 00125, pp. 2814–2822. Curran Associates, Inc. (2013)
2. Cho, K., et al.: Learning Phrase Representations using RNN Encoder-Decoder for Statistical Machine Translation. arXiv:1406.1078 [cs, stat], June 2014
3. Clevert, D.A., Unterthiner, T., Hochreiter, S.: Fast and accurate deep network learning by exponential linear units (ELUs). arXiv:1511.07289 [cs], November 2015
4. Glorot, X., Bengio, Y.: Understanding the difficulty of training deep feedforward neural networks, vol. 03417, p. 8 (2010)
5. Goodfellow, I., Bengio, Y., Courville, A.: Deep learning. In: Adaptive Computation and Machine Learning, The MIT Press. Cambridge (2016)

6. Goodfellow, I.J., et al.: Generative adversarial networks. arXiv:1406.2661 [cs, stat], June 2014
7. Hjorth, B.: EEG analysis based on time domain properties. Electroencephalogr. Clin. Neurophysiol. **29**(3), 306–310 (1970). https://doi.org/10.1016/0013-4694(70)90143-4
8. Hochreiter, S., Schmidhuber, J.: Long short-term memory. Neural comput. **9**(8), 1735–1780 (1997)
9. Kaur, E.T., Singh, B.: Brain computer interface: a review. Int. Res. J. Eng. Technol. **04**(04), 9 (2017)
10. Kingma, D.P., Ba, J.: Adam: a method for stochastic optimization. arXiv:1412.6980 [cs], December 2014
11. Lawhern, V.J., Solon, A.J., Waytowich, N.R., Gordon, S.M., Hung, C.P., Lance, B.J.: EEGNet: a compact convolutional neural network for EEG-based brain-computer interfaces. J. Neural Eng. **15**(5), 056013 (2018)
12. Lotte, F., Bougrain, L., Cichocki, A., Clerc, M., Congedo, M., Rakotomamonjy, A., Yger, F.: A review of classification algorithms for EEG-based brain-computer interfaces: a 10 year update. J. Neural Eng. **15**(3), 031005 (2018). https://doi.org/10.1088/1741-2552/aab2f2
13. Lotte, F., Congedo, M., Lécuyer, A., Lamarche, F., Arnaldi, B.: A review of classification algorithms for EEG-based brain-computer interfaces. J. Neural Eng. **4**(2), R1–R13 (2007). https://doi.org/10.1088/1741-2560/4/2/R01. 01903
14. Mao, W., Zhu, J., Li, X., Zhang, X., Sun, S.: Resting state EEG based depression recognition research using deep learning method. In: Wang, S., Yamamoto, V., Su, J., Yang, Y., Jones, E., Iasemidis, L., Mitchell, T. (eds.) BI 2018. LNCS (LNAI), vol. 11309, pp. 329–338. Springer, Cham (2018). https://doi.org/10.1007/978-3-030-05587-5_31
15. McFarland, D.J., Wolpaw, J.R.: Brain-computer interfaces for communication and control. Commun. ACM **54**(5), 60 (2011). https://doi.org/10.1145/1941487.1941506. 06351
16. Nicolas-Alonso, L.F., Gomez-Gil, J.: Brain computer interfaces, a review. Sensors **12**(2), 1211–1279 (2012). https://doi.org/10.3390/s120201211
17. Nijholt, A.: BCI for games: a 'state of the art' survey. In: Stevens, S.M., Saldamarco, S.J. (eds.) ICEC 2008. LNCS, vol. 5309, pp. 225–228. Springer, Heidelberg (2008). https://doi.org/10.1007/978-3-540-89222-9_29
18. Pascanu, R., Mikolov, T., Bengio, Y.: On the difficulty of training Recurrent Neural Networks. arXiv:1211.5063 [cs], November 2012
19. Pfurtscheller, G., Neuper, C.: Motor imagery and direct brain-computer communication. Proc. IEEE **89**(7), 1123–1134 (2001). https://doi.org/10.1109/5.939829
20. Ramadan, R.A., Vasilakos, A.V.: Brain computer interface: control signals review. Neurocomputing **223**, 26–44 (2017). https://doi.org/10.1016/j.neucom.2016.10.024
21. Schirrmeister, R.T., Gemein, L., Eggensperger, K., Hutter, F., Ball, T.: Deep learning with convolutional neural networks for decoding and visualization of EEG pathology. arXiv:1708.08012 [cs, stat], August 2017
22. Smith, S.L., Kindermans, P.J., Ying, C., Le, Q.V.: Don't decay the learning rate, increase the batch size. arXiv:1711.00489 [cs, stat], November 2017
23. Sun, M., Wang, F., Min, T., Zang, T., Wang, Y.: Prediction for high risk clinical symptoms of epilepsy based on deep learning algorithm. IEEE Access 1–1 (2018). https://doi.org/10.1109/ACCESS.2018.2883562

24. Tan, C., Sun, F., Zhang, W., Chen, J., Liu, C.: Multimodal classification with deep convolutional-recurrent neural networks for electroencephalography. arXiv:1807.10641 [cs], July 2018
25. Tan, C., Sun, F., Zhang, W., Chen, J., Liu, C.: Multimodal classification with deep convolutional-recurrent neural networks for electroencephalography. In: Liu, D., Xie, S., Li, Y., Zhao, D., El-Alfy, E.S. (eds.) ICONIP 2017. LNCS, vol. 10635, pp. 767–776. Springer, Cham (2017). https://doi.org/10.1007/978-3-319-70096-0_78
26. Tangermann, M., et al.: Review of the BCI competition IV. Front. Neurosci. **6**, (2012). https://doi.org/10.3389/fnins.2012.00055
27. Vaid, S., Singh, P., Kaur, C.: EEG signal analysis for BCI interface: a review. In: Fifth International Conference on Advanced Computing & Communication Technologies (ACCT), 2015, pp. 143–147. IEEE (2015)
28. Wang, P., Jiang, A., Liu, X., Shang, J., Zhang, L.: LSTM-based EEG classification in motor imagery tasks. IEEE Trans. Neural Syst. Rehabil. Eng. **26**(11), 2086–2095 (2018). https://doi.org/10.1109/TNSRE.2018.2876129

Data Communication in Electromagnetic Nano-networks for Healthcare Applications

Hanen Ferjani[1,2]([⊠]) and Haifa Touati[1,2]

[1] Hatem Bettaher IResCoMath Research Unit, Gabès, Tunisia
[2] Faculty of Science of Gabes, University of Gabes, Gabès, Tunisia
ferjanihanen1@gmail.com, haifa.touati@cristal.rnu.tn

Abstract. One of the most promising applications of nanotechnology is their use in health care scenarios to monitor, in real-time, several parameters inside the human body such as cancer biomarker detection, glucose level, etc. However, real-time medical parameters communication is constrained by the tiny size of nano-nodes and their extremely limited energy. Ongoing efforts in this area are in their very early stage of development. Therefore further research is required to propose a suitable communication model. In this paper, we study the deployment of nano-networks in a living biological environment, and we focus on communication protocols challenges that must be overcome. We also proposed a multi-hop data dissemination approach that transmits sensed data from nano-nodes moving inside an artery to an outside controller while optimizing energy consumption.

Keywords: Nano-network · Healthcare applications ·
Electromagnetic communication · Communication protocols

1 Introduction

Nanotechnology is undoubtedly an emerging technology that will have a major impact in our daily lives in the near future. According to the famous scientist Robert Floyd Curl Jr, winner of the Nobel Prize in Chemistry in 1996, nanotechnology has been used for two thousand years.

Recently, because of the growing interest in atomic and subatomic particles, the scientific community has begun to question the viability of a deterministic disposition of these nano-particles. As a result, nano-science has taken off and many sub-disciplines are now focusing their efforts on assembling nano-particles to produce much more qualified nano-materials and nano-devices.

A nano-network is formed by connecting nano-devices; therefore, it is able to perform more complex tasks such as drug administration, health surveillance and the detection of biological or chemical attacks in nano-scale environments through the cooperation of nano-machines. Nano-networks connected to Internet

© Springer Nature Switzerland AG 2019
E. Renault et al. (Eds.): MSPN 2019, LNCS 11557, pp. 140–152, 2019.
https://doi.org/10.1007/978-3-030-22885-9_13

gateways enables a new network paradigm called *Internet of Nano-Things* or IoNT.

The IoNT has a great potential for advanced health services and applications. Integration of IoNT with other healthcare network systems will expand the range of services that can be provided to patients as well as health decision-makers. But the efficient dissemination of data in a nano-network poses several challenges to communication protocols.

The main contribution of this paper, is to study the applicability of the evolving nano-network technology for heathcare monitoring from a communication protocols perspective. Nano-communication challenges in healthcare applications are identified and the main architecture of our energy efficient communication approach is presented.

The reminder of this paper is organized as follows: In Sect. 2, we define some nanotechnology related concepts. Then, Sect. 3, presents the communication challenges related to the application of nanotechnology in healthcare applications and details recent proposed communication protocols. The proposed architecture is presented in Sect. 4. Finally, concluding remarks are given in Sect. 5.

2   An Overview of Nano-network Architecture

The concept of nanotechnology was described in detail by the physicist Richard Feynman in his famous lecture entitled *"There is a lot of room for substance"* in 1959. The development of nanotechnologies has a considerable potential for advances in knowledge and positive transformations in our daily lives. Some examples of the benefits they can bring are: New medical diagnostic tools, better targeted drugs to combat cancer tumors or other serious illnesses such as AIDS, technological leaps with new breakthroughs in information and communication technologies, materials that are both stronger, more resilient and better formable or deformable, openness to substantial progress in the area of energy savings and new energies that will condition our future, etc.

The progress of nanotechnology improves the development of new nano-materials that is known in literature as *nano-machine*. Throughout this paper, we use the terms '*nano-machine*', and '*nano-device*' interchangeably. The size of these nano-machines ranges from one to few hundred of nano-meters and they can perform only simple computation, sensing and actuation tasks. A network of nano-machines is called a *nano-network*. This later expands the capabilities of a single nano-device by providing a way to cooperate and share information. Finally, *nano-communication* is defined as the exchange of information at the nano-scale on the basis of any wired or wireless interconnection of nano-machines in a nano-network.

2.1   Different Components of a Nano-machine

A nano-machine is an integrated device formed of one or more components incorporated into each other in different levels of complexity. It ranges from a simple

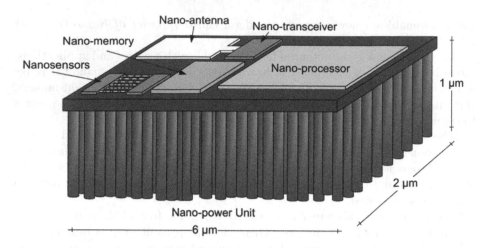

Fig. 1. Nano-machine units [2]

miniaturization machine to high-end and sophisticated nano-robotics. As shown in Fig. 1, a Nano-machine is composed by the following units [2]:

- **Processing unit:** Nano-processors are activated by the development of smaller FET transistors in different forms. The smallest transistor experimentally tested to date is based on a thin graphene strip. Despite being small, the transistors are able to operate at higher frequencies.
- **Data storage unit:** Nano-memories store a single bit on a single atom by nano-material and new technologies. The atomic memories have been currently introduced which consider the presence of one silicon atom as storing bit 1 (or 0) and its absence as storing bit 0 (or 1).
- **Power unit:** The supply of nano-machines requires new types of nano-batteries [16,17] as well as nano-scale energy recovery systems [18]. One of the most promising techniques is to convert vibratory energy into electricity. This energy can then be stored in a nano-battery and consumed dynamically by the device.
- **Communication unit:** Nano-antennas units together with transceiver schemes will enable the communication among nano-devices.
- **Sensing unit:** A nano-sensor is not just a tiny sensor, but a device that makes use of the novel properties of nano-materials to identify and measure new types of events in the nano-scale, such as the physical characteristics of structures just a few nano-meters in size, chemical compounds in concentrations as low as one part per billion, or the presence of biological agents such as virus, bacteria or cancerous cells. Those tiny sensors can be classified into three types which are *physical, chemical* and *biological* nano-sensors and they have been developed by using graphene and other nano-materials [15,19]. Nano-sensors types will be detailed in the following sub-section.

2.2   Types of Nano-sensors

The various nano-sensors can be loosely grouped into three broad categories:

- **Physical nano-sensors:** these are used to measure magnitudes such as mass, pressure, force, or displacement. Their working principle is usually based on the fact that the electronic properties of both nano-tubes and nano-ribbons change when these are bent or deformed.
- **Chemical nano-sensors:** these are used to measure magnitudes such as the concentration of a given gas, the presence of a specific type of molecules, or the molecular composition of a substance.
- **Biological nano-sensors:** these are used to monitor bio-molecular processes such as antibody/antigen interactions, DNA interactions, enzymatic interactions or cellular communication processes, among others.

2.3   Nano-machine Development Techniques

In order to develop nano-machines, there are basically three main techniques (i) Top down approach, (ii) Bottom-up approach and (iii) Bio Hybrid Approach [1].

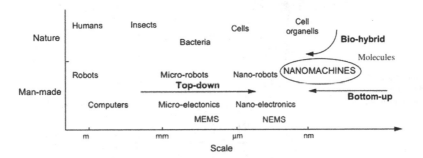

Fig. 2. Approaches for the development of nano-machines [1].

- *The top-down approach:* is focused on the development of nano-scale objects by downscaling current existing micro-scale level device components. To achieve this goal, advanced manufacturing techniques, such as electron beam lithography and micro-contact printing, are used. Resulting devices keep the architecture of preexisting micro-scale components such as micro-electronic devices and Micro-Electro-Mechanical Systems (MEMS).
- *The bottom up approach:* focused on the design of nano-machines using individual molecules. This approach is nominated as molecular manufacturing. Example: Nano-machines like molecular switches, molecular shuttles, etc.
- *The bio hybrid approach:* focused on the design of new nano-machines, also known as biological nano-machines, based on molecular signalling. Example: Bio-nano robots, nano-biosensors, biological storing components etc.

3   Wireless Nano Sensors Networks

3.1   Wireless Nano Sensors Network Architecture

In the previous section, nano-machines have been defined as autonomous units capable of performing simple tasks. The number of tasks that these devices can perform and their range of operation is greatly limited by their size. To facilitate communication between nano-machines, Akyildiz et al. have defined in [3] a new architecture for the nano-sensor-network. They mentioned that a network of nano-sensors should be composed of three types of nodes that can be fixed or mobile, as shown in Fig. 3: The *nano-nodes*, the *nano-routers* and the *nano-micro-interface*, in addition to the *gateway*.

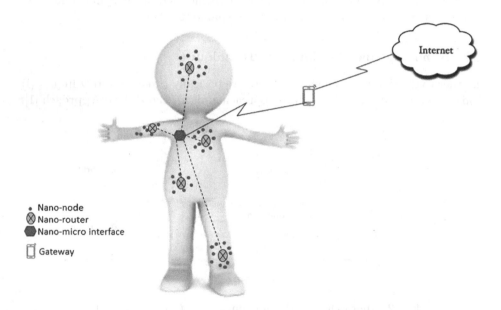

Fig. 3. Wireless nano sensor networks components

– **Nano-nodes:** Nano-nodes are regarded as the smallest and simplest nano-machines which perform various tasks like computation and transmission of the data over short distances and have less memory.
– **Nano-routers:** Nano-routers have large computational power in comparison to nano-nodes and can aggregate and process information coming from nano-nodes. They also control nano-nodes by the exchange of control commands.
– **Nano-micro interface devices:** These devices perform the task of aggregation of information coming from nano-routers and transmit it to the micro-scale and vice versa. They act as hybrid devices to communicate in nano-scale using Nano-communication techniques and also with traditional communication networks using classical network protocols.

- **Gateway:** It enables the remote control of the entire nano-network over the Internet. For example, in health monitoring application, an advanced cellphone can receive the information from a nano-micro interface and forward data to a health-care center.

3.2 Nano-sensor Networks' Communication Paradigms

Since existing conventional communication paradigms can not be applied directly to this domain without taking into account the new constraints of nano-devices, new communication paradigms have been proposed over the past decade. Two main representatives of this field can be cited: (i) *molecular* communications and (ii) *electromagnetic* communications.

Molecular Communication: Molecular communication is defined as the transmission and reception of information encoded in molecules. Molecular communication is a new and interdisciplinary field that spans nano, bio and communication technologies [4]. Molecular communication consists of nano-machines, nano-receptors, carrier molecules, information molecules and the environment in which they operate. Emitters and receivers are biologically and artificially created Bio-Nano-machines that have the ability to emit and capture information molecules. The information data is moved from the sender to the recipient by the carriers. The carriers in this system are molecular motors, hormones or neurotransmitters. Since molecular communication works in the biological system, the information to be transmitted is proteins, ions or DNAs. The environment is the aqueous solution that is inside and between cells.

As illustrated in Fig. 4, the five phases in the operation of molecular communication are as follows:

- **Encoding:** This is the phase in which the bio-nano-source machine, or transmitter codes the information into information molecules that are detected by the bio nano receiving machine.
- **Sending:** This is the phase by which a bio-nano-emitting machine emits these molecules of information into the environment. This is done by untying the information molecules from the sender's bio-nano-machine.
- **Propagation:** Propagation is a common method present in all communication technologies. Propagation is the phase in which information moves from the source to the destination. This is similar for molecular communication where information molecules move from the bio-nano-emitting machine to the bio-nano-machine
- **Reception:** As the word implies, this is the phase in which the bio-nano-receiving machine captures the information molecules that propagate in the bio-nano-environment
- **Decoding:** Encoding and decoding are the most important phases in communication methods. In molecular communication during decoding, the bio nano-receiver machine captures the information molecules and decodes the received molecules into a chemical reaction.

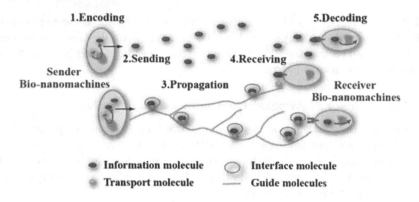

Fig. 4. Molecular communication system [22]

Electromagnetic Communication: The electromagnetic (EM) communication is based on the transmission of information through modulation and demodulation of electromagnetic waves by components that are manufactured by novel nano-materials. Extremely high electromagnetic frequencies (expected in the THz band) are used for communication among nano-devices. This frequency band (0.1–10 THz) can potentially provide very large bandwidths. Recent advancements in molecular and carbon electronics have opened the door to a new generation of electronic nano-components such as nano-batteries, nano-memories [6], logical circuitry in the nano-scale and even nano-antennas [7]. In this paper, we focus on applications based on electromagnetic communications.

4   Nanotechnology for Health-Care Applications

The world of nanotechnology offers fields of application of a crazy diversity. Among the areas in which nanotechnology already plays an important role and will have a decisive role in the future, health is of course in the lead. Different challenges against protocols design are still being investigated with no currently fully developed solutions.

4.1   Communication Challenges

The limited processing and storage capabilities of nano-machines require that **routing design** should take into account the random and dynamic topology of the network inside the body because of the uncontrolled properties of the biological communication medium. Moreover, the routing process should limit to a minimum the collaboration between the nano-machines.

The communication range for IoNT systems should be between $1cm$ and $1m$ for terahertz electromagnetic communication [8]. This implies that the transmission range is very limited, which makes multi-hop communication and routing a critical aspect of nano-networks. In addition, the direction of a communication channel is not deterministic and depends on the speed of the nano-machines inside the body, which can cause a delay in communication. The mobility of nano-machines can be used for routing to reduce delays due to packet propagation but this will require efficient systems for creating and managing multi-hop paths.

Designing a **channel access** procedure is a very difficult task for any wireless technology. Since the WNSN network has a very large number of nano-nodes, it becomes even more difficult. In this context, protocols requiring synchronization between nodes are generally not recommended [9].

In addition, since the most suitable transmission techniques are based on pulse communications, approaches based on carry-over detection strategies, such as carrier-based multiple access (CSMA), can not be applied in the same way because of the absence of a signal to detect.

At the **physical layer level**, since the in-vivo medium contains bio-materials and fluids, e.g., blood, the THz signal could be contaminated. A recent study made by Ahmed et al. in [20] has shown that RBC concentration in the blood widely affects path loss and communication quality. Thus investigating the blood's spreading and absorption spectrum and proposing adequate electromagnetic model for the blood in the THz band is necessary.

4.2   Literature Review of WNSN Communication Protocols

To resolve the above communication challenges and adapt communication protocols to WNSN constraints, several solutions have been recently proposed. In this section, we summarize the key contributions on MAC and routing protocols for WNSN in the electromagnetic communication model.

Greedy energy-harvesting aware and **optimal energy harvesting aware** are two forwarding schemes, based on energy, proposed in [10] for nano-sensors moving uniformly in an environment following human blood directions. In greedy forwarding scheme, the neighbor with the highest energy level is nominated by the greedy energy-harvesting scheme as a relay node. Whereas, the optimal energy-harvesting scheme chooses the node that can maximize the network energy level as a relay node.

A centralized routing framework based on hierarchical clustering architecture is introduced in [11]. The authors introduce a routing framework for WNSNs that uses a hierarchical cluster-based architecture to offload the network operation complexity from the individual nano-sensors towards the cluster heads, or nano-controllers.

Piro et al. Proposed in [12] two routing algorithms along with two MAC protocol for electromagnetic WNSN. In this work, the authors propose and evaluate two routing strategies, specifically the **selective flooding routing** and the **random routing**.

- In the **selective flooding** routing, when a nano-node receives a packet, it broadcasts the message to all the devices within its transmission range. Therefore, a packet generated by a nano-node is propagated into the network.

- In the **random routing** approach, to send a packet to the nano-micro interface, a nano-node selects randomly one neighboring node to forward the data.

In addition to these two routing approaches, Piro et al. introduced two different asynchronous MAC strategies, namely the **transparent-MAC** and **Smart-MAC**:

- In **transparent-MAC**, the packet is simply forwarded from the network layer to the physical layer without executing any kind of control.
- In **Smart-MAC**, the packet received from the upper layer is kept in a queue until delivery to physical layer. Before sending out a packet, the MAC layer starts a handshaking process to find the neighbors of the node. If there is one or more node within its transmission range, it sends the packet to the physical interface. Therefore, if the network layer has not already determined the next-hop, the MAC layer will select it randomly among neighboring nano-nodes. Moreover, if a nano-node haven't any neighbor, the nano-node waits a random back off time, and then it starts the handshaking process to find the nano-nodes in its transmission region.

To evaluate their proposals, Piro et al. implemented the Nano-Sim simulator [13], an NS-3 module to model WNSNs [12] which is currently widely used as a reference simulator.

In [14], a **Probabilistic-Based Broadcasting** for electromagnetic WNSN algorithm is proposed. The algorithm determines the rebroadcast probability by considering the network density. In this way, for low-density nodes, the rebroadcast probability is increased while it is decreased for high density nodes.

5   Our Proposed Communication Architecture

Currently, flooding is the principal protocol used to disseminate data between nano-machines. However, this scheme is inefficient in term of resources usage since it results in bandwidth waste and collision due to excessive messages transmission. Therefore, an urgent challenge for Wireless Nano Sensor Networks is to adapt data dissemination protocols to the energy constraint of the nano-devices while minimizing packet loss ratio, energy consumption, collision and average latency. For this purpose, we present a novel communication architecture to disseminate sensed data inside an artery to an outside controller using a WNSN.

The targeted scenario is a health-monitoring application where multiple nano-devices are deployed in an artery as shown in Fig. 5. Sensing Data are generated by nano-nodes. Data packets are usually sent from nano-nodes (sources) to the nano-micro interface (destination). We assume that, nano-nodes are moving with a constant velocity and following a given direction while the nano-routers and nano-micro interface are stationary nodes. The nano- micro-interface is placed at the middle of the artery. We place the nano-routers in a way that each nano-router has at least one nano-router in its transmission range.

The main idea of our data dissemination scheme is inspired by the geographic routing, which is widely used in VANET [21], WSN [23] and IoT [24] networks.

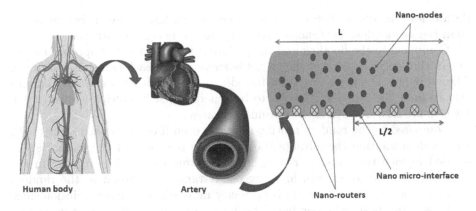

Fig. 5. Proposed communication architecture

As shown in Fig. 6, to avoid energy harvesting the key feature is to reduce the number of relaying nodes (especially relaying nano-nodes) for a given transmission. To that end, we propose to associate each nano-node to one nano-router, called nearest router $(N.R)$. The nearest nano-router $(N.R)$ is chosen based on its location from the sender nano-node (S). Once reaching the $N.R$, the DATA packet will be forwarded only by nano-routers until it reaches the nano-micro-interface. In other words, a message sent by a nano-router will never be relayed by a nano-node, which save the energy of the nano-nodes.

To reach its nearest nano-router, the sender node (S) selects the best neighbor nano-node $(B.N)$ based on its distance to the chosen nearest nano-router $(N.R)$. The DATA packet is forwarded from best neighbor to best neighbor until it reaches the nearest nano-router $(N.R)$. This scheme guarantees that in each transmission range only one nano-node forwards the DATA packet.

Compared to recent routing protocols proposed in the literature for WNSN (see Sect. 4.2), our approach is clearly more energy efficient due two important conceptual features: First, the association to the nearest router, which guarantees that a minimum number of nanonodes will be involved in the multi-hop transmission to reach the nanorouter. Second, once reaching a nano-router, the

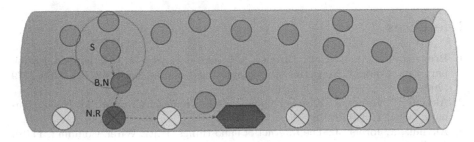

Fig. 6. Principal of our data dissemination algorithm

data is forwarded only between nanorouters, which have more energy resources than the nanonodes. This choice saves nanonodes' energy resources.

Compared to the flooding and the probabilistic schemes, our approach guarantees that only one copy of the packet is forwarded in each transmission range. The probabilistic scheme, even if it introduces a rebroadcast probability parameter to limit the number of copies to be generated, still multiple copies of the packets are forwarded in each transmission range.

Compared to the random routing solution, even if our approach shares with the random solution the advantage of that only one copy of the packet is forwarded in each transmission range, it outperforms the random routing in the choice of the forwarder, which, we recall, is randomly chosen in the random routing. The forwarder selection is obviously more efficient in our solution since it chooses the best neighbor based on its geographic position to the nearest router. This choice reduces hop count and avoids network loops in multi-hop connection, which is the main drawback of the random routing.

Finally, compared to the centralized routing framework, our approach operates in a distributed manner where the routing process is managed by all the nodes in the network, whereas in the centralized approach the life time of the nano-controllers could be a real challenge.

6 Conclusion and Future Scope

In healthcare, the use of nanotechnology is being explored in the fight against diseases such as cancer, glucose etc. That is why, in this paper, we tackle the problem of the applicability of a nano-network to monitor some parameters inside the human body from the data communication perspective. We focus on electromagnetic communication protocols challenges in healthcare applications that must be overcome and we highlight some recent proposals for these communication challenges. Finally, we propose a communication architecture based on a geographic routing approach, to disseminate data between nano-machines while reducing energy consumption. A qualitative comparison to existing solutions highlights the efficiency of our proposal.

As a future work, we plan to carry out a quantitative study to analyze the performance of our approach using simulations.

References

1. Brunetti, F., Akyildiz, I., Blzquez, C.: Nanonetworks: a new communication paradigm. Comput. Netw.: Int. J. Comput. Telecommun. Netw. **52**(12), 2260–2279 (2008)
2. Akyildiz, I., Jornet, J.: Electromagnetic wireless nanosensor networks. Nano Commun. Netw. **1**, 319 (2010)
3. Akyildiz, I., Jornet, J.: The Internet of nano-things. IEEE Wirel. Commun. **17**(6), 58–63 (2010)

4. Moore, M., et al.: A design of a molecular communication system for nanomachines using molecular motors. In: Proceedings of the Fourth Annual IEEE International Conference on Pervasive Computing and Communications (PerCom 2006), March 2006

5. Dragoman, M., Dragoman, D.: Graphene-based quantum electronics. Progress Quantum Electron. **33**(6), 165–214 (2009)

6. Rutherglen, C., Burke, P.: Nanoelectromagnetics: circuit and electromagnetic properties of carbon nanotubes. Small **5**(8), 884–906 (2009)

7. Burke, P., Rutherglen, C., Yu, Z., Burke, P.: Nanotubes and Nanowires. World Scientific (2007)

8. Agoulmine, N., Kim, K., Kim, S., Rim, T., Lee, J.-S., Meyyappan, M.: Enabling communication and cooperation in bio-nanosensor networks: toward innovative healthcare solutions. IEEE Wirel. Commun. **19**(5), 42–51 (2012)

9. Akyildiz, I., Jornet, J.: The Internet of nano-things. IEEE Wireless Commun. **17**(6), 58–63 (2010)

10. Boggia, G., Piro, G., Grieco, L.A.: On the design of an energy harvesting protocol stack for body area nano-networks. Nano Commun. Netw. **6**(2), 74–84 (2014)

11. Akkari, N., Almasri, S., Pierobon, M., Jornet, J.M., Akyildiz, I.: A routing framework for energy harvesting wireless nanosensor networks in the terahertz band. Wirel. Netw. **20**(5), 1169–1183 (2014)

12. Piro, G., Grieco, L.A., Boggia, G., Camarda, P.: Nano-Sim: simulating electromagnetic-based nanonetworks in the network simulator 3. In: Proceedings of The SimuTools, pp. 203–210 (2013)

13. Grieco, L., Boggia, G., Piro, G., Camarda, P.: Simulating wireless nano sensor networks in the NS-3 platform. In: Proceedings of The Workshop on Performance Analysis and Enhancement of Wireless Networks, Barcelona, Spain (2013)

14. Oukhatar, A., Bakhouya, M., Ouadghiri, D.E., Zine-Dine, K.: Probabilistic Based Broadcasting for EM-based Wireless Nanosensor Networks. In: MoMM 2017, 4–6 December 2017

15. Hierold, C., Jungen, A., Stampfer, C., Helbling, T.: Nano electromechanical sensors based on carbon nanotubes. Sens. Actuators. A: Phys. **136**(1), 51–61 (2007)

16. Ji, L., et al.: Multilayer nanoassembly of Sn-nanopillar arrays sandwiched between graphene layers for highcapacity lithium storage. Energy Environ. Sci. **4**(9), 3611–3616 (2011)

17. Stoller, M.D., Park, S., Zhu, Y., An, J., Ruoff, R.S.: Graphene-based ultracapacitors. Nano Lett. **8**(10), 3498–3502 (2008)

18. Wang, Z.L.: Towards self-powered nanosystems: from nanogenerators to nanopiezotronics. Adv. Funct. Mater. **18**(22), 3553–3567 (2008)

19. Yonzon, C.R., Stuart, D.A., Zhang, X., McFarland, A.D., Haynes, C.L., Duyne, R.P.V.: Towards advanced chemical and biological nanosensors-an overview. Talanta **67**(3), 438–448 (2005)

20. Salem, A., Azem, A.M.A.: The effect of RBCs concentration in blood on the wireless communication in Nano-networks in the THz band. Nano Commun. Netw. **18**, 34–43 (2018)

21. Kardi, A., Touati, H.: NDVN : named data for vehicular networking. Int. J. Eng. Res. Technol. IJERT **4**(4) (2015)

22. Nakano, T., Moore, M.J., Wei, F., Vasilakos, A.V., Shuai, J.: Molecular communication and networking: opportunities and challenges. IEEE Trans. Nanobiosci. **11**(2), 135–148 (2012)

23. Aboud, A., Touati, H.: Geographic interest forwarding in NDN-based wireless sensor networks. In: Proceedings of the 13th ACS/IEEE International Conference on Computer Systems and Applications (AICCSA), November 2016
24. Aboud, A., Touati, H., Hnich, B.: Efficient forwarding strategy in a NDN-based Internet of things. Cluster Comput. (2018). https://doi.org/10.1007/s10586-018-2859-7

A Distributed Ensemble of Deep Convolutional Neural Networks with Random Forest for Big Data Sentiment Analysis

Badr Ait Hammou[1(✉)], Ayoub Ait Lahcen[1,2], and Salma Mouline[1]

[1] LRIT, Associated Unit to CNRST (URAC 29), Rabat IT Center,
Faculty of Sciences, Mohammed V University, Rabat, Morocco
badr.aithamou@gmail.com, ayoub.aitlahcen@univ-ibntofail.ac.ma,
salma.mouline@um5.ac.ma
[2] LGS, National School of Applied Sciences (ENSA),
Ibn Tofail University, Kenitra, Morocco

Abstract. Big data has become an important issue for a large number of research areas. With the advent of social networks, users can express their feelings about the products they bought or the services they used every day. Also, they can share their ideas and interests, discuss current issues. Therefore, Big Data sentiment analysis has become important in decision-making processes. In this paper, we propose a novel distributed ensemble of deep convolutional neural networks with random forest for sentiment analysis, which is tailored to handle large-scale data and improve classification accuracy. Experimental results on two real-world data sets confirm the claim.

Keywords: Big data · Distributed deep learning ·
Natural language processing · Word2Vec · Random forest ·
Sentiment analysis · Twitter

1 Introduction

Big data has become an important issue for a large number of research areas. The main challenge for big data lies in processing the huge amount of data and extracting useful information for specific objectives. Several big data frameworks have been developed for massive data processing and enabling the efficient utilization of data mining methods [6].

With the advent of social networks, big data analytics played an important role in decision-making processes. For instance, Twitter has evolved to become a source of varied kind of information. This is due to the fact that people post real-time messages about their opinions on a variety of topics, share ideas and interests, discuss current issues and express positive or negative sentiment for products they utilize in daily life [21,28,29]. In order to analyze these data

© Springer Nature Switzerland AG 2019
E. Renault et al. (Eds.): MSPN 2019, LNCS 11557, pp. 153–162, 2019.
https://doi.org/10.1007/978-3-030-22885-9_14

properly, the traditional analytic techniques require an adaptation according to the new big data paradigms emerged for massive data processing.

Sentiment analysis represents a practical technique, which is widely used to allow businesses, politicians, organizations, researchers, and governments to know about people's sentiments and understand their behaviors for specific purposes [12, 26, 27].

Recently, deep learning models have achieved remarkable success in various natural language processing tasks, such as text classification and sentiment analysis [19, 25]. However, the exponential growth of data generated in social networks has created serious problems for sentiment analysis due to their high computational complexity, especially in the context of big data. Moreover, improving the performance in terms of classification accuracy is very important in real-world sentiment analysis applications.

In this paper, we propose a novel distributed ensemble of deep convolutional neural networks with random forest for big data sentiment analysis. It is tailored to increase the classification accuracy, and processing large-scale data efficiently.

The rest of the paper is organized as follows. Section 2 presents the related work. Section 3 introduces the convolutional neural networks for text classification. Section 4 details the proposed methodology. Section 5 describes the experimental results. Finally, Sect. 6 concludes this paper.

2   Related Work

In recent years, deep learning models have played an important role in natural language processing. Indeed, several deep learning models for natural language processing have been designed based on employing word vector representations [12]. Mikolov et al. [8] proposed the Word2Vec algorithm, a deep learning model for vector representations of the words, which is intended to convert words into meaningful vectors. Rezaeinia et al. [12] proposed a novel method called Improved Word Vectors (IWV), which is dedicated to improving the accuracy of pre-trained word embeddings in sentiment analysis.

On the other hand, Zhang et al. [25] conducted a sensitivity analysis of one-layer CNNs for sentence classification. This analysis is specifically intended to investigate the effect of architecture components on the model performance. Socher et al. [21] developed a machine learning framework based on semi-supervised recursive autoencoders for predicting sentiment distributions. While, Socher et al. [22] proposed a model called the Recursive Neural Tensor Network (RNTN), which is designed for semantic compositionality over a human annotated sentiment treebank. Ren et al. [24] designed a topic-enhanced word embedding approach for Twitter sentiment classification. Irsoy et al. [23] developed a deep recursive neural network, which relies on stacking multiple recursive layers for sentiment analysis tasks. Kim [19] proposed three deep learning models, which are designed based on convolution neural network and pre-trained word2vec vectors for sentence classification.

3 Deep Convolutional Neural Networks for Text Classification

This section presents the word embedding and convolutional neural networks for text classification.

3.1 Word Embedding

Recently, several natural language processing tasks have been considerably improved via deep learning models. Word2Vec represents one of the most popular word embedding techniques based on neural networks, which is developed by Tomas Mikolov in 2013 at Google. It is specifically designed to learn high-quality vector representations of words from large amounts of textual data [8,9]. These representations of words are helpful for several problems, such as text classification and clustering [10–12].

Generally, there are two variants of word2vec to generate distributed representations of words, namely, skip-gram and continuous bag-of-words (CBOW) models. Skip-gram aims to predict the context given a word, while CBOW aims to predict a word given its context. The main assumption behind them is that words close in meaning are near in the word embedding space [11]. In this step, Google News pre-trained model is adopted to extract continuous vector representations of words. As each word is represented as a D-dimensional vector, all the word embeddings are stacked in a $V \times D$ matrix, where each row is related to a single word, V is the vocabulary size, and D is embedding vector size.

3.2 Deep Convolutional Neural Networks

Deep convolutional neural networks (CNNs) have demonstrated good performance in various Natural Language Processing tasks. In particular, each CNN architecture is based on the following blocks:

Convolutional Layer

The convolutional layer represents the most important building block of convolutional neural network architectures. It is mainly based on the convolution operation.

Let S be a review that consists of N words after padding. To process this review using CNN, it is necessary to transform textual data into numerical vectors. Based on the word embeddings, each review S can be converted into a $N \times D$ matrix denoted X_S, where each word is represented by a vector of size D.

Given X_S the input of CNN, $\{b_1, b_2, \ldots, b_k\}$ the biases values, and $\{W_1, W_2, \ldots, W_k\}$ the k convolution weight matrices of size $f \times D$. The convolution process can be expressed as follows:

$$Y_i = A(X_S * W_i + b_i) \tag{1}$$

Where $*$ represents the convolution operation, $A(.)$ is the activation function [13–15].

Pooling Layer

The pooling layer stands for the second common building block of CNN. Indeed, after the convolution process, the pooling layer is intended to subsample the outputs generated by the convolutional layers.

Let Y_i be the output obtained by the ith convolution layer. The max-pooling selects the maximum value of the convolution layer. This process can be expressed as follows:

$$MY_i = max(Y_i) \tag{2}$$

where MY_i is the maximum value of Y_i.

Fully Connected Layer

After the concatenation of the maximum values provided by the k convolution layers, the set of relevant features representing each sentence is denoted as follows:

$$F = (MY_i, \ i = 1, \ldots, k) \tag{3}$$

where F depends to each sentence.

Then, the fully connected layer processes the features to produce the final output. In particular, it outputs the estimated class probabilities.

4 Proposed Methodology for Big Data Sentiment Analysis

In this section, we present our proposal, a distributed ensemble of deep convolutional neural networks with random forest using Tensorflow and Spark, for sentiment analysis in the context of big data. The main purpose is to enhance the prediction accuracy. Figure 1 depicts the general flowchart of our proposed method.

4.1 Text Pre-processing

Text pre-processing is an important stage in text mining. It represents the process of preparing the reviews for text classification. As the reviews are usually composed of noisy and poorly structured sentences, it is essential to transform the content of each review to reduce the negative impact of the noise and facilitate the sentiment analysis task. The main objective of this step is to perform a series of pre-processing such as removing the numbers, URLs, hashtags.

After data cleaning and tokenization, each text review consists of a sequence of words. Each word is transformed into a vector using Word2Vec. As a result, each review in the data set is represented as a matrix.

4.2 Feature Extraction

Let $E = (CNN_1, \ldots, CNN_c)$ be an ensemble of CNNs, which consists of c convolutional neural networks. Each CNN architecture stacks several convolutional

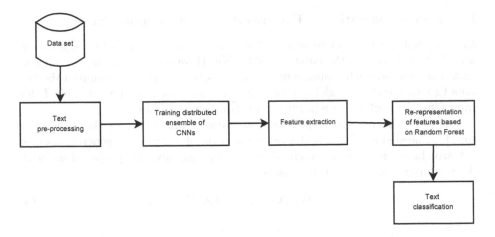

Fig. 1. Proposed methodology.

layers with Rectified Linear Unit (ReLU) as activation function, then the max-pooling and the softmax layer.

To extract the relevant features for each sentence, the c convolutional neural networks are trained based on the training data set. The layers of each CNN architecture are defined as follows:

- **Input:** Each review is represented as a matrix of size $N \times D$.
- **Convolutional layer 1:** The first convolutional layer filters the sentences using 150 kernels. Each kernel is of size $2 \times D$.
- **Convolutional layer 2:** The second layer is a convolutional layer which filters each sentence using 150 kernels of size $3 \times D$.
- **Convolutional layer 3:** The third convolutional layer filters the sentences using 150 kernels. Each kernel is of size $4 \times D$.
- **Convolutional layer 4:** The fourth convolutional layer filters each sentence using 150 kernels, where each kernel is of size $5 \times D$.
- **Max-pooling layer:** This layer applies the max-pooling process. It produces a feature vector of size 1×600 for each sentence.
- **Fully connected layer:** This layer outputs the estimated probabilities of labels.

After training all the CNNs, the high-level features learned by each CNN are combined to produce a global representation of the ensemble E as follows:

$$E_F = (F_j, \; j = 1, \ldots, c) \tag{4}$$

Where $F_j \in \mathbb{R}^k$ and $E_F \in \mathbb{R}^{k|E|}$ stand for the features generated by CNN_j, and the ensemble E, respectively.

4.3 Re-representation of Features Based on Random Forest

As described in the previous section, the extraction of features for each review is performed based on the ensemble of CNNs. However, finding an appropriate representation for each sentence may lead to better results. Therefore, this step aims to re-represent the global representation generated by the ensemble E for improving the performance in terms of prediction accuracy.

Let β be the parameter of re-representation, which defines the number of functions needed to obtain better representation of features. In general, in order to learn the appropriate representation for each sentence, our proposed methodology adopts β functions as follows:

$$(L_1(X_1), \ldots, L_\beta(X_1)) \tag{5}$$

where

$$X_i = \begin{cases} E_F & if \ i = 1 \\ (X_{i-1}, L_{i-1}(X_1)) & if \ 1 < i \le \beta \end{cases} \tag{6}$$

Each function $L_i(X_1)$ is considered as a classification problem, which can be resolved based on a random forest classifier. The output of this step is expressed as follows:

$$E_F^* = (X_\beta, L_\beta(X_1)) \tag{7}$$

where E_F^* represents the optimal representation for a review.

4.4 Text Classification

Text classification can be defined as the problem of learning classification model from reviews with pre-defined labels. The learned model can be employed to classify future reviews [7].

Random forest is one of the most powerful and popular machine learning algorithms. It is a supervised learning algorithm, which is widely used for both classification and regression problems. The random forest is typically an ensemble of decision trees, where the training process is generally based on the bagging method [1–5].

Let $T = \{(x_i, y_i), i = 1, \ldots, |T|\}$ be the training data set, which consists of $|T|$ reviews. Each $x_i \in \mathbb{R}^{|E_F^*|}$ and $y_i \in \mathbb{R}$ denote the appropriate representation of features E_F^* and the class label of a review i, respectively. The main objective of this step is to exploit the appropriate representation of features generated in the previous step for performing the sentiment analysis task, i.e., training a random forest model based on the training data set T. Then, using the learned model to classify the reviews.

5 Experimental Results

In this section, we present the data sets used in this work and experimental results to show the effectiveness of our proposed method.

5.1 Data Sets

In this work, the experiments are conducted on two benchmark data sets. The detailed descriptions of these datasets are as follows:

- **MR:** This is a Movie reviews data set. It was collected from IMDb movie review website. It consists of 10662 movie reviews with equal number of positive and negative reviews, i.e., 5331 positive and 5331 negative [16].
- **Sentiment140:** This is a Twitter sentiment analysis data set, which is originated from Stanford University. This particular data set contains 1600000 classified tweets. In this work, we have randomly selected 70000 tweets as the original data set [17].

5.2 Implementation Detail

All the experiments have been executed on a cluster which is composed of two nodes: one master node, and a slave node.

We have adopted 300-dimension word2vec embeddings trained on Google News [20]. We have implemented the deep learning models using the several frameworks, like Apache Spark 2.1.0, Tensorflow 1.5.0, Apache Hadoop-2.7.4, Python 3.5.2.

5.3 Results and Discussions

In this work, we have tested our approach on two benchmark data sets. All the data sets have been divided into two parts. The training set for training the model and the test set for evaluating the model's performance. The training set contains 90% of the reviews, while the test set includes 10% of the reviews.

Since CNN architectures have proved a remarkable success in several NLP tasks. The comparison of our work with one of the benchmark model based on CNN is important to prove the ability of the proposed method to improve existing works such as [12,19].

We have compared our method with the following models:

- **MNB-TF-IDF**: Multinomial Naive Bayes with Term Frequency-Inverse Document Frequency (TF-IDF).
- **CNN-non-static** [19]: CNN architecture with pre-trained word embeddings and fine-tuning optimizing strategy.
- **Proposed-CNN**: The proposed CNN architecture, which is composed of 4 convolutional layers.
- **Ensemble-CNN-non-static**: The proposed distributed ensemble based on CNN-non-static architecture and Random Forest.
- **Ensemble-Proposed-CNN**: The proposed distributed ensemble based on Proposed-CNN architecture and Random Forest.

For both data sets, we have adopted the Rectified Linear Unit (ReLU) as activation function. For our proposed architecture Proposed-CNN, the filter size of each CNN for the four convolutional layers are 2, 3, 4 and 5 with 150 feature maps each. While for the benchmark deep learning architecture CNN-non-static [19], the filter size of the three convolutional layers are 3, 4 and 5 with 100 feature maps each. In general, the deep learning models were optimized using Adam optimization algorithm. The batch size was set to 64. The dropout rate was fixed at 0.5. The number of CNNs adopted in each ensemble was set to 5. The number of random forests adopted for each ensemble is $\beta = 10$. The number of trees was fixed at 200.

Based on several previous works such as [18,19], we have used the accuracy as the evaluation metric to measure the overall sentiment classification performance. Table 1 shows the experimental results on the two data set MR and Sentiment140.

Table 1. Experimental results on both data sets.

Model	Data set	
	MR	Sentiment140
MNB-TF-IDF	0.7760	0.7682
CNN-non-static [19]	0.8114	0.7953
Proposed-CNN	0.8086	0.7942
Ensemble-CNN-non-static	**0.8208**	**0.8031**
Ensemble-Proposed-CNN	0.8198	0.8018

In particular, this table presents the comparative results in terms of classification accuracy. To highlight the best result of each, we mark in bold the best value.

From Table 1, it can be observed that Ensemble-CNN-non-static substantially outperforms the other competitors on both data sets. Also, it is obvious that our proposed method Ensemble-CNN-non-static shows higher accuracy than the original model CNN-non-static [19]. Ensemble-Proposed-CNN improves the performance of Proposed-CNN.

As a result, it is reasonable to conclude that the proposed approach can improve the performance of several existing approaches based on convolution neural networks for sentiment analysis in the context of big data.

6   Conclusion

In this paper, we have proposed a novel distributed ensemble of Deep Convolutional Neural Networks with Random Forest for sentiment analysis in the context of big data. It is designed based on Tensorflow and Apache Spark for processing large-scale data efficiently.

The experiments carried out have proved that the proposed approach outperforms other competitors, and it is able to improve existing deep convolutional neural networks work for natural language processing. In addition, it can be successfully applied to large data sets.

As future work, we will consider improving the performance of our method using more complex CNN architectures.

References

1. Chen, X., Ishwaran, H.: Random forests for genomic data analysis. Genomics **99**(6), 323–329 (2012)
2. Wyner, A.J., Olson, M., Bleich, J., Mease, D.: Explaining the success of adaboost and random forests as interpolating classifiers. J. Mach. Learn. Res. **18**(1), 1558–1590 (2017)
3. Breiman, L.: Random forests. Mach. Learn. **45**(1), 5–32 (2001)
4. Genuer, R., Poggi, J.M., Tuleau-Malot, C., Villa-Vialaneix, N.: Random forests for big data. Big Data Res. **9**, 28–46 (2017)
5. Chen, J., Li, K., Tang, Z., Bilal, K., Yu, S., Weng, C., Li, K.: A parallel random forest algorithm for big data in a spark cloud computing environment. IEEE Trans. Parallel Distrib. Syst. **28**, 919–933 (2017)
6. Hammou, B.A., Lahcen, A.A., Mouline, S.: APRA: an approximate parallel recommendation algorithm for big data. Knowl.-Based Syst. **157**, 10–19 (2018)
7. Liu, B.: Web Data Mining: Exploring Hyperlinks, Contents, and Usage Data. Springer, Heidelberg (2007). https://doi.org/10.1007/978-3-540-37882-2
8. Mikolov, T., Sutskever, I., Chen, K., Corrado, G.S., Dean, J.: Distributed representations of words and phrases and their compositionality. In: Advances in Neural Information Processing Systems, pp. 3111–3119 (2013)
9. Mikolov, T., Chen, K., Corrado, G., Dean, J.: Efficient estimation of word representations in vector space. arXiv preprint arXiv:1301.3781 (2013)
10. Xie, Y., Le, L., Zhou, Y., Raghavan, V.V.: Deep Learning for Natural Language Processing. Handbook of Statistics (2018)
11. Kim, H.K., Kim, H., Cho, S.: Bag-of-concepts: comprehending document representation through clustering words in distributed representation. Neurocomputing **266**, 336–352 (2017)
12. Rezaeinia, S.M., Rahmani, R., Ghodsi, A., Veisi, H.: Sentiment analysis based on improved pre-trained word embeddings. Expert Syst. Appl. **117**, 139–147 (2019)
13. Jaderberg, M., Vedaldi, A., Zisserman, A.: Speeding up convolutional neural networks with low rank expansions. arXiv preprint arXiv:1405.3866 (2014)
14. Krizhevsky, A., Sutskever, I., Hinton, G.E.: Imagenet classification with deep convolutional neural networks. In: Advances in Neural Information Processing Systems, pp. 1097–1105 (2012)
15. Ciresan, D.C., Meier, U., Masci, J., Maria Gambardella, L., Schmidhuber, J.: Flexible, high performance convolutional neural networks for image classification. In: IJCAI Proceedings-International Joint Conference on Artificial Intelligence, vol. 22, no. 1, p. 1237, July 2011
16. Pang, B., Lee, L.: Seeing stars: exploiting class relationships for sentiment categorization with respect to rating scales. In: Proceedings of the 43rd Annual Meeting on Association for Computational Linguistics, pp. 115–124. Association for Computational Linguistics, June 2005

17. Sentiment140. https://cs.stanford.edu/people/alecmgo/trainingandtestdata.zip. Accessed 31 Jan 2018
18. Chen, T., Xu, R., He, Y., Wang, X.: Improving sentiment analysis via sentence type classification using BiLSTM-CRF and CNN. Expert Syst. Appl. **72**, 221–230 (2017)
19. Kim, Y.: Convolutional neural networks for sentence classification. arXiv preprint arXiv:1408.5882 (2014)
20. Word2Vec. https://code.google.com/archive/p/word2vec/. Accessed 31 Jan 2018
21. Socher, R., Pennington, J., Huang, E.H., Ng, A.Y., Manning, C.D.: Semi-supervised recursive autoencoders for predicting sentiment distributions. In: Proceedings of the Conference on Empirical Methods in Natural Language Processing, pp. 151–161. Association for Computational Linguistics, July 2011
22. Socher, R., et al.: Recursive deep models for semantic compositionality over a sentiment treebank. In: Proceedings of the 2013 Conference on Empirical Methods in Natural Language Processing, pp. 1631–1642 (2013)
23. Irsoy, O., Cardie, C.: Deep recursive neural networks for compositionality in language. In: Advances in Neural Information Processing Systems, pp. 2096–2104 (2014)
24. Ren, Y., Wang, R., Ji, D.: A topic-enhanced word embedding for Twitter sentiment classification. Inf. Sci. **369**, 188–198 (2016)
25. Zhang, Y., Wallace, B.: A sensitivity analysis of (and practitioners' guide to) convolutional neural networks for sentence classification. arXiv preprint arXiv:1510.03820 (2015)
26. Jianqiang, Z., Xiaolin, G.: Comparison research on text pre-processing methods on Twitter sentiment analysis. IEEE Access **5**, 2870–2879 (2017)
27. Wang, H., Can, D., Kazemzadeh, A., Bar, F., Narayanan, S.: A system for real-time twitter sentiment analysis of 2012 us presidential election cycle. In: Proceedings of the ACL 2012 System Demonstrations, pp. 115–120. Association for Computational Linguistics, July 2012
28. Cambria, E., Rajagopal, D., Olsher, D., Das, D.: Big social data analysis. Big Data Comput. **13**, 401–414 (2013)
29. Pandarachalil, R., Sendhilkumar, S., Mahalakshmi, G.S.: Twitter sentiment analysis for large-scale data: an unsupervised approach. Cogn. Comput. **7**(2), 254–262 (2015)

Road Safety Against Sybil Attacks Based on RSU Collaboration in VANET Environment

Said Benkirane(✉) (iD)

SAEDD Laboratory, EST Essaouira, Cadi Ayyad University,
Marrakesh, Morocco
sabenkirane@gmail.com

Abstract. Vehicular Ad-hoc Network (VANET) is a special case of an Ad hoc mobile network formed by vehicles communicating directly with each other or via a wireless infrastructure called the Road Side Unit (RSU). Like all similar networks, VANET is more concerned with Sybil attacks where a malicious attacking node sends messages with multiple identities to other nodes in the network. Thus, causing a general malfunction of the network, which gives the illusion of a problem of traffic like traffic jam or a virtual accident. So, honest vehicles change their path or leave the road for the benefit of 'attacker'. In this paper, we present an effective solution against this severe threat by using a distributed and collaborative technique between RSUs allowing the detection of Sybil vehicles based on their real positions.

Keywords: ITS · VANET · Security · Sybil attack · Multi-agent system · Trilateration

1 Introduction

Intelligent Transportation Systems (ITS) refers to the integration of new information and communication technologies into the transportation domain. The vehicles have been made "Intelligent" by adding new hardware and software systems to understand their environment, to communicate with other vehicles through wireless radio interfaces, to process this information and make decisions on the behavior of the vehicle via an onboard calculator. Radio interfaces allow vehicles to communicate with one another (Vehicle-to-Vehicle Communication, V2V) or with roadside units based on V2I (Vehicle-to-Infrastructure Communications). During these communications, vehicles broadcast a range of very sensitive information, such as position, speed and direction [1].

VANETs are characterized mainly by a rapid change in the topology and high speed of vehicles. They are based on two main types of applications: applications to improve road safety and applications deployed for passenger comfort [2].

Ad hoc networks in general, and VANETs in particular, are more vulnerable and highly susceptible to different attacks than wire networks because of the rapid mobility

É. Renault et al. (Eds.): MSPN 2019, LNCS 11557, pp. 163–172, 2019.
https://doi.org/10.1007/978-3-030-22885-9_15

of nodes that makes detection of anomalies difficult (such as the announcement of false routes) and lack of infrastructure and centralized administration.

Security is therefore one of the most difficult problems of the VANET network due to their particular characteristics. Identity attacks are a particular class of attacks that exploit the identity of a vehicle to carry out a malicious action. There are two types of identity attacks: Spoofing which consists in stealing the identity of a vehicle and using it to carry out the malicious action, and Sybil [3], which uses several different identities in the network [4].

In this work, we are dealing with the type of Sybil attack that poses a dangerous threat to VANETs networks producing multiple identities that compromise the availability or integrity of the network. We are also introducing our security solution to prevent this type of attack and allow the network to easily detect Sybil vehicles.

The rest of this paper is organized as follows. Section 2 describes the related work in the same field. We provide an overview of the Sybil Attack in Sect. 3. In Sect. 4, we present our avoidance technique. The performance evaluation is described in Sect. 5. Finally, we conclude the paper in Sect. 6.

2   Related Work

Network security in general and VANETs in particular, have always taken a great interest by researchers. Many works in the literature propose several techniques and solutions to overcome different attacks in VANET.

Authors in [5] have presented a global survey on possible attacks in VANETs and the consistent detection approaches that are proposed in the literature. They have classified and explained the effects of attacks and presented the equivalent solutions with their advantages and disadvantages.

Manvi et al. [6] have provided a taxonomy of authentication schemes, and discussed their mechanisms, advantages, disadvantages, performance and scope of research. They have also presented issues of open security in VANET authentication.

Authors in [7] have presented an overview on the main security threats and attacks in VANETs. They have also discussed corresponding security solutions reported in the recent literature to mitigate those attacks, especially, security issues namely: anonymity, key management, privacy, reputation and location. They have provided a summary of the different attacks in the VANETs and their proposed solutions.

In order to detect Sybil attacks in vehicular networks, Golle et al. [8] have proposed a heuristic approach, called adversarial parsimony, which depends on sensor data, collected by nodes in the VANET, shared with immediate neighbors, and propagated to a neighboring region. The sensor data provides redundant information, allowing each individual node to process the sensor data and detect or remove malicious information. Individual nodes use a model of the VANET to check the validity of the sensor data, and when inconsistencies arise, an adversarial model is used to search for explanations of the errors, ranking explanations using a parsimony approach, and using the best clarification to correct the consequences of the attack.

In [9] the authors have proposed a Detection Technique against a Sybil Attack protocol (DTSA) which produces to vehicles secure information for the road situation and the traffic flow among vehicles and allows the detection of Sybil attack. This mechanism uses SKC (Session Key based Certificate) to verify the IDs among vehicles, which generates a vehicle's anonymous ID, a session key, the expiration date and a local server's certificate for the detection of a Sybil attack. In conclusion, this DTSA reduces not only the detection time against a Sybil attack but also the verification time for ID by using a hash function and an XOR operation.

Xiao et al. [10] have presented a lightweight security scheme for detecting and localizing Sybil nodes in VANETs, based on statistical analysis of signal strength distribution. In this approach, each vehicle on a road can perform the detection of potential Sybil vehicles nearby by verifying their claimed positions based on signal-strength. To increase accuracy, authors have proposed a technique to prevent Sybil nodes from covering up for each other. In this technique, traffic patterns and support from roadside base stations are used for advantage. They also proposed two statistic algorithms to enhance the correctness of position verification. The algorithms can detect potential Sybil attacks by observing the signal strength distribution of a suspect node over a period of time.

Zhou et al. [11] have presented a lightweight and scalable protocol to detect Sybil attacks in VANET. In this protocol, a malicious user pretending to be multiple vehicles can be detected in a distributed manner through passive overhearing by set of fixed nodes called roadside boxes (RSBs). The detection of Sybil attacks in this manner does not require any vehicle in the network to disclose its identity; hence, privacy is preserved at all times. Authors also have discussed some improvements on their scheme.

In [12] authors have proposed a cooperative method to verify the positions of Sybil nodes, they have used a Random Sample Consensus (RANSAC)-based algorithm to make this cooperative method more robust against outlier data fabricated by Sybil nodes. However, several inherent drawbacks of this cooperative method prompt us to explore additional approaches. They have introduced a statistical method and design a system which is able to verify where a vehicle comes from. The system is termed the Presence Evidence System (PES) enabling improvement the detection accuracy using statistical analysis over an observation period.

Feng et al. [13] have proposed an approach called EBRS (Event Based Reputation System), in which dynamic reputation and trusted value for each event are employed to suppress the spread of false messages. EBRS detects Sybil attack with fabricated identities and stolen identities in the process of communication by establishing a reputation threshold and trust threshold for each event message, the dissemination of false message is restricted no matter it is from forgery identities or legitimate identities; it also defends against the conspired Sybil attack since each event has a unique reputation value and trusted value. In EBRS, a trusted RSU is used to issue the certificate of vehicles in its communication range.

3 Overview of Sybil Attack

The Sybil attack is one of the most severe attacks in an ad hoc network. It is an attack in which a malicious node presents itself in the network with multiple identities, which gives the illusion that there are several legitimate nodes. The purpose of the malicious node, source of the Sybil attack, is tampering with the neighborhood and entire network malfunction (Fig. 1).

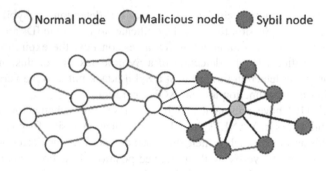

Fig. 1. Sybil attack mechanism

The "Sybil" attack is difficult to be detected it via radio resources because the attacker has multiple identities and may appear in several places at the same time. The probability of choosing this false node is high, which leads to a degradation of the guarantee of the quality provided by the multi-jump protocols [14].

The Sybil Attack causes many problems in Ad hoc networks. For example:

- Routing: Sybil attacks disrupt routing protocols because they rely on the paths and links between nodes because malicious nodes appear at more than one place at a time.
- Vote and Reputation System: A Sybil attack can create enough malicious identities to report repeatedly and then remove legitimate nodes from the network, which falsifies the voting result.
- Aggregation of Data: A Sybil identity may be able to report malicious readers and report incorrect sensor readings thereby influencing the overall calculated total.
- Traffic congestion in VANETs: A malicious vehicle can create the illusion of traffic congestion by producing an arbitrary number of non-existent (virtual) vehicles and transmit false information in the network to give a fake impression of traffic congestion.
- Distributed Storage: A Sybil attack causes huge data damage in a network where the storage is distributed since the data will be given to virtual nodes.
- Resource Allocation: The allocation of resources, like the TDMA Schedule, is based on knowledge of the network topology; this allocation will be poorly distributed when there are fictitious nodes.

4   Sybil Attack Avoidance Technique

In a Sybil attack situation, the malicious vehicle delivers valid messages and false messages that contain a false identity and a false position. Other vehicles receiving these messages will be misled because they believe there are several vehicles and can make life-threatening decisions such as overtaking. Figure 2 shows an example of Sybil attack in VANET environment.

Our solution is based on calculating the real positions of each vehicle in the road and comparing them with those included in the messages sent. The calculation of these positions is entrusted to the RSUs without integration of any other vehicle (because we cannot predict the number of vehicles in a road).

We adopt the following assumptions:

- Each vehicle in the road is linked to 3 reliable RSUs at a given time;
- Only one malicious vehicle creates 2 more Sybil nodes;
- When a vehicle broadcasts a message to other vehicles, the 3 RSUs also receive this message;
- Vehicle position is assumed to be known (GPS system);
- The identities of the vehicles are known;
- RSUs communicate and exchange information with each other.

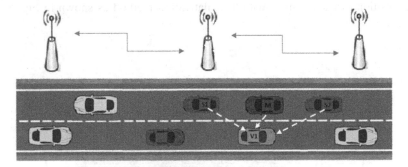

Fig. 2. Sybil vehicle situation

The Fig. 2 above shows a situation where a malicious vehicle (M) sends three different messages (m, m_1 and m_2) to V1 including one valid (m) and two false messages (m_1 and m_2), containing three different identities and positions. Receiving the messages, V1 believes that there are three vehicles S1, S2 and M.

When an RSU receives a message sent by a malicious vehicle (M) it will save it in its local database of this format (Table 1):

Table 1. Message of a malicious vehicle

Id	Position	RSSI	Message
M	P_M	R	m
S1	P_1	R	m_1
S2	P_2	R	m_2

Based on the Received Signal Strength Indication (RSSI) measurements made by the three RSUs, we can easily have the distances that separate each vehicle to the three RSUs at a given time according to free space transmission formula [15]:

$$\frac{P_r}{P_t} = G_r G_r (\frac{\lambda}{4\pi d})^2$$
(1)

- P_r: Power at the receiving antenna
- P_t: Output power of transmitting antenna
- G_r, G_r: Gain of the transmitting and receiving antenna, respectively
- λ: Wavelength
- d: Distance between the antennas (transmitter and receiver)

Physically, there is only one vehicle (M) while the others are Sybil vehicles. So, obviously each RSU receives the same values RSSI (M, S1 and S2).

Now, for each vehicle we will have three distances d_i, which separate them from the 3 RSUs. Since the positions of the three RSUs are known, it is easy to calculate the actual position of each vehicle with the trilateration method as shown in Fig. 3.

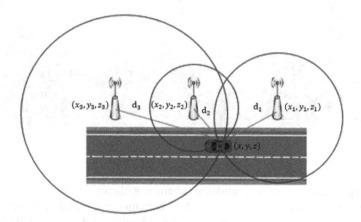

Fig. 3. Trilateration technique

We will have the following system:

$$\begin{cases} (x_1 - x)^2 + (y_1 - y)^2 + (z_1 - z)^2 = d_1^2 \\ (x_2 - x)^2 + (y_2 - y)^2 + (z_2 - z)^2 = d_2^2 \\ (x_3 - x)^2 + (y_3 - y)^2 + (z_3 - z)^2 = d_3^2 \end{cases}$$
(2)

From (2) we will have:

$$Ap = B$$
(3)

Where:

$$A = \begin{bmatrix} 2(x_1 - x_3) & 2(y_1 - y_3) & 2(z_1 - z_3) \\ 2(x_2 - x_3) & 2(y_2 - y_3) & 2(z_2 - z_3) \end{bmatrix} \tag{4}$$

$$B = \begin{bmatrix} x_1^2 - x_3^2 + y_1^2 - y_3^2 + z_1^2 - z_3^2 + d_1^2 - d_3^2 \\ x_2^2 - x_3^2 + y_2^2 - y_3^2 + z_2^2 - z_3^2 + d_2^2 - d_3^2 \end{bmatrix} \tag{5}$$

$$p = \begin{bmatrix} x \\ y \\ z \end{bmatrix} \tag{6}$$

The coordinates of p will be calculated by the following formula:

$$p = (A^T A)^{-1} A^T B \tag{7}$$

A simple comparison between the positions (sent and calculated) makes it easy to detect Sybil vehicles.

5 Simulation

The simulation is performed with our application developed with Java language using the Java Framework Development Framework [16] to perform the communication between the different nodes (vehicles and RSUs). The architecture used is that shown in Fig. 4 below.

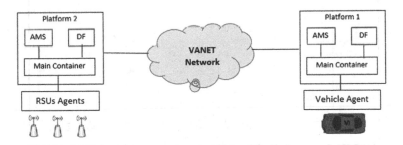

Fig. 4. Multi-agent platforms used

The chosen scenario is the one shown in Fig. 2 where a malicious vehicle (M) produces two Sybil vehicles. According to our proposed solution described above, the collaboration of the three RSUs makes it possible to detect the virtual vehicles (Sybil) and to block them.

The experiment is in a linear road with the fixed length of 500 meters consisting 3 Roadside Units, as shown in Fig. 5, and the radio range of both vehicles and RSUs is chosen so that there will be communication along the road.

A malicious vehicle produces several virtual vehicles but all have the same real position and the same RSS, so we focus on a test on a single vehicle to test the validity of calculations.

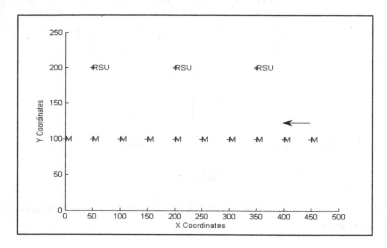

Fig. 5. Path traveled by a vehicle M

M *Position from vehicle,* O *Position from trilateration*

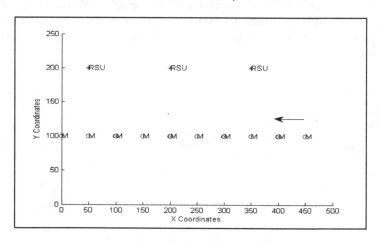

Fig. 6. Provided and calculated positions (Color figure online)

Based on the calculation of the actual positions of each vehicle, our technique allows communication in the network only with real vehicles (not fictitious).

Figure 6 below shows the positions provided by the vehicle M denoted by the (M) and those calculated by the trilateration method denoted by the red circles. We can notice the high accuracy of result obtained by the calculations.

The location error represents the distance between the calculated positions and those provided by the vehicle, as shown in Fig. 7 below. This error is of the order of

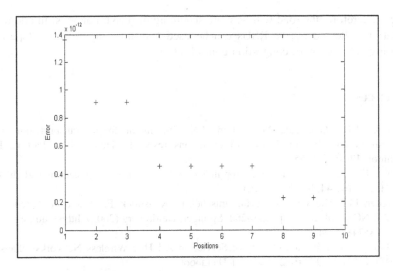

Fig. 7. Error of calculated positions

10^{-12}. So, it is very negligible and will have no influence on the effectiveness of our technique especially that vehicles are bulky objects and not points.

The average of the error is given by the formula (8). It depends on the numbers of the positions taken by each vehicle and the number of RSUs. Indeed, the more RSUs there are, the more accurate the trilateration

$$Average\ Error = \frac{\sum_{j \neq i} \sqrt{(x_i - x_j)^2 + (y_i - y_j)^2}}{(NoP + NRSU)} \tag{8}$$

Where:

NoP: Number of positions taken (here we took 10)
NRSU: Number of RSU (here we have 3)

$$Average\ Error = 4.2195e - 013(m)$$

6 Conclusion

In this paper, we have proposed a technique based on a distributed collaboration of Road Side Units allowing to have a local database containing instantaneous information on the vehicles circulating in the road. This information includes their positions with which they communicate and the actual calculated positions based on the trilateration between 3 RSUs by exploiting the strength of the received signal (RSS). The comparison between these positions makes it easy to detect Sybil vehicles and block them. With this technique, we will never have fictitious vehicles produced by malicious vehicles. Therefore, the road will be more secure against Sybil attacks. In addition, the information collected by the RSUs can be used for future applications (speed limit monitoring, vehicle theft, congestion control, etc.).

References

1. Crainic, T.G., Gendreau, M., Potvin, J.Y.: Intelligent freight-transportation systems: assessment and the contribution of operations research. Transp. Res. Part C: Emerg. Technol. **17**(6), 541–557 (2009)
2. Cunha, F., et al.: Data communication in VANETs: protocols, applications and challenges. Ad Hoc Netw. **44**, 90–103 (2016)
3. Douceur, J.R.: The Sybil attack. In: Druschel, P., Kaashoek, F., Rowstron, A. (eds.) IPTPS 2002. LNCS, vol. 2429, pp. 251–260. Springer, Heidelberg (2002). https://doi.org/10.1007/3-540-45748-8_24
4. Mishra, A.: Security and Quality of Service in Ad Hoc Wireless Networks (chaps. 1, 3) (2008). ISBN 13 978-0-521-87824-1 Handbook
5. Sakiz, F., Sen, S.: A survey of attacks and detection mechanisms on intelligent transportation systems: VANETs and IoV. Ad Hoc Netw. **61**, 33–50 (2017)
6. Manvi, S.S., Tangade, S.: A survey on authentication schemes in VANETs for secured communication. Veh. Commun. **9**, 19–30 (2017)
7. Isaac, J.T., Zeadally, S., Camara, J.S.: Security attacks and solutions for vehicular ad hoc networks. Commun. IET **4**(7), 894–903 (2010)
8. Golle, P., Greene, D., Staddon, J.: Detecting and correcting malicious data in VANETs. In: Proceedings of the 1st ACM International Workshop on Vehicular Ad Hoc Networks, VANET 2004, Philadelphia, PA, USA, pp. 29–37. ACM (2004)
9. Lee, B., Jeong, E., Jung, I.: A DTSA (detection technique against a Sybil attack) protocol using SKC (session key based certificate) on VANET. Int. J. Secur. Appl. **7**(3), 1–10 (2013)
10. Xiao, B., Yu, B., Gao, C.: Detection and localization of Sybil nodes in VANETs. In: Proceedings of the 2006 Workshop on Dependability Issues in Wireless Ad Hoc Networks and Sensor Networks, DIWANS 2006, Los Angeles, CA, USA, pp. 1–8. ACM (2006)
11. Zhou, T., Choudhury, R.R., Ning, P., Chakrabarty, K.: P2DAP-Sybil attacks detection in vehicular ad hoc networks. IEEE J. Sel. Areas Commun. **29**(3), 582–594 (2011)
12. Yu, B., Xu, C.Z., Xiao, B.: Detecting Sybil attacks in VANETs. J. Parallel Distrib. Comput. **73**(6), 746–756 (2013)
13. Feng, X., Li, C., Chen, D., Tang, J.: A method for defending against multi-source Sybil attacks in VANET. Peer-to-Peer Netw. Appl. **10**(2), 305–314 (2017)
14. Newsome, J., Shi, E., Song, D., Perrig, A.: The Sybil attack in sensor networks: analysis & defenses. In: Proceedings of the 3rd International Symposium on Information Processing in Sensor Networks, IPSN 2004, pp. 259–268. ACM, New York (2004)
15. Friis, H.T.: A note on a simple transmission formula. Proc. IRE **34**, 254–256 (1946)
16. Bellifemine, F., Poggi, A., Rimassa, G.: Developing multi-agent systems with a FIPA-compliant agent framework. Softw. Pract. Exp. **31**, 103–128 (2001)

A New Alert Message Dissemination Protocol for VANETs Based on Leach Routing Protocol and Simulation in Random Waypoint Model Scenario

Hamid Barkouk[1(✉)], El Mokhtar En-Naimi[1(✉)], Mounir Arioua[2(✉)], and Aziz Mahboub[1(✉)]

[1] Department of Computer Sciences, LIST Laboratory, FST of Tangier,
Abdelmalek Essaâdi University, Tangier, Morocco
barkouk@gmail.com, ennaimi@gmail.com,
amahboub@uae.ac.ma
[2] Team of New Technology Trends, National School of Applied Sciences,
Abdelmalek Essaâdi University, Tangier, Morocco
m.arioua@m.ieee.org

Abstract. The intelligent Transportation system (ITS), through its derivative system named Vehicle Ad hoc NETwork (VANET) allows vehicles to exchange information relating to safety and comfort of drivers and passengers. Communication equipment fixed in the vehicles makes it possible to send and receive messages. Two categories of VANET communication used: vehicle-to-vehicle (V2V) and vehicle to infrastructure named vehicle-to-road (V2R). In the V2V communication, vehicles act as relay nodes to ensure the exchange of messages between them. In V2R communication, road-side units (RSU) act as relay nodes to transmit information to nearby vehicles and RSUs.

The vehicle knows the roads status by receiving an alert message broadcasted by other vehicles that have detected the event.

The main goal of our work is firstly to inject the alert functionality to one of existing VANETs routing protocols that is the Low-Energy Adaptive Clustering Hierarchy (LEACH). We have used only the basic routing functionalities of LEACH protocol. We have integrated five procedures to the LEACH protocol, which will ensure the following features:

– Procedure 1: Event point detection.
– Procedure 2: Search for close neighbors.
– Procedure 3: Sending of messages to nearby neighbors.
– Procedure 4: Communications From vehicles to Infrastructure.
– Procedure 5: Communications From infrastructure to Vehicles.

The second goal is to simulate our protocol functionality on a random waypoint model and to examine the impact of varying density on the number of sent/received packets and average delay. The results of the number of packets sent/received and of the low average delay prove that our proposed algorithm is reliable.

© Springer Nature Switzerland AG 2019
É. Renault et al. (Eds.): MSPN 2019, LNCS 11557, pp. 173–187, 2019.
https://doi.org/10.1007/978-3-030-22885-9_16

Keywords: LEACH · Vanet · Routing · Setdest · Cbrgen · ITS · Random waypoint mobility model

1 Introduction

Personal transport and goods vehicles are becoming increasingly intelligent and well equipped to ensure the comfort and safety of the driver and passengers. To this end, these vehicles are equipped with:

For comfort:

- Rain Sensors, Brightness Sensors, Radar/Reversing Camera, etc.
- Parking assistance systems.
- Onboard computers.
- Automated driving

For the safety:

- To overcome driving errors.
- Increase the safety of passengers in case of accidents.
- Improve vehicle maintenance.
- Decrease the ecological impact.
- Cruise control (speed controller)
- Speed regulator.
- Alert in case of breakdowns.

The above-mentioned intelligence elements remain unique to each vehicle independently of other vehicles sharing the same route, which increases the likelihood of accidents.

To increase the comfort and safety of drivers, passengers as well as pedestrians, the communication between the different vehicles has become imperative and one of the research subject launched a few years ago under the name of intelligent transport system (ITS) [8]. Vehicular Ad-Hoc Network, or VANet, is a kind of adaptation of the Mobile Ad-hoc Network (MANet) to vehicles whose nodes are vehicles and roadside units [11].

VANet provides connectivity and communication between multiple vehicles using different types of sensors:

Exteroceptive that provides a measure on the environment:

- Raw data.
- Elaborated data.
  ⇒ sent to a central site (database).
  Example: road traffic management, traffic information, etc.
  Proprioceptive that provides a measurement on the inside of the vehicle:

- In order to provide elaborated information to the driver as well as possibly to his passengers.
- In order to take immediate action (examples: braking, warning, etc.)
- To transmit elaborated information to other vehicles or to a central site.

All these data are exchanged by GSM (sending data to a central site) or by WIFI (802.11p) in communication mode between vehicles V2V (Vehicle to Vehicle) or in communication mode between vehicle and Road Side Unit (RSU) V2I (Vehicle to Infrastructure).

One of the main motivations for the development and study of vehicular communications is the reduction in the number of road accidents, which presents a huge challenge to improve road safety. Many propositions of new software and hardware are developed by academic institutions, industries and governments to reduce the number of road accident. The alert message dissemination protocols are one of the most important VANET protocols, which must have most attentions of researchers to improve roads security [11]. In order to be able to anticipate and act in order to avoid an accident, the driver must be offered a driving aid by informing him, for example, that a vehicle has just passed a red light or that a pedestrian is crossing the road. Alert messages must be exchanged efficiently, quickly and with reasonable use of resources. VANet vehicles can exchange information such as road condition alert, overtaking aid (distances calculation, verification blind spot), braking alert and collision warning. The SOS service is one of the alert applications currently deployed on high-end vehicles. In the event of an accident, a message is sent to warn the nearest rescue center, which minimizes the emergency time [1, 2, 11].

In a Vehicle to Vehicle warning system, several pieces of information are collected to help the system and the driver to take the appropriate decisions. The following steps show the process of engaging an alert message:

Step 1: Detect obstacle or risk of collision
Step 2: Generate alert messages
Step 3: Alert the driver

The figure below shows a dissemination example of alerts on VANET networks (Fig. 1):

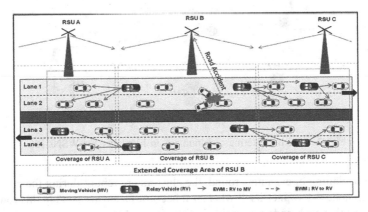

Fig. 1. Dissemination alerts on VANET network [7].

The remainder of the paper is organized as follows: Sect. 2 is a brief presentation of LEACH protocol. Section 3 is a detailed presentation of our algorithm. Sections 4 and 5 show the results of the simulation of our algorithm.

2 LEACH Protocol

LEACH is a variant of clustering which means '(Low - Energy Adaptive Clustering Hierarchy)'. This Protocol is based on a network of sensors that use a clustering method which divides the network into two levels: the Cluster Heads and member nodes.

As with conventional clustering protocols, as in LEACH, the sensor network is divided into individual clusters and the nodes of a cluster communicate but with one excellent node named cluster head (CH).

Cluster Heads then pass data from all other nodes in the cluster to the base station. The group heads being used as relay stations consume a lot of energy. However, the LEACH protocol attempts to evenly distribute energy consumption in the sensor network by not keeping the same cluster heads, but by changing them randomly [3, 4].

LEACH is divided into rounds; each round is divided into two phases:

Setup phase: consists of forming the clusters and determining the cluster heads.
Steady phase: the data is then forwarded from the member nodes via the cluster heads to the base station.

The setup phase lasts longer than the steady phase to minimize the overhead required to create the clusters. The two phases of LEACH will be discussed in detail in what follows (Fig. 2).

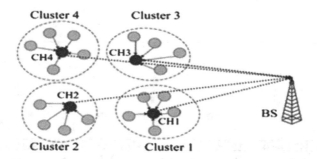

Fig. 2. Leach clustering communication hierarchy for WSNs [6].

At the beginning of each new round, the clusters are rebuilt during the construction phase. Each node determines itself whether it becomes a cluster head in this round. And given the fact that each node can decide individually whether it becomes a cluster head, which means that it does not have to communicate with its neighbors, the choice of cluster heads requires little energy. The decision is based on a fixed proportion of nodes, which must be cluster heads, and which had already been so many times.

In order to decide whether a node becomes a cluster head, it selects a random number in the interval [0, 1], and then compares it to a threshold value T (n). If the number is below the threshold T (n), the node becomes a cluster head for the current round. T (n) is calculated as follows:

$$T(n) = \begin{cases} \frac{P}{1 - \left[r * mod\left(\frac{1}{P}\right) \right]} & if n \in G \\ 0 & otherwise \end{cases}$$

- G denotes the set of nodes that were not selected as a cluster head in last 1/P rounds
- r is the current round
- P is the desired percentage to become a cluster head

If this threshold is used, each node of the 1/P rounds becomes the cluster head once. If the cluster heads are determined, they send a notification message with fixed transmission power. The remaining nodes receive these messages and decide which group they want to join in this round. They respond to the group head whose notification message measures the highest signal strength. Assuming symmetric channels, a node reaches this cluster head with the lowest transmission power.

The cluster head now creates a Time Division Multiple Access (TDMAS) scheduler in which a fixed time slot is assigned to each node for communication with the cluster head. It also chooses a Code Division Multiple Access (CDMA) code allocated to each communication. Because each cluster chooses a different CDMA code, it is possible to communicate simultaneously within clusters without causing interference between two clusters.

Once the clusters are formed and the TDMA schedules are distributed to the nodes, the communication phase begins. Nodes now send their data in the time slot reserved for them at the cluster head. They use the knowledge of the signal strength of the notification message to send it with minimal energy. After the cluster leader receives the data from each cluster node, it aggregates them and sends the result to the base station. Because it is far, this transmission must be done with a lot of energy [3–6].

The advantages of LEACH are that the energy consumption is evenly distributed over the sensor nodes by the rotation of the cluster head. Another advantage is that this idea of classification can be applied in several stages resulting in a hierarchical classification. A disadvantage of LEACH is that it implicitly assumes that all nodes have the same opportunities to reach the base station, which is not the case for most sensor networks. Another disadvantage of this protocol is that in the event of a cluster head failure, the base station will no longer receive one-round data from all nodes in the cluster.

3   New Proposed Algorithm

3.1   Description

Whenever an event is triggered, the vehicle that detects it should search for close neighbors to whom the alert message will be sent, which is ensured by our algorithm and is illustrated in the following steps (Fig. 3):

Fig. 3. Proposed algorithm steps

These steps were decorticated as five procedures detailed below and were injected into the Leach routing protocol.

3.2   Description of the Above Algorithm Steps

1. We must have a trigger event to send alert message. For this, we created a random point with the two coordinates X and Y in the map that was created as a vehicle movement location.
2. If a vehicle approaches this point with a distance equal to 200 m, he starts looking for his neighbors back to warn them of this event.
3. After the list of neighbors is obtained, the vehicle triggers the sending of the message.
4. When a vehicle receives this message, it will redo the search for close neighbors to broadcast the message.
5. The direction of the sending of the warning message is in the opposite direction to the movements of the vehicles.

3.3   Vehicle to Vehicle Communication

Each vehicle has a GPS receiver for localization of the event point and other vehicles in the network.

Procedure 1: Detection of Event point.

```
incircle1 : distance between the current vehicle and
the event point.
K: X coordinate of the event point.
B: Y coordinate of the event point.
x : X coordinate of the current vehicle.
y : Y coordinate of the current vehicle.
nodeID : current vehicle near the event point.
Now : current time.
round : tour
next_change_time_ : time of the end of round 1 and the
beginning of the next round.
Procedure detect_event
Begin
Obtaining coordinates X and Y of the current vehicle.
Calculates the distance between the current vehicle
and the event point.
If (incircle1 < 200)
   If(x < K || y < B)
# the current vehicle detects that it is close to the
event point, it will search its close
 neighbors and send them the alert message.
    Call the procedure NeighborsNode
EndIf
EndIf
Increment round
for each next_change_time_ repeat these steps.
End
```

Procedure 2: Search of Close Neighbors

```
upstream_: neighbors list.
x : X coordinate of the sender vehicle.
y : Y coordinate of the sender vehicle.
nx : X coordinate of other vehicles.
ny : Y coordinate of other vehicles
incircle : distance between the sender vehicle and the
other nodes.
```

```
nodeID : ID of the sender vehicle.
max_dist : the maximum distance among the distances of
the close neighbors.
i : ID of other vehicle.
NextHope : variable used to store the identifier of
the neighboring vehicle.
dist_ : variable used to save the incircle distance.
# dist_ is initialized to 0
dist_ = 0
Begin
# Assign to  each sender node a unique code.
If (nodeID != i)
     If (((nx == x) && (ny < $y)) || ((ny == y) && (nx
<x)))
        If (incircle <200)
            If (dist_ < incircle)
max_dist = incircle
                else
max_dist = dist_
            EndIf
NextHope = i
dist_ = incircle
# sender vehicle adds the vehicle (NextHope) to its
 list of neighbors
            upstream_
          EndIf
EndIf
EndIf
# If the list of neighbors is obtained, the sender ve-
hicle call the SendData
procedure to its neighbors in multicast mode with ar-
guments: lists of neigh
bors and the distance between the sender and these ve-
hicles.
If(upstream_ != "")
   Call proceduresendData (upstream_ max_dist)
EndIf
Dist_ = 0
End
```

Procedure 3: Sends Alerts to Near Neighbors

```
# variables used
Liste : list of neighbors.
nodeID : ID of sender vehicle
msg : message to send.

dist_ : the distance between the sending vehicle and
the receiving vehicle.
SenderCode : code of sender vehicle.
Sender vehicle « nodeID » send the message   « msg »
to close neighbors
« Liste » by using send procedure of Leach protocol.
This procedure takes as a parameter the mac address of
the sender vehicle,
sender code SenderCode , the distance that separates
it from neighboring
dist_, and the message to send rmsg.
```

3.4 Vehicle to Infrastructure and Infrastructure to Vehicle Communication

Procedure 4: Vehicle to Infrastructure communication proposed algorithm
To add the V2I communication in our proposed algorithm, we have added one condition on alert message receiver.

```
# Changes to Neighbors Node procedure.
distB : distance between the sending vehicle and the
base station SB
upstream_: list of neighbors sender vehicle.
dist_ : the distance between the sender node and the
receiver vehicle.
If (upstream_ != "")
If (distB < dist_ )
# the sender vehicle is close to the SB
Call of the procedure sendDataToBS
else
        call the procedure sendData (upstream_
dist_)
EndIF
Else
# the sender vehicle has no close neighbors
        Call the proceduresendDataToBS
EndIF
```

Procedure 5: Infrastructure to Vehicle communication

After receiving the alert message from de vehicle, the base station broadcast it to all network vehicles by eliminating the sender vehicle.

```
procedure BsSendData
sender : the ID of the sender vehicle of the alert
message.
bsID : the identifier of the base station SB.
dist : distance between the vehicle and the SB
send_to : the vehicle to which the message will be
sent.
Begin
If (send_to != sender)
The base station transmits the alert message to all
network vehicles
EndIf
End
```

We created a procedure, recvDataBS that takes as a parameter the message sent, so that, the vehicle can receives the broadcasted alert message by the base station. This procedure has the same structure as the RecvDATA procedure of Leach, but we changed the type of messages that the node can distinguish it from the message sent by the nodes.

4 Simulations

The delay of sending and receiving an alert message must be very short, otherwise it will be useless. We will proceed below in our article to the analysis of the results of sending, reception and average delay, generated in a random waypoint model scenario [9, 13, 14].

Average Delay: Is the time taken for a packet to be transmitted across a network from source to destination. The average of the lowest end-to-end shows the best performance of the routing protocol. It is calculated as follows [8, 10]:

$$\text{Average Delay (ms)} = \frac{\sum(\text{RPT} - \text{PTT})}{\sum \text{RP}} * 1000$$

- PRT: Packet Reception Time
- PTT: Packet Transmission Time
- RP: Received Packets.

4.1   Simulation Tools

For compatibility and interoperability reasons we realized our simulation using the following tools:

- Ubuntu 10.04 as operation system.
- NS2.34 as network simulator [10, 11].
- Setdest and cbrgen for mobility and traffic nodes generation.

4.2   Nodes Movement Generation

As mentioned in the introduction, our simulation scenario is based on random waypoint model [9, 14]; it will be generated by using a node-movement generator tool named "setdest" developed by Carnegie Mellon University (CMU) and it's available under "∼ns/indep-utils/cmu-scen-gen/setdest/".

Setdest generates a random movement of the nodes with a maximum speed in a fixed zone. The node can be set to stop for a certain amount of time (pause time) when it arrives the movement location [12, 14].

Setdest is used to:

- Create hops between the nodes.
- Create mobility for nodes.
- Move from one place to another place.

4.3   Nodes Traffic Generation

We have generated random traffic connections between nodes by using a traffic-scenario generator script called cbrgen.tcl available under "∼ns/indep-utils/cmu-scen-gen" [12, 14].

Cbrgen.tcl is used to:

- To create connections between the nodes.
- To create the type of agents between the nodes (cbr or tcp)
- Rate at which the packets are transmitted.

4.4   Simulation Parameters

The table below shows network parameters we have used for our simulation (Table 1):

Table 1. Simulation parameters

Parameter	Value
Topology area	1000 m * 800 m
Protocol	Our new alert protocol based on leach
Simulation time (s)	600 s
Mobile nodes	70, 90
Initial energy	300 J

5 Simulation Results and Analysis

5.1 Results of Sent Packets

- Case of 70 vehicles (Fig. 4).

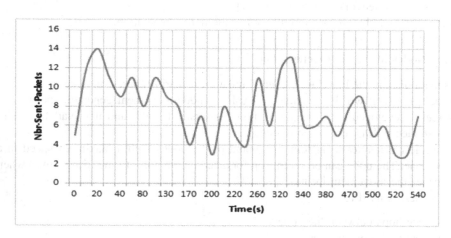

Fig. 4. Number of sent packets in the case of 70 vehicles

- Case of 90 vehicles (Fig. 5).

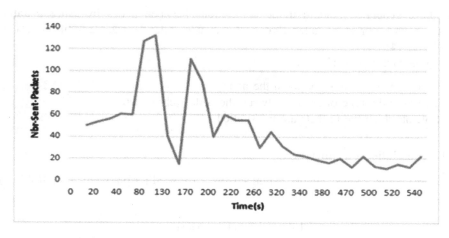

Fig. 5. Number of sent packets in the case of 90 vehicles

The graph and trace file of the simulations in the two cases, 70 and 90 nodes shows that the communication between the nodes is reliable. For the duration of the simulation, we see that the vehicles react and send an alert to its close neighbors or to the base station.

5.2 Results of the Received Packets

- Case of 70 vehicles (Fig. 6).

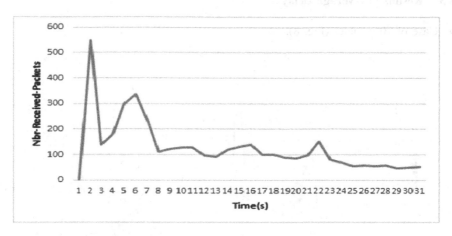

Fig. 6. Number of received packets in the case of 70 vehicles

- Case of 90 vehicles (Fig. 7).

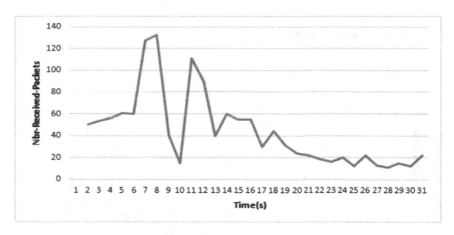

Fig. 7. Number of received packets in the case of 90 vehicles

In the two cases, 70 V and 90 V nodes, the reception in our protocol is reliable. Each packet sent is well received. The number of packets received has increased compared to the number of packets sent because we have used broadcast messages based on distances. That is, the signal of the sending message covers the maximum distance between the sending vehicle and its receiving neighbors. It is observed that in some cases, vehicles enter this interval, even if they are not in the list of neighbors when the vehicle that detected the event point starts sending the alert. This is due to the mobility of the latter which brings them closer to the sending vehicle.

5.3   Results of Average Delay

• Case of 70 vehicles (Fig. 8).

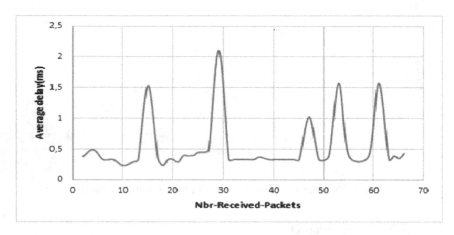

Fig. 8. Average delay VS number of received packets in the case of 70 vehicles

• Case of 90 vehicles (Fig. 9).

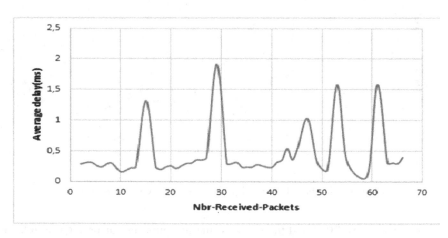

Fig. 9. Average delay VS number of received packets in the case of 90 vehicles

The graphs in the two cases, 70 and 90 vehicles, shows that the average delay does not exceed 2,1 ms in both simulations. The packets arrive at the destination at a short time. We notice that the proposed protocol is well suited to dense networks because the average time in the case of 90 vehicles is often lower than in the case of 70 vehicles.

6 Conclusion and Perspectives

In this work, we have integrated five procedure to leach protocol to create a new alert message dissemination protocol. As shown in the simulations and results, we have noticed that our protocol is reliable and is better suited to dense network.

The evaluation parameters studied in our work are not surely sufficient and further performance evaluation is required. On the other hand we planify in future work to compare our protocol with other alert protocols.

References

1. Srinivetha, R., Gopi, R.: Alert message dissemination protocol for VANET to improve road safety. Int. J. Emerg. Technol. Adv. Eng. **4**(1) (2014). ISSN 2250-2459
2. Maheswari, R., Kiran Kumar, T.V.U.: Efficient way of emergency message dissemination and reliable broadcast in vehicular ad-hoc network. Int. J. Adv. Res. Electr. Electron. Instrum. Eng. **4**(1) (2015). ISSN 2278-8875 (Online)
3. Tandel, R.I.: Leach protocol in wireless sensor network: a survey. (IJCSIT) Int. J. Comput. Sci. Inf. Technol. **7**(4), 1894–1896 (2016). ISSN 0975-9646
4. Gill, R.K., Chawla, P., Sachdeva, M.: Study of LEACH routing protocol for wireless sensor networks. In: International Conference on Communication, Computing & Systems (ICCCS) (2014)
5. Saxena, S., Babulal, K.S.: SURVEY: increasing energy of node by modified leach protocol. Int. J. Recent. Innov. Trends Comput. Commun. **3**(9) (2015). ISSN 2321-8169
6. Syed, K., Fathima, A., Sumitha, T.: To enhance the lifetime of WSN network using PSO. Int. J. Innov. Res. Comput. Commun. Eng. **2**(1), (2014). ISSN 2320-9801
7. https://journals.plos.org/plosone/article?id=10.1371/journal.pone.0143383
8. Barkouk, H., En-Naimi, E.: Performance analysis of the vehicular ad hoc networks (VANET) routing protocols AODV, DSDV and OLSR. In: 5th International Conference on Information & Communication Technology and Accessibility (ICTA 2015), Marrakech, Morocco, 21–23 December 2015 (2015)
9. Agrahari, S., Chinara, S.: Simulation of random waypoint mobility model using colored PetriNets. IPCSIT **47** (2012). https://doi.org/10.7763/ipcsit.2012.v47.13
10. Singh, A., Verma, A.K.: Simulation and analysis of AODV, DSDV, ZRP in VANET. IJFCST **3**(5), 13–26 (2013)
11. Berradj, A.: Contrôle de la diffusion multi-saut pour la dissémination de messages. Thesis, UT3 Paul Sabatier, October 2015
12. Fall, K., Varadhan, K.: The ns Manual. The VINT Project collaboration between researchers at UC Berkeley, LBL, USC/ISI, and Xerox PARC, April 2001
13. Bettstetter, C., Hartenstein, H., Pérez-Costa, X.: Stochastic properties of the random waypoint mobility model. Wirel. Netw. **10**, 555–567 (2004)
14. Sandhya Rani, M., Rekha, R., Sunitha, K.V.N.: Performance evaluation of MANET routing protocols using random waypoint mobility model. IJIARCSSE J. **4**(4) (2014). ISSN 2277 128X

Towards Semantic Integration
of Heterogeneous Data Based
on the Ontologies Modeling

Cheikh Ould El Mabrouk[(⊠)] and Karim Konaté[(⊠)]

Department of Mathematics and Computing, University Cheikh Anta Diop,
Dakar, Senegal
cheikhmab@yahoo.fr, kkonate911@yahoo.fr

Abstract. The integration of the heterogeneous data is a major problem encountered today by the users of the Web. A typical integration scenario is that two heterogeneous systems A and B are built for different business purposes for different users at different times by different software developers using different information models. The two systems often have heterogeneous semantics, data structures and business rules are different.

It involves in particular the differences between systems infrastructures, the conceptual schematizations of the data and its meanings. Indeed, the ontology specifies its systems of knowledge representation. It allows the modeling of knowledge in an explicit and formal way by concepts and relations between these concepts. The semantic integration comes after syntactic integration and the mechanisms of translation connection.

In this paper, we proceeded to a semantic integration of the heterogeneous data based on the management of the heterogeneousness and the semantic ontology of the knowledge.

Keywords: Integration · Ontologies · Semantic Web · Heterogeneousness · Distribution

1 Introduction

The integration process of heterogeneous information sources in the ontologies context of the semantic Web rely on several approaches. For that purpose, the last years have seen the several researches works realization in the Web databases domains and the ontologies concerning the integration design realization of different databases in open environments such as Semantic Web.

This new Web generation is an important evolution compared to the other previous generations will be based on ontologies and semantic knowledge management. Furthermore, the ontologies are used in several areas of information processing. In addition to, the semantic Web infrastructure has to allow their integration giving the impression to the user that it uses a homogeneous system. However, the typologies information distribution systems are generally based on software and sources of heterogeneous data on several computers. Often, within a company, there are several heterogeneous systems that are not designed to integrate data or applications. Then, the development and

© Springer Nature Switzerland AG 2019
É. Renault et al. (Eds.): MSPN 2019, LNCS 11557, pp. 188–200, 2019.
https://doi.org/10.1007/978-3-030-22885-9_17

deployment tools evolve over time. This raises integration problems, because infrastructures information systems do not easily exchange computerized data. In particular, the semantic integration problems become then ontological integration problems [1, 2].

A machine and human readable language is therefore preferred to model both the semantics of the systems and the heterogeneity between them. Data Semantics models can be expressed in various forms ranging from schemas to system documentation. Some well-known information modeling languages are evaluated below for the criteria of machine and human readability. Gathered data often comes from heterogeneous (different) sources; therefore, integration activities are needed and very important. In a business context, integration activities are commonly referred to as Enterprise Integration. This means the ability to integrate information and functionalities of different Information Technology systems.

In this paper, we divide our work as follows: the first part is this introduction. The second part constituted by the problem of data integration. The third part makes a state of the art on the heterogeneousness of the information system. The fourth part formulated the set of heterogeneousness management approaches. The fifth part of this article focuses mainly on a conception of the ontology models and the data integration. Finally, the sixth part summarizes all of our works and gives some perspectives for their continuation.

2 Problem of Data Integration

The systems of the information (SI) consist of Hardware and Software such as: operating systems, communication protocols, local area network, network links, DATABASE MANAGEMENT SYSTEM (DBMS), programs and software packages. Data integration addresses problems related to the provision of interoperability to information systems by the resolution of heterogeneity between systems on the data level. The heterogeneousness of the information system is an inevitable problem in the fact that the data and the applications of SI can be developed and deployed in independent ways and according to approaches and different methodologies of design and realization [3].

Data integration is an area of research that addresses a pervasive challenge faced in applications that need to query across multiple autonomous and heterogeneous data sources.

In this context, the systems of integration have to allow the user to access, via a single access interface, data stored in several sources of data. These sources have been independently designed by different designers. It entails the heterogeneousness of data, that is to say, that the data relating to the same meaning are differently represented on different information systems [4]. This heterogeneousness systems from different choices which are made to represent facts of the real world in a scheme of design and development.

3   State of the Art on the Heterogeneousness of the Information System

Heterogeneous (means from Greek "other" or heteros and geneous or "nature") is the characteristic to contain dissimilar constituents. A common use of this word in terms of information technology is to describe a product as a measure to contain or to be a part of a «heterogeneous hardware/ software», made up of various manufacturers products that can (interoperate) [5].

In this context, the heterogeneousness of data concerns at the same time the physical system, the syntactic and semantic structure. This informational heterogeneousness results from the fact that the sources of data may have different structures and/or different formats to represent their data. And the sources of data are independently designed, by different designers, having different application objectives. Everyone can, thus, have a different point of view on the same concept and the object [2]. As a result, it exists several types of heterogeneousness are due to the technical differences of management of SI such as the differences between the physical hardware, the software systems. The authors' work [3, 6, 7, 27, 28] can distinguish mainly three types of heterogeneousness as below:

- Technical heterogeneousness: refers to the difference between physical hardware, network infrastructure, cables, operating systems and application platforms. It refers to the resolution of structural heterogeneity; for instance, the heterogeneity of data models, query and data access languages, protocols, and hardware platforms.
- Syntactic heterogeneousness: corresponds to the different presentations in the data formats and interfaces of the applications. It refers to the resolution of semantic mismatch between schemata. A mismatch of concepts appearing in such schemata may be due to a number of reasons. For instance, different schemas may represent the same information in different ways. The major issues that make integrating data difficult include. The similar semantics of data representation might be quite different in each data source. Moreover, they may contain conflicting data. In addition, heterogeneity may also occur at lower levels, including access methods, underlying operating systems, etc.
- Semantic heterogeneousness: corresponds to the differences related to the interpretation or the explanation in the sense associated with the data and functions of an application. Data sources are independent elements that are not designed for a data integration system. They cannot be forced to act in certain ways. As a natural consequence of this, they can also change their data or functionality unannounced.

4   Approaches to Heterogeneousness Management

The web services development today has allowed the putting on line of an imaginable number of heterogeneous and distributed information (data, files, video, images, sound …). Each type of information offers autonomous access interfaces of other types and often heterogeneous between different web technologies (HTML, PHP, JAVA, Web Services ….), and by the communication infrastructure of the information system (Systems,   Networks,   DBMS   (DATABASE   MANAGEMENT   SYSTEM)) heterogeneous [8]. Therefore, the integration and the exchange of the heterogeneous data allow having a logical integration at the level of the access to the data.

In this case, the logical integration of the data takes place at the level access to the data. At the global level, the applications have a uniform view of the data physically distributed, through a representation of the data. At the local level, information systems keep their autonomy of the data representation (identification, type, length ...), and to allow access the data via other applications [2, 9]. These approaches aim to solve the above-mentioned heterogeneous problems and to move to the limits semantic integration ontologies.

4.1 Management of the Technical Heterogeneousness

The management of the technical heterogeneousness allows opening a dynamic management of the tasks and the human-machine interface. The evolution of the material and the IT software have led to new needs in terms of adapted networks and highly distributed architecture (offering to all the possibility of enriching the company's information system) [10].

In this context, software allows in this case to launch several tasks invited on host machines and be placed next to several completely isolated operating systems. Then, facilitate communications between the protocols of operating systems and networks.

For that purpose, all the potential machines are provided with linking network cards which are in fact processors producing the option to exchange information with the outside in order to establish easily effective interactions between the systems. As a result, several technical solutions are used for the operation of the heterogeneous hardware and software. The HAL stands for "Hardware Abstraction Layer", or hardware (or software) abstraction layer, whose function is to isolate the specificities of the hardware through a number of hardware-specific functions: [11, 12].

(1) - Partitioning, isolation of the physical and/ or software resources.
(2) - The ability to manipulate remote machines by transcribing data, pausing, stopping and starting, remote programming capabilities...
(3) - Possibility of "logical" networking of remote machines but also interfacing them with physical networks.
(4) - The high availability for backup security: outsourcing and third-party centralization can be applied to any SI.

4.2 Management of the Syntactic Heterogeneousness

The syntactic heterogeneousness is when data of interest is available in various formats, different representation schema or a query translation [13]. Thus, the interaction between several information systems requires efficient management of the exchange of computerized data between the heterogeneous applications of these latters.

The difficulty mainly arises from the data representations incompatibility. As for example, «id-student of alphabetical type and length 10A» and «code-student of digital type and length 6 N» are two different representations from the same meaning identification of a student.

The authors' work [6] proposed mechanisms of translation between the diagrams of representations of data (designation, type, length…).

To resolve this problem of syntactic heterogeneity, translation mechanisms between data representations must be implemented. We have proceeded to prove by recurrence the two approaches presented by [6] (in position by type of distribution architectures point-to-point, EAI (Enterprise Application Integration) and ESB (Enterprise Service Bus)).

We distinguish two approaches according to the architecture of distribution (Fig. 1):

A) - A point-to-point architecture for data translation approach

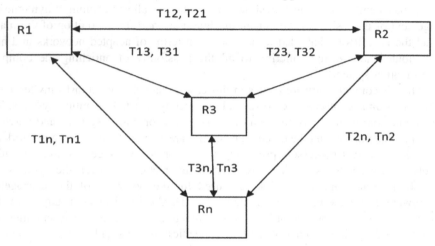

Fig. 1. Data translation by point-to-point architecture

In this approach to data representation of point-to-point architecture, the translations are directly established between two representations. To link two representations (R_i, R_j), two translations T_{ij} (from representation i to representation j) and T_{ji} (from representation j to representation i) carry out the syntactic correspondences.

As a result, each representation (R_i) there are translations as follows:

$$T_{ij}, \ j = 1, 2, .., i-1, \ i+1, .., n$$

$$T_{ji}, \ j = 1, 2, .., i-1, \ i+1, .., n$$

Therefore; for each (R_i) in (n) representations of the data: $(n-1) + (n-1) = 2*(n-1)$.

The principle of this approach: for (n) representations there exists $n * (n-1)$ translation mechanisms.

We suppose that valid for $(n-1)$ representations and we prove by the recursion for (n) representations.

For $(n-1)$, the representation number is $(n-1) * (n-2)$

For "n^{th}" the representation number is 2 * (n−1)
So, the number of representation this sum of:
(n−1) * (n−2) + 2 * (n−1)
As a result, to represent (n) there must exist [n * (n−1)] translation mechanisms.

b) An approach of data translation by architectures EAI, ESB

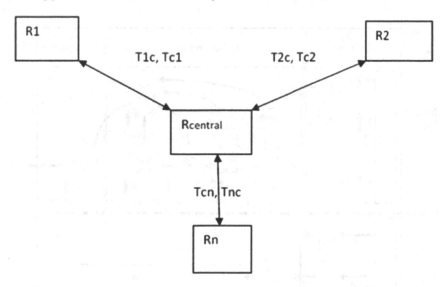

Fig. 2. Data translation by central mediation EAI, ESB

In this approach of the data representation of the EAI (Enterprise Application Integration), ESB (Enterprise Service Bus) architectures they are necessary to translate the entire source representation to a central representation and then translate this central representation to the target representation scheme (Fig. 2).

Consequently, for each representation scheme (R_i) there are two translation mechanisms from and to the central representation scheme ($R_{central}$): T_{ic}, T_{ci}.

The principle of this approach is that for (n) diagrams of representation there must be (2 * n) translation mechanisms.

We suppose that valid for (n-1) representations and we prove by the recursion for (n) representations.

For (n−1), the representation number is 2 * (n−1)
For n «n^{th}» the number of representation is 2
So, the number of representation this sum of:
2 * (n−1) +2 = 2 * (n−1 + 1) = 2 * n
Finally, to represent n there must exist [2 * n] translation mechanisms.

4.3   Management of the Semantic Heterogeneousness

The semantic heterogeneousness means resources of the data highly varied and more or less structured information sources (databases, XML documents, texts); whereas, in homogeneous sources from the viewpoint of their level of constitution but nevertheless coherent. The semantic heterogeneousness describes the difference in the meaning of the data between the various sources of the data [6, 14] (Fig. 3).

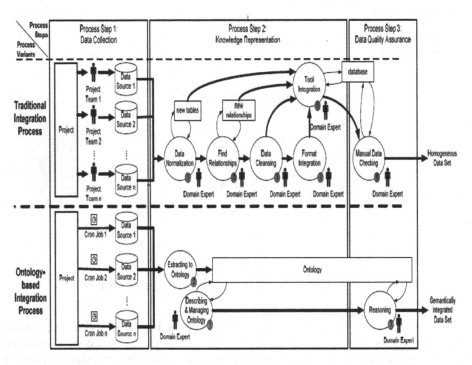

Fig. 3. Comparison of traditional and ontology integration processes [27].

The Extraction of integration rules is based on the heterogeneity analysis of the different systems. Therefore the quality of the heterogeneity description decides directly the quality of integration rules. In order to describe the heterogeneity, semantics of the source systems need to be described first. Machine readable semantic models are preferred compared to only human understandable semantic models because machine readability provides the possibility of utilizing automated reasoning and thereby the possibility of automation of the integration rules extraction.

In the ontology-based approach, the knowledge representation is done by designing and implementing an initial ontology that captures all data models and requirements in advance. The designer defines the classes, attributes and relations of ontology that will be populated automatically by using tool during the data collection step. In the ontology, the designer should also define restrictions, rules and axioms that are used for data quality assurance to check the syntax and the constraint of the data [26].

In this context, Semantic web is an integrative vision of many problems of heterogeneous data and ontological knowledge and of indexing and the communication of information. However, ontologies as information server interrogation interfaces and a tool for combining data from heterogeneous data sources and where core semantic Web applications and as well as rules and axioms that cover a rich data management.

According to the authors [15–17, 23, 25]; they are based on the three approaches:

- The acquisition: identify all the different sources of the knowledge and the concepts and its logical relations in a specific field.
- The modeling: to indicate the set of data or knowledge that fixes the linguistic meaning of the concepts in a specific domain.
- The representation: define the set of concepts linked by specific relations.

Finally, heterogeneity managing approaches are limited in terms of modeling ontological for each domain of knowledge.

5 Ontology Models and Data Integration

Ontology models are used to facilitate the integration and the exchange of heterogeneous data. In association with the syntactic translation and the semantic management almost one-to-one object, class, type entity and the converter to the attribute, property, type value and contribute to the accurate modeling of the properties, and classes for the semantic integration of information [18, 22].

In this context, Ontologies have been extensively used in data integration systems because they provide an explicit and machine-understandable conceptualization of a domain.

5.1 Modeling Ontological Knowledge

Knowledge modeling involves depositing the entities of different identical concepts, retaining the concepts and the relationships, in determining their domain, and indicating the set of data or knowledge that sets the linguistic meaning of the concepts for each type of semantic ontology and logical link.

The works of the authors [19, 20, 24] proposed ontologies ranking approaches before semantic integration:

- The regional ontology is seen as a tree of semantic concepts and its relationships. Its interpretation is constrained by the differential principles associated with the elements constituted of the tree: root, ancestor, branch, leaf...
- The referential ontology describes a set of referential (or formal) concepts that are characterized by a term/ designation whose semantics is defined by an extension of objects.
- The computational ontology deals with computational concepts that are characterized by the operations that can be applied to them to generate inferences. The global ontology provides a conceptual view over the schematically-heterogeneous source schemas.

5.2   Semantic Integration

The semantic integration focuses on the intended meaning of the concepts, and to establish the semantic relationships between the concepts of the modeled ontologies. This process of semantic integration based on two ontological approaches: [2, 21].

- A posteriori: to perform in a manual or semi-automatic manner and to establish the correspondence between the basic concepts of the ontologies.

  For [n] ontologies one has to create [n * (n−1)] correspondence.

- A priori: allows to automatically integrating each ontology source [Oi] of the semantic relations as a subset of the global ontology.

  For each [Oi] of the global ontology of [n] elements one has to create [(n−1)] correspondence.

5.3   A Semantic Integration Procedure

In this procedure we have proceeded to an approach of our semantic integration by: Proposed algorithm, schema simulation of syntactic and semantic representations, table of semantic integration results of heterogeneous data, and discussion.

(A) -Algorithm "Sematic Integration"

```
     BEGIN
  ➢  management of technical heterogeneity
         Web Services "connection of heterogeneous and distributed systems"
  ➢  management of syntactic heterogeneousness
      IF Architecture Type = Point-to-Point THEN
         Translation number = n * (n-1)
           ELSE Translation number = 2 * n
      END IF
  ➢  management of semantic heterogeneousness
         Creating, Modeling and Representing Semantic Data
  ➢  Semantic ontology modeling
         Classification of ontologies by type
         Definition of ontological relationships
      BEGIN
      IF type of information Automatic THEN number of matches = 2 * (n-1)
         ELSE number of matches = n * (n-1)
      END IF
      END
     END
```

(B) - Algorithm Simulation
Table 1

Table 1. Schema of syntactic and semantic representations

Number	Syntactic heterogeneousness		Semantic heterogeneousness	
	Point-to-point	Mediation	Manual or semi- automatic	Automatic
1	0	2	0	0
2	2	4	2	1
3	6	6	6	2
4	12	8	12	3
..				
N	N*(N-1)	2*N	N*(N-1)	(N-1)

(C) - Result

- Manual semantic integration by point-to-point representation MP = $(N * (N-1))^2$
- Manual semantic integration by representation Mediation MM = $2 * (N-1) * N2$
- Automatic semantics integration by point-to-point representation AP = $N * (N-1)^2$
- Automatic semantics integration by representation Mediation AM = $2 * N * (N-1)$
  (Table 2).

Table 2. Result of heterogeneous semantic integration data

N	MP	MM	AP	AM
1	0	0	0	0
2	4	8	2	4
3	36	36	12	12
4	144	96	36	24
5	400	200	80	40
6	900	360	150	60
7	1764	588	252	84
8	3136	896	392	112
9	5184	1296	576	144
10	8100	1800	810	180

(D) – Discussion
The solution we propose offers a heterogeneity management algorithm that resembles all the necessary processes for the syntactic and semantic integration of heterogeneous information. In our algorithm, we have combined the two approaches: [6] and [21], integrating the identification and description of data that existing web services

capabilities into models for integration direct and effective interesting parts that implement the web service of the information environment.

The process begins with the management of technical heterogeneity, which is considered as a preparatory step of the integration phase, where we will decide whether it is possible or even recurring to continue composing the information environment towards an integrated environment. This step is very important to manage the heterogeneity of an integrated data environment, hence the clear and deep understanding of the translation mechanism and the management of syntactic and semantic heterogeneity.

In the same run, we calculate the two last phases of translation and the representation of the data. From these, we distinguish the types of architectures that exist in the system and that must be exchanged the translation mechanism to other representations. The integration of information environments is realized by the integration of their applications via web services interfaces. The final step is the integration of web data into a central control flow of the information system.

6 Conclusion

The integration of heterogeneous data is an important problem in the current and future times. To this end, the ontology of the semantic web has been proposed to solve this problem. An important evaluation of the web generations shows that it produces a semantic integration of heterogeneous data.

In this paper, we have shown the semantic integration process based on the management of heterogeneity and semantic ontology of knowledge and we discussed the main issues and the proposal solutions.

This proposal presents a limited syntactic integration approach towards semantic integration, calculations of the different models translation mechanism and the information representation.

Our future works concerns the semantic evolution problems towards knowledge integration. The advantages and disadvantages for each proposed approach, the queries optimization approaches of the heterogeneous web data, and to explore other ontologies models to develop the semantic integration process towards global integration.

References

1. Hasan, M.K., et al.: A community-driven approach for missing background knowledge in Semantic matching. Int. J. Eng. Sci. Technol. 2(10), 5921–5928 (2010)
2. Nguyen Xuan, D.: Intégration de bases de données hétérogènes par articulation apriori d'ontologies application aux catalogues de composants industriels, thèse (2006)
3. Sneed, H.M.: Integrating legacy software into a service oriented architecture, discussion paper. In: Lehner, F., Nösekabel, H., Kleinschmidt, P. (eds.) Multikonferenz Wirtschaftsinformatik 2006, Band 2, XML4BPM Track, GITO-Verlag Berlin, pp. 345–360 (2006)
4. Bellatreche, L., et al.: An a priori approach for automatic integration of heterogeneous and autonomous databases. In: International Conference on Database and Expert Systems Applications (DEXA 2004), pp. 475–485, September 2004

5. What is heterogeneous? Conférence CIO-MIDMARK 20000. http://searchcio-midmarket. techtarget.com/definition/heterogeneous. Accessed 31 Jan 2019

6. Touzi, A.C.J.: Aide à la conception de Système d'Information Collaboratif support de l'interopérabilité des entreprises, thèse Doctorat Ecole des Mines (2007)

7. Wiederhold, G.: Mediators in the architecture of future information systems. IEEE Comput. 25(3), 38–49 (1992)

8. Hacid, M.-S., et al.: L'intégration de sources de données. http://leo.saclay.inria.fr//publifiles/ gemo/GemoReport-416.pdf. Accessed 30 Jan 2019

9. David, R., et al.: Virtual integration for improved system design. In: The First Analytic Virtual Integration of Cyber-Physical Systems Workshop, pp. 57–64, Avicps (2010)

10. Zhao, X., et al.: Web services in distributed information systems: availability, performance and composition. Int. J. Distrib. Syst. Technol. 1(1), 1–16 (2010)

11. Remus, D.B.: Transparent high availability for database systems. In: Minhas, U.F. et al. (eds.) Proceedings of the VLDB Endowment the 37th International Conference on Very Large Data Bases, Seattle, Washington, 29th August 3rd September 2011, vol. 4, no. 11 (2011)

12. La Virtualisation: machine virtuelle ou hyperviseur New Technologies System Virtualisation. http://www.ntsysv.com/index.php/la-virtualisation-machine-virtuelle-ou-hyperviseur. Accessed 17 Jan 2019

13. Abrouk, L., DiJorio, L., Fiot, C., Hérin, D., Teisseire, M.: «Enrichissement d'ontologie basé sur les motifs séquentiels». 23èmes Journées Bases de Données Avancées, BDA 2007, Marseille, 23–26 October 2007

14. Laublet, P., Reynaud, C.: Ontologies et Gestion de l'Hétérogénéité Sémantique conférence GDR, INRI, 3 juillet, Grenoble, France, vol. 13, p. 5 (2007)

15. Ouksel, A.M., Jurca, O., Podnar, I., Aberer, K.: Efficient probabilistic subsumption checking for content-based publish/subscribe systems. In: Middleware, pp. 121–140 (2006)

16. Nagiba, A.M., et al.: AISIGHTED: a framework for semantic integration of heterogeneous sensor data on the Internet of things. Proc. Comput. Sci. 83 529–536 (2016). The 7th International Conference on Ambient Systems, Networks and Technologies (ANT 2016)

17. Bachimont, B.: Engagement Sémantique et Engagement Ontologique: Conception et Réalisation D'ontologies En Ingénierie Des Connaissances, chap. 19, pp. 305–324. Eyrolles (2000)

18. Gruber, T.: A translation approach to portable ontology specifications Knowl. Acquisition 5 (2), 199–220 (1993)

19. Chandrasekaran, B., Josephson, J.R., Benjamins, V.R.: What are ontologies and why do we need them? IEEE Intell. Syst. 14(1), 20–26 (1999)

20. Brisson, L.: Mesures d'intérêt subjectif et représentation des connaissances. Rapport technique, Laboratoire I3S, Université Sophia Antipolis, Nice France, Octobre 2004. http:// www.i3s.unice.fr/mh/RR/2004/RR-04.35-L.BRISSON.pdf. Accessed 10 Jan 2019

21. Mellal, N.: Réalisation de l'interopérabilité sémantique des systèmes, basée sur les ontologies et les flux d'information, thèse (2007)

22. Wang, J., et al.: Integrating heterogeneous data source using ontology. J. Softw. 4(8), 843–850 (2009)

23. Noy, N.F., et al.: Semantic integration: a survey of ontology-based approaches. ACM SIGMOD Rec. 33(4), 65–70 (2004)

24. Shi, L., et al.: SBVR as a semantic hub for integration of heterogeneous systems - a case study and experience report -. Statsbygg, Pb. 8106 Dep, 0032 Oslo, Norway. http://ceur-ws. org/Vol-1004/paper10.pdf

25. Cruz, I.F., Xiao, H.: ADVIS, the role of ontologies in data integration, Lab Department of Computer Science University of Illinois at Chicago, USA. www.cs.uic.edu/~advis/ publications/dataint/eis05j.pdf

26. Olaru, M.O.: Heterogeneous data warehouse analysis and dimensional integration Ph.D. dissertation, International Doctorate School in Information and Communication Technologies XXVI Cycle. www.dbgroup.unimo.it/tesi/Tesi_Phd/phdOlaru.pdf
27. Biffl, S., et al.: Semantic integration of heterogeneous data sources for monitoring frequent-release software projects. In: 2010 International Conference on Complex, Intelligent and Software Intensive Systems, pp. 360–367 in p. 365. IEEE Computer Society (2010)
28. Macura, M., et al.: Integration of data from heterogeneous sources using ETL technology. Comput. Sci. 15(2), 109–132 (2014)

A Comparison Between MADM Methods and Utility Functions in the Network Selection Context

Mouad Mansouri$^{(\boxtimes)}$ ⓘ and Cherkaoui Leghris ⓘ

L@M Lab, RTM Team, Computer Sciences Department, FST Mohammedia,
Hassan II University, Casablanca, Morocco
mansouri.mouad@yahoo.com, cleghris@yahoo.fr

Abstract. The vertical handover is the communication switch from a source point of attachment, to a destination one, using a different access typology, for some quality, cost, load balancing or security requirements. In fact, mobile users often walk through wireless multi-access environments and need diverse services. Thus, devices must smartly pick out the best target network to transfer the communications to, from those available anytime. The network selection must consider different parameters together, like the available bandwidth, the energy consumption, the cost, the security, etc. The works in the literature propose many techniques to tackle this decision issue, such as MADM methods and utility functions. These methods can consider multiple attributes together when evaluating the alternatives. This work aims to compare some combinations of these two decision-making techniques in the network selection context. The results show that the compared utility functions outperform MADM methods in some situations, and make steadier decisions to ensure the session continuity.

Keywords: MADM methods · Network selection · Utility functions · Vertical handover · Wireless multi-access environments

1 Introduction

In the IoT era, more and more mobile users (MUs) require services on internet. Nowadays, mobile devices (MDs) are equipped with powerful interfaces, allowing them to access heterogeneous wireless networks, from both IEEE and 3GPP groups [1], as they are omnipresent. Thus, MUs tend to access the best available wireless technology anytime (i.e. always best connected "ABC"), which leads to a big vertical handover (VH) probability. The VH is switching the point of attachment (PoA) between two heterogeneous wireless access technologies (e. g. from 4G to WLAN). In opposition, the horizontal handover means changing the PoA within homogeneous networks (i.e. between base stations for 3GPP or access points for WLANs) [2], while still using the same access type.

© Springer Nature Switzerland AG 2019
É. Renault et al. (Eds.): MSPN 2019, LNCS 11557, pp. 201–210, 2019.
https://doi.org/10.1007/978-3-030-22885-9_18

There exist many classifications of VHs in the literature, depending on the aspects the authors treat in their works. In our works, we try to consider the most desirable options and qualities of a VH. Indeed, the VH must be "seamless" or "Soft", which means it should not cause any connectivity ruptures or disruptions. This imposes the VH process to be fast to reduce the transfer time, and profitable to avoid useless handovers that lead to poor quality of service (QoS), which could disturb the communications.

IEEE 802.21 or Media Independent Handover (MIH) standard outlines the two first stages of the VH, each one with its steps [3], without imposing the how. It includes messages and features contained in the MIH Function (MIHF), which is implemented between Layer two and three. It defines the events, commands, information and triggers that help the MD performing the VH. MIH divides the VH process into three main stages which are: The VH initiation, the VH preparation and the VH execution. Figure 1 is a scheme illustrating the different phases and steps of the VH.

Fig. 1. Different steps of the vertical handover process

The network selection comes in the first stage of the VH (i.e. initiation), whose steps are:

1. VH discovery: After it is triggered by "weak Received signal strength (RSS)" or "Link going down" of the current PoA through MIHF triggers, the MD gathers data and link states of the near available wireless networks via MIHF information services (Neighbor map and metrics of different wireless access networks).
2. VH decision-making (Network selection): In this step, the MD must decide, which available wireless access technology is the best, by evaluating different attributes of each alternative.
3. VH negotiation: After selecting the best available wireless network, the MD must decide whether to continue the VH process to the preparation and execution phases or not, the instructions are passed via MIHF command services.

The second stage (preparation) is transitory, in which the MD sets up the link and IP settings, to arrange the communication transfer. MIH doesn't provide specifications of the third stage (execution), during which the MD exchanges signaling and context information, and starts transmission/reception of packets. The MD automatically executes the second and third stages after the VH is triggered and the initiation is complete. MIH supports the "make before break" link transfer, to avoid session ruptures. The VH can either be "Terminal-Controlled" or "Network-Controlled". In our contributions, we focus on the "Terminal-Controlled" "Network-Assisted" VH. First, the MD launches the VH process when needed. Then, the network-side provides the MD with the necessary information about the near PoAs' configurations and link states to help the MD managing the VH.

In our works, we focus on optimizing the network selection step, to reduce the number of unnecessary VHs, using Multi Attributes Decision-Making (MADM) and fuzzy MADM methods. We propose in this contribution to study two utility functions, in the network selection context, and compare their results with those of the best known MADM methods.

We organize this paper as follows: The second section presents the state of the art and the methods used to optimize the VH decision-making phase. Section three explains how we designed the simulation scenario, implementing our scheme to handle the network selection steps, and how we compared the results in this work. Section four illustrates the results of our simulation and discuss them and finally, we conclude and give future ways of research, related to this contribution.

2   State of the Art

The network selection is a crucial issue in the future internet, it requires an efficient and fast strategy to reach the "seamless VH" goal [2]. MIH is the standard for the VH initiation and preparation, it proposes the VH steps, but doesn't give well-defined methods for each step. Meanwhile, IETF made the mechanisms for the VH execution, such as Mobile IPv.6 (MIPv.6) and fast MIPv.6 (FMIPv.6), ensuring the session continuity. Thus, the network selection step is the most treated subject in the literature, from the VH initiation steps, supposing that we can simulate data gathered in the discovery phase.

We found many works treating the network selection issue in the literature, they adopt different techniques and strategies to designate the best wireless network from those available everywhere, the considering multiple attributes together. In [4], the authors present a survey of the existing techniques and architectures to support the mobility management and handovers. They classify these strategies following the techniques used to deal with this issue and list the desired criteria to be considered in comparing these strategies. In [5], the authors give an overview of the VH process and its steps, present some selection parameters used to select the best available wireless network in a heterogeneous environment and classify the VH strategies based on the techniques used for the VH decision, they list the different criteria used to evaluate a VH decision strategy. They finally propose some combinations of VH decision techniques that could give better results and allow better connectivity. In [6], the authors present an overview of the VH decision architectures, they classified them into five different decision making groups, focusing on the main characteristics of each one, to finally propose their own intelligent and context-aware architecture, using multi-criteria decision-making that take into account multiple network attributes, as well as fuzzy logic and context-aware policies that consider the MT state and movement, for solving the network selection issue in a loose-coupled heterogeneous environment (i.e. 3G and WLAN). In [7], the authors present a survey of VH decision approaches using different methods, such as the basic algorithms, based on the sensed network conditions, the cost function that can aggregate more than one condition, the MADM methods, the artificial intelligence and neural networks algorithms, and context-aware algorithms. They also outlined the requirements for developing new optimized algorithms that could minimize the signaling cost and packet delay, very desired in real-time applications.

In [8], the authors present a review and a classification of the most significant MADM algorithms in the context of network selection in heterogeneous wireless environments, focusing on the positive and negative points of each decision-making scheme. They also discussed the criteria choice and its impact on the decision-making, and finally, they give an overview of the current research trend in the application of MADM algorithms to network selection problems. Our previous work in [9] presents a comparison between different MADM methods used in VH network selection, based on three evaluation criteria: The total VH number, the rank reversal rate, and the QoS delivered during all the simulated movement trajectory. We concluded that the Technique for Ordering Preferences by Similarity to the Ideal Solution (TOPSIS), is the best MADM method in this context, using the Fuzzy Analytic Network Process (FANP) to weight the attributes.

In [10], the authors present utility models for the network selection in heterogeneous wireless environments, they use the additive aggregation of linear and exponential utility functions to choose the best available network, differentiating between profit $(u(x))$ and cost $(1 - u(x))$ attributes; $u(x)$ is the utility function for attribute x. Then, they propose the logarithmic transformation: $v(x) = ln(u(x))$, as the function is linear, and state that the weights reflect better the user preferences, they also highlighted the limitations of such methods in this context.

The authors in [11] propose a utility-based algorithm to evaluate the available wireless networks. They discuss the existing utility functions and the types of aggregations (additive, multiplicative, and mixed), used to calculate the overall performance of a candidate network, while considering the user satisfaction as well. The authors in [12] present a tutorial on mathematical modelling for network selection in heterogeneous wireless environment, they studied the most used mathematical theories in this context and present an overview of the use of different utility functions, normalization and weighting methods. They finally compare these different schemes and propose a MADM based network selection solution. The authors of [13] (2016) propose a context-aware and utility-based scheme for the wireless access network selection, that considers the users' satisfaction and the delivered QoS in a WLAN/LTE environment. This strategy enables seamless connectivity and an effective resource management following the required services. The authors in [14] use a Cost function with Signal to Noise Ratio (SINR) prediction method in the network selection context, the simulation results show that the proposed method enhances the prediction accuracy and ensures the best tradeoff between the network conditions and the user preferences and offers a better QoS to the end-users, which improves their satisfaction. In [15], the authors propose a cost function based network selection solution, combined with fuzzy logic and Particle Swarm Optimization (PSO), the studied cost function is similar to the additive aggregation of utility functions proposed before.

All of these works propose utility/cost-based algorithms for the network selection in wireless heterogeneous environments. In this contribution, we compare two utility functions with the best MADM methods in the same context. We basically study the additive aggregation of linear and logarithmic utility functions for attributes in this work.

3 Our Methodology

As introduced before, we mainly focused in our works on evaluating the decisions that every combination of methods will make in different situations. We designed a dataset that contains simulated data gathered during the discovery step of the VH (D matrices filled with the metrics of available networks in every decision point), we compute this data and output the selected wireless network every time, using different combinations based on the use-case scenario described in [3].

In this contribution, we consider four heterogeneous decision zones (DZs), each one has multiple decision points, we variate data to simulate the real metrics fluctuations. We note $t = t_0$ to $t = t_8$, the times that the location of the mobile user (MU) or the networks characteristics change:

1. A MU goes home from somewhere outside, from $t = t_0$ to $t = t_1$ (DZ_1);
2. He stays a while until $t = t_4$ (DZ_2);
3. He leaves his house to the airport at $t = t_4$, he reaches the destination at $t = t_6$ (DZ_3).
4. The MU stays at the airport until $t = t_8$ (DZ_4).

The MD senses the networks configurations in different situations, where multiple wireless technologies are available. We normalize and compute this same dataset using different MADM and utility functions-based combinations, named uF1 and uF2, to see which one is relatively the best, in selecting the best available networks in the MU's trajectory. We take the input data, which constitute D matrices in the dataset, from the possible values in Table 1, every time a wireless technology is available (in every DZ), we variate data from the min to the max value to take into account some other effects (e.g. the ping-pong effect) during the decision.

We consider nine wireless networks in different decision points, as they are present in most places. These nine wireless technologies are GPRS, EDGE, UMTS, HSxPA, LTE, 802.11 a/b/g, 802.11 n, 802.11 ac and WiMAX. We decided to consider eight attributes, which are the throughput (T), the availability (Av), the security (S), the packet delay (D), the loss rate (L), the energy consumption (Ec), the cost (C) and the jitter (J). The attributes' choice is a large debate subject, every author opts for considering different benefit/cost attributes. We carefully designed a dataset with values from Table 1, to simulate the real-life fluctuation of metrics. This dataset is computed using different combinations, to finally compare their results.

Table 1. Possible values of attributes used during the simulation of numeral method

Attributes	T (Kbps)	Av (%)	S (%)	D (ms)	L ($*10^6$)	EC (1–7)	C (1–7)	J (ms)/Networks
GPRS	21.4–171.2	50–100	50	50–70	50–80	2	1	3–20
EDGE	43.2–345.6	40–100	50	20–60	25–70	2	2	3–20
UMTS	144–2000	40–100	60	20–40	15–65	4	4	3–20
HSxPA	14 Mbps	50–100	60	10–50	10–80	4	5	3–20
LTE	10–300 Mbps	40–100	65	10–30	10–40	7	7	3–20
Wi-Fi abg	8–54 Mbps	40–100	60	130–200	30–70	3	1	3–20
Wi-Fi n	72–450 Mbps	30–100	65	100–140	20–60	3	1	3–20
Wi-Fi ac	433–1300 Mbps	50–100	70	90–100	10–40	5	2	3–20
WiMAX	70 Mbps	40–100	60	60–100	10–70	7	5	3–20

We mainly focus in this work on comparing new utility-based combinations with the best MADM ones in the network selection context, without differentiating between service classes. Both utility functions and MADM methods must normalize the data gathered during the discovery phase, to compute them and score the alternatives. Figure 2 shows the general steps of the two groups of methods.

We compare two utility functions with the best MADM methods in the network selection context using different normalizations. The Eqs. 1 and 2 describe these two functions as well as their aggregation methods:

1. The first utility function (uF1) uses Eq. 1:

$$uF1(x)_i = N(x) \quad \text{For benefit criteria.}$$
$$= 1 - N(x) \quad \text{For cost criteria.} \tag{1}$$

2. The second utility function (uF2) uses Eq. 2:

$$uF2(x)_i = log(N(x)) \quad \text{For benefit criteria.}$$
$$= 1 - log(N(x)) \quad \text{For cost criteria.} \tag{2}$$

Where $N(x)$ is the normalized value of attribute x, we used the sum aggregations to compute the final score for each alternative.

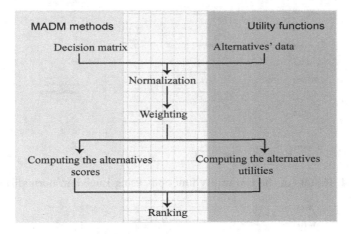

Fig. 2. Flowchart of the network selection process using different compared methods

4   Results and Discussion

We run the simulations as described in the previous section, and we recorded the decisions made by every combination of methods. We illustrate the results of the two best combinations of MADM methods: TOPSIS using FANP for weighting and GRA (with Sum normalization) using FAHP in Fig. 3. Figures 4 and 5 show the results of the two best combinations of utility functions, named uF1 and uF2, using the Euclidian and the Sum normalizations respectively. Figure 6 illustrates the total number of VHs and rank reversals occurred during the whole simulation using the different combinations.

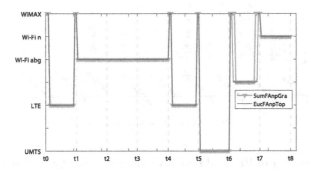

Fig. 3. Results of the best MADM combinations

The results in the illustrated figures show that seeing the delivered QoS (i.e. the selected wireless networks ensure a good connectivity), the results of uF2 in Figs. 4 and 5 are better than those of MADM methods in Fig. 3, in DZ4, while in DZ3 the function performs worse than MADM methods. Although the

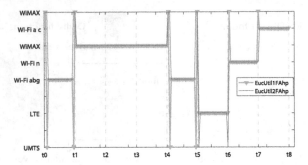

Fig. 4. Results of the two utility functions using Euclidian normalization

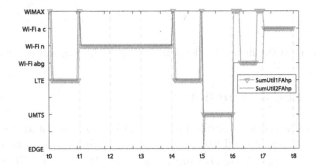

Fig. 5. Results of the two utility functions using Sum normalization

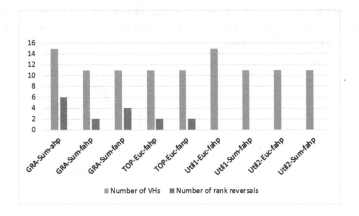

Fig. 6. Total number of VHs and rank reversals performed by the best combinations

total number of VHs is the same, the decisions of uF2 are steadier in DZ4 with one VH, compared with uF1 and MADM methods with 3 VHs. The opposite happens in DZ3. In the other DZs, the performance of uF2 and MADM methods are the same. We notice that uF1 using the Sum normalization is better than when using the Euclidian one, seeing the number of VHs.

FAHP is the best weighting method for utility function, they perform better when using it. Moreover, utility functions perform no rank reversals, which is a desired criterion. Even though, the selection strategy must be further improved to reduce the VH number and ensure a better QoS.

5 Conclusion

The network selection is an important issue in the next generation networking. In fact, mobile devices must, in real time, determine the best available wireless network. Moreover, they must be able to transfer communications to the selected network, without impacting the QoS, which imposes an efficient and fast enough decision strategy. In this paper, we propose to compare combinations of two utility functions with the best MADM ones, in the network selection in wireless multi-access environments. The results show that the utility-based combinations make more efficient decisions, leading to a steadier connection in some defined situations, while MADM combinations still give convincing results and maintain the sessions as well. We must adjust the weights to avoid the unnecessary VHs caused by imprecisions in weighting, add more constraints during the discovery and negotiation steps, and try more combinations, to have more optimal VH decision strategy.

References

1. Tuysuz, M.F., Trestian, R.: Energy-efficient vertical handover parameters, classification and solutions over wireless heterogeneous networks: a comprehensive survey. Wirel. Pers. Commun. **97**, 1155–1184 (2017)
2. Fernandes, S., Karmouch, A.: Vertical mobility management architectures in wireless networks: a comprehensive survey and future directions. IEEE Commun. Surv. Tutor. **14**(1), 45–63 (2012)
3. Gupta, V.: IEEE 802.21 Media Independent Handover. IEEE P802.21 Tutorial (2008). http://www.ieee802.org/21/Tutorials/802%2021-IEEE-Tutorial.ppt. Accessed Sept 2018
4. Ferretti, S., Ghini, V., Panzieri, F.: A survey on handover management in mobility architectures. Comput. Netw. **94**, 390–413 (2016)
5. Johal, L., Singh, A.: An overview of vertical handover process and techniques. Indian J. Sci. Technol. **9**, 14 (2016)
6. Kassar, M., Kervella, B., Pujolle, G.: An overview of vertical handover decision stratgies in heterogeneous wireless networks. Comput. Commun. **31**, 2607–2620 (2008)
7. Bhute, H., Karde, P., Thakare, V.M.: A vertical handover decision approaches in next generation wireless networks: a survey. Int. J. Mob. Netw. Commun. Telematics **4**, 33–43 (2014)
8. Obayiuwana, E., Falowo, O.E.: Network selection in heterogeneous wireless networks using multi-criteria decision-making algorithms: a review. Wirel. Netw. **23**, 2617–2649 (2016)
9. Mansouri, M., Leghris, C.: The use of MADM methods in the vertical handover decision making context. In: International Conference on Wireless Networks and Mobile Communications (WINCOM 2017), pp. 1–6 (2017)

10. Nguyen-Vuong, Q., Ghamri-Doudane, Y., Agoulmine, N.: On utility models for access network selection in wireless heterogeneous networks. In: NOMS 2008-2008 IEEE Network Operations and Management Symposium, pp. 144–151, April 2008
11. Lai, Y., Chait, K.K., Chen, Y.: A utility-based intelligent network selection for 3G and WLAN heterogeneous networks. In: IET International Conference on Wireless Communications and Applications (ICWCA 2012), pp. 1–6, October 2012
12. Wang, L., Kuo, G.G.S.: Mathematical modeling for network selection in heterogeneous wireless networks - a tutorial. IEEE Commun. Surv. Tutor. **15**(1), 271–292 (2013)
13. Drissi, M., Oumsis, M., Aboutajdine, D.: A context-aware access network selection based on utility-function for handover in WLAN-LTE environment. In: El-Azouzi, R., Menasché, D.S., Sabir, E., Pellegrini, F.D., Benjillali, M. (eds.) Advances in Ubiquitous Networking 2. LNEE, vol. 397, pp. 57–66. Springer, Singapore (2017). https://doi.org/10.1007/978-981-10-1627-1_5
14. Yu, H.W., Zhang, B.: A hybrid MADM algorithm based on attribute weight and utility value for heterogeneous network selection. J. Netw. Syst. Manag. **27**(3), 756–783 (2019)
15. Ahuja, K., Singh, B., Khanna, R.: Network selection in wireless heterogeneous environment by CPF hybrid algorithm. Wirel. Pers. Commun. **98**(3), 2733–2751 (2018)

A Robust Blind 3-D Mesh Watermarking Technique Based on SCS Quantization and Mesh Saliency for Copyright Protection

Mohamed Hamidi[1]([✉]), Aladine Chetouani[2], Mohamed El Haziti[1],
Mohammed El Hassouni[1,3], and Hocine Cherifi[4]

[1] LRIT - CNRST URAC29, Rabat IT Center, Faculty of Sciences,
Mohammed V University in Rabat, Rabat, Morocco
hamidi.medinfo@gmail.com, elhazitim@gmail.com,
mohamed.elhassouni@gmail.com
[2] PRISME Laboratory, University of Orleans, Orléans, France
aladine.chetouani@univ-orleans.fr
[3] LRIT - CNRST URAC29, Rabat IT Center, FLSH,
Mohammed V University in Rabat, Rabat, Morocco
[4] Le2i, UMR 6306 CNRS, University of Burgundy, Dijon, France
hocine.cherifi@u-bourgogne.fr

Abstract. Due to the recent demand of 3-D meshes in a wide range
of applications such as video games, medical imaging, film special effect
making, computer-aided design (CAD), among others, the necessity of
implementing 3-D mesh watermarking schemes aiming to protect copyright has increased in the last decade. Nowadays, the majority of robust
3-D watermarking approaches have mainly focused on the robustness
against attacks while the imperceptibility of these techniques is still a
serious challenge. In this context, a blind robust 3-D mesh watermarking
method based on mesh saliency and scalar Costa scheme (SCS) for Copyright protection is proposed. The watermark is embedded by quantifying
the vertex norms of the 3-D mesh by SCS scheme using the vertex normal
norms as synchronizing primitives. The choice of these vertices is based
on 3-D mesh saliency to achieve watermark robustness while ensuring
high imperceptibility. The experimental results show that in comparison with the alternative methods, the proposed work can achieve a high
imperceptibility performance while ensuring a good robustness against
several common attacks including similarity transformations, noise addition, quantization, smoothing, elements reordering, etc.

Keywords: 3-D mesh watermarking · Scalar Costa scheme (scs) ·
Mesh saliency · Copyright protection

1 Introduction

Nowadays, the transfer of multimedia contents such as image, audio, video and
3-D model has been increased considerably due to the increase in network band-

ⓒ Springer Nature Switzerland AG 2019
E. Renault et al. (Eds.): MSPN 2019, LNCS 11557, pp. 211–228, 2019.
https://doi.org/10.1007/978-3-030-22885-9_19

width and the rapid development of digital services. These contents can be copied or modified easily. Therefore, the necessity to protect their copyright becomes crucially important. Digital watermarking has been found as an efficient solution to overcome this problem. Its underlying concept is to embed an auxiliary information named watermark into multimedia content to protect its ownership. It is worth noticing that only 3-D meshes are considered in the proposed work. 3-D meshes have been widely used in several applications including medical images, computer aided design (CAD), video games, virtual reality, film special effect making, etc. A 3-D mesh is defined as a collection of polygonal facets that aim to give an approximation of a real 3-D object. It contains three primitives: vertices, edges and facets. A mesh can be also described by two kinds of information: geometry information that represents the positions of vertices and connectivity information which describes the adjacency relations between the different components.

Three major requirements must be satisfied in each watermarking system: imperceptibility, capacity and robustness. Imperceptibility represents the similarity between the original 3-D mesh and the watermarked one while the capacity refers to the maximum amount of information that can be embedded in the 3-D mesh. Robustness means the ability of extracting the watermark bits even if the stego model has incurred manipulations named attacks. These attacks can be divided into two main groups. Connectivity attacks, that include subdivision, cropping, remeshing, and simplification. Geometric attacks including local deformation operations, similarity transformations as well as signal processing operations. The applications of 3-D mesh watermarking include authentication, indexation, content enhancement, copyright protection, etc.

It is worth mentioning that compared to the maturity of image, audio and video watermarking methods [1], there are only few 3-D mesh watermarking techniques that have been proposed [2]. This is mainly due to the challenges in three dimensional geometry related to its irregular and complex topology as well as the gravity of attacks that 3-D meshes can be exposed to [3]. Moreover, in contrast with 2-D image, there is no obvious robust intrinsic ordering for 3-D mesh elements, which make the use of spectral analysis watermarking of 2-D images impossible.

The majority of 3-D watermarking methods have mainly focused on the robustness against attacks while few ones based on saliency have been proposed [4]. Nakazawa et al. [5] presented a 3-D watermarking method based on visual saliency. First, the perceptually conspicuous regions have been identified using the mesh saliency of Lee et al. [6]. Next, the norm of each vertex is calculated and its histogram is constructed. Finally, the watermark is embedded in each bin by normalizing the associated vertex norms. In [7], Zhan et al. proposed a blind 3-D mesh watermarking method based on curvature. The authors calculated the root mean square curvature for all vertices and the watermark is embedded by modulating the mean of the root mean square curvature fluctuation of vertices. Rolland-Neviere et al. [8] proposed a 3-D mesh watermarking method where the watermark embedding is formulated as a quadratic programming problem. In

[9], Jeongho Son et al. proposed a 3-D watermarking technique that aims to preserve the appearance of the 3-D watermarked model. The authors used the distribution of the vertex norm histogram as a watermarking primitive which has been already introduced by Cho et al. [10]. The latter embeds the watermark by modifying the mean or variance of the vertex norms histogram.

In this paper, a 3-D robust and blind watermarking method based on mesh saliency and scalar Costa scheme (SCS) quantization is proposed. The watermark is embedded in the 3-D mesh by quantizing its vertices norms according to the mesh saliency. The vertex normal norms are sorted in the descending order and chosen as synchronizing primitives. This order is found to be robust to geometric attacks and element reordering. Taking the full advantages of mesh saliency as well as SCS scheme, the proposed method can ensure both high robustness to common attacks and good imperceptibility. The rest of this paper is organized as follows. Section 2 presents the 3-D mesh saliency. Section 3 gives a description of the proposed method composed by embedding and extraction. The experimental setup, evaluation metrics and experimental results are discussed in Sect. 4. Finally, Sect. 5 concludes the paper.

2   3-D Mesh Saliency

Nowadays, saliency detection becomes an interdisciplinary scientific study of computer science and human perception. It allows to detect perceptually important points or regions of a 3-D mesh automatically [11]. Mesh saliency can be defined as a measure that captures the importance of a point or local region of a 3-D mesh in a similar way to human visual perception. This technique generally merges perceptual criteria inspired by human visual system (HVS) with mathematical measures based on geometry. The visual attention of Human is usually directed to the salient shape of the 3-D model. The evaluation of mesh saliency used in the proposed scheme is Lee et al. [6]. Lee's method evaluates the saliency of each vertex using the difference in mean curvature of the 3-D mesh surfaces from those at other vertices in the neighborhood. The first step is computing surface curvatures. The computation of the curvature at each vertex v is performed using Taubin's method [12]. Let $Curv(v)$ the mean curvature of a mesh at a vertex v. The Gaussian-weighted average of the mean curvature can be expressed as follows:

$$G(Curv(v), \sigma) = \frac{\sum_{x \in N(v, 2\sigma)} Curv(x) exp(\frac{-\|x-v\|^2}{2\sigma^2})}{\sum_{x \in N(v, 2\sigma)} exp(\frac{-\|x-v\|^2}{2\sigma^2})} \tag{1}$$

where x is a mesh point and $N(v, \sigma)$ denotes the neighborhood for a vertex v which represents a set of points within an Euclidean distance σ calculated as:

$$N(v, \sigma) = \{x| \parallel x - v \parallel < \sigma\} \tag{2}$$

The saliency $S(v)$ of a vertex v is calculated as the absolute difference between the Gaussian-weighted averages computed at fine and coarse scale.

$$S(v) = |G(Curv(v), \sigma) - G(Curv(v), 2\sigma)| \tag{3}$$

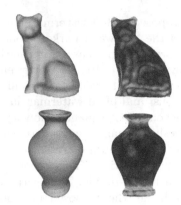

Fig. 1. 3-D meshes and their corresponding mesh saliency using Lee's method [6]: (left) Original 3-D meshes, (right) 3-D mesh saliency.

Figure 1 reported an example of mesh saliency of Cat and Vase object using Lee's method [6].

3   Proposed Scheme

The majority of 3-D robust watermarking approaches have focused on the resistance to attacks. Only few methods have investigated the visual impact caused by the watermark embedding. In this context, a robust and blind 3-D mesh watermarking method based on mesh saliency and SCS quantization for Copyright protection is proposed. In this work, the watermark is embedded by quantifying the salient vertex norms of the 3-D object using mesh saliency proposed by Lee et al. [6] and SCS quantization. Lee's method is used to obtain candidate vertices in order to ensure high imperceptibility and to improve the robustness performance. The choice of these points is motivated by the fact that these primitives are relatively stable even after that 3-D meshes suffered from different attacks such as additive noise, similarity transformations, quantization, smoothing, etc. Figure 4 illustrates the Lee's [6] mesh saliency of Bimba model after applying different attacks. The flowcharts of embedding and extraction processes are given in Figs. 2 and 3 respectively.

3.1   Watermark Embedding

In order to ensure both robustness and imperceptibility, the proposed method exploits the full advantages of the mesh saliency and SCS quantification. The watermarking bits are embedded by quantizying the vertex norms of the 3-D model using mesh saliency. The SCS quantization is used since it is blind and provides a good tradeoff between robustness and capacity [13]. First, the mesh saliency is computed based on a threshold fixed automatically to define the salient points. In fact, for each object, the 70% maximum values of saliency vector

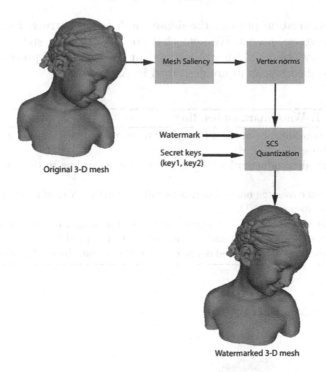

Fig. 2. The proposed embedding scheme.

represent the salient points while the other points are considered non-salient. Second, the norms of salient points are calculated according to this threshold. The watermark bits are embedded by quantifying the vertex norms of salient points using Lee's mesh saliency [6]. Next, the quantization step Q_S is fixed to N_{av}/λ, where N_{av} is the average of the verices normal norms while λ is a parameter which adjusts the tradeoff between robustness and imperceptibility. This parameter is tuned experimentally and chosen in such a way that ensures both good robustness and high imperceptibility. The quantization of the salient vertex norms (NV) is carried out using the 2-symbol scalar Costa scheme (SCS) [13] where a random code is established for each vertex norm using Eq. 4.

$$\beta_{x_i, t_{x_i}} = \bigcup_{l=0}^{1} \left\{ u = zQ_S + l\frac{Q_S}{2} + t_{x_i} \right\} \tag{4}$$

where $z \in \mathbb{Z}^+$, $l \in \{0, 1\}$ represents the watermark bit, Q_S is the quantization step, t_{x_i} is an additive pseudo-random dither signal generated using a secret key (key1). Next, we look for the nearest codeword $\beta_{NV_i}^J$ to NV_{i^J} in the codebook that implies the correct watermark bit. The quantized value $NV_i'^J$ is calculated according to (5). The perfect security is achieved when $\gamma = 0.5$ as explained in details in [14].

$$NV_i'^J = \left\| NV_i^J \right\| + \gamma(\beta_{NV_i^J} - \left\| NV_i^J \right\|) \tag{5}$$

After the quantization process, the dense mesh is reconstructed starting from the modified vertex norms. We note that the quantization step is used as an extra secret key (key2) which will be used in the extraction process. For more details, the embedding steps are described in Algorithm 1.

Algorithm 1. Watermark embedding

1- Compute the saliency of the 3-D original mesh using Lee's method [6] and extract salient vertices.
2- Sort in the descending order the salient vertices according to their normal norms.

3- Calculate the average normal norms of salient vertices N_{Av} of normals and set the quantization step as N_{av}/λ.
4- Calculate the norms of the salient vertices and quantize them using 2-symbol scalar Costa quantization scheme (4) according to the predefined order.
5- Reconstruct the watermarked dense mesh starting from the modified vertex norms.

3.2 Watermark Extraction

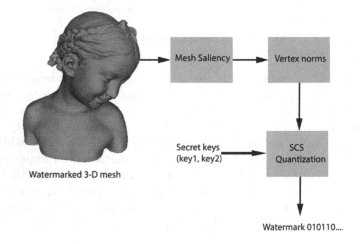

Fig. 3. The proposed extracting scheme.

The exaction process is blind since we doesn't need the original mesh. Only the secret keys (key1 and key2) are needed. Firstly, mesh saliency of the 3-D watermarked mesh is calculated in order to extract salient vertices according to the same threshold used in the embedding process. This parameter is chosen automatically since it represents the 70% maximum values of the mesh saliency. Secondly, the norms of salient vertices are calculated. Afterwards, we reestablish the vertex order (the norms of vertices normals sorted in the descending order).

Next, we recalculate the quantization step and reconstruct the codebook. Finally, we search the nearest codeword to the vertex norm in the reconstructed codebook with the aim of finding the watermark bits. For more details, the extraction steps are described in Algorithm 2.

Algorithm 2. Watermark extracting

1- Calculate the saliency of 3-D watermarked mesh.
2- Extract salient vertices and calculate their corresponding norms.
3- Reestablish the vertices order according to the normal norms of salient vertices.
4- Recalculate the quantization step and reconstruct the codebook.
5- Extract the watermark bits by looking for the nearest codeword to the vertex norms.

---

4 Experimental Results

4.1 Experimental Setup

Several experiments were carried out to assess the performance of the proposed watermarking method on 3-D meshes with different shape complexities: Flower (2523 vertices, 4895 faces), Vase (2527 vertices, 5004 faces), Cup (9076 vertices, 18152 faces), Ant (7654 vertices, 15304 faces), Bimba (8857 vertices, 17710 faces) and cat (3534 vertices, 6975 faces). Figure 5(a), (c), (e), (g) shows the above mentioned objects. We note that for comparison purpose the imperceptibility and robustness have been evaluated using the 3-D meshes: Bunny (34835 vertices, 69666 faces), Horse (112642 vertices, 225280 faces) and Venus (100759 vertices, 201514 faces). The quantification step is chosen in such a way that ensures the best imperceptibility-robustness tradeoff. This parameter has been tuned experimentally and we kept $Q_S = 0.08$.

4.2 Evaluation Metrics

Several experiments were conducted to assess the performance of the proposed method in terms of imperceptibility and robustness. The distortion introduced by the watermark embedding is evaluated objectively and visually using the maximum root mean square error (MRMS), hausdorff distance (HD) and mesh structural distortion measure (MSDM) respectively. The robustness of the proposed scheme is evaluated using the normalized correlation ($Corr$).

Imperceptibility

In order to evaluate the imperceptibility of the proposed method several metrics have been used to measure the amount of distortion introduced by the embedding process. This distortion can be measured geometrically or perceptually. The maximum root mean square error (MRMS) proposed in [15] is used to calculate the objective distortion between the original meshes and the watermarked ones.

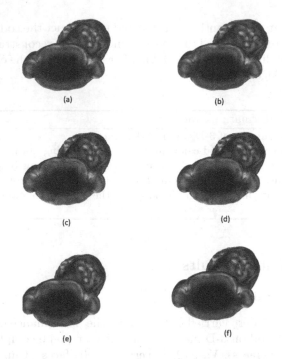

Fig. 4. Mesh saliency of Bimba before and after attacks: (a) before attack, (b) additive noise 0.3%, (c) Similarity transformation 1, (d) Simplification ratio, (e) Quantization 9 bits, (f) Smoothing $\lambda = 0.1$ (30 iterations).

The MRMS which refers to the maximum between the two root mean square error (RMS) distances calculated by:

$$d_{MRMS} = max(d_{RMS}(M, Mw), d_{RMS}(Mw, M)) \tag{6}$$

$$d_{RMS}(M, Mw) = \sqrt{\frac{1}{|M|} \int \int_{p \in M} d(p, Mw)^2 dM} \tag{7}$$

where p is a point on surface M, $|M|$ represents the area of M, and $d(p, Mw)$ is the point-to-surface distance between p and Mw. It is worth noticing that surface-to-surface distance, as the MRMS metric, does not represent the visual distance between the two meshes [16]. So, another perceptual metric is needed to measure the distortion caused by the watermark insertion.

The mesh structural distortion measure (MSDM) metric is chosen to measure the visual degradation of the watermarked meshes [16]. The MSDM value is equal 0 when the original and watermarked 3-D objects are identical. Otherwise, the MSDM value is equal to 1 when the objects are visually very different. The global MSDM distance between the original mesh M and watermarked mesh Mw having n vertices respectively is defined by:

$$d_{MSDM}(M, M_w) = \left(\frac{1}{n}\sum_{i=1}^{n} d_{LMSDM}(a_i, b_i)^3\right)^{\frac{1}{3}} \in [0,1) \tag{8}$$

d_{LMSDM} is the local MSDM distance between two mesh local windows a and b (in mesh M and Mw respectively) which is defined by :

$$d_{LMSDM}(a, b) = (0.4 \times Curv(a, b)^3 + 0.4 \times Cont(a, b)^3 + 0.2 \times Surf(a, b)^3)^{\frac{1}{3}} \tag{9}$$

$Curv$, $Cont$ and $Surf$ refers to curvature, contrast and structure comparison functions respectively.

Table 1. Watermark imperceptibility measured in terms of MRMS, HD and MSDM.

Model	MRMS (10^{-3})	HD (10^{-3})	MSDM
Flower	0.60	4.13	0.21
Vase	0.38	3.14	0.41
Cup	0.96	2.98	0.42
Ant	0.71	4.33	0.57
Cat	0.67	1.2	0.18
Bimba	0.37	1.62	0.11

Robustness

The robustness is measured using the normalized correlation ($Corr$) between the inserted watermark and the extracted one as given by the following equation:

$$Corr = \frac{\sum_{i=1}^{m}(w_i' - \overline{w}^*)(w_i - \overline{w})}{\sqrt{\sum_{i=1}^{m}(w_i' - \overline{w}^*)^2 . \sum_{i=1}^{m}(w_i - \overline{w})^2}} \tag{10}$$

where $i \in \{1, 2, \ldots, m\}$, m is the length of the watermark, $\overline{w}^*$ and $\overline{w}$ are the averages of the watermark bits respectively (Fig. 6).

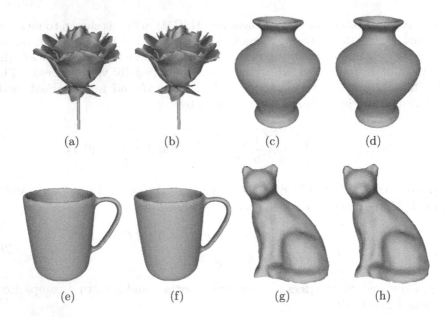

Fig. 5. (a) Flower, (b) Watermarked Flower, (c) Vase, (d) Watermarked Vase, (e) Cup, (f) Watermarked Cup, (g) Ant, (h) Watermarked Ant, (i) Cat, (j) Watermarked Cat.

Fig. 6. Saliency of 3-D meshes using Lee's method [6] (a) Flower, (b) Vase, (c) Cup, (d) Ant, (e) Cat, (f) Bunny.

4.3   Results and Discussion

Imperceptibility. Figure 5 illustrates the original and watermarked 3-D meshes. We can see that the distortion is very imperceptible. This is due to the saliency adjustment. In addition, according to Table 1, it can be observed that the proposed method can achieve high imperceptibility in terms of MRMS, HD and MSDM. We believe that this performance is obtained thanks to the exploitation of mesh saliency to avoid serious distortions. It can be also observed that the imperceptibility results in terms of MRMS, HD and MSDM are different from a mesh to another. This difference is mainly due to the curvature nature of each one of these 3-D meshes.

Table 2. Watermark imperceptibility without using saliency measured in terms of MRMS, HD and MSDM compared to the proposed method.

Model	MRMS (10^{-3})	HD (10^{-3})	MSDM
Flower	0.89/0.60	5.03/4.13	0.88/0.21
Vase	0.58/0.38	4.76/3.14	0.76/0.41
Cup	1.02/0.96	3.45/2.98	0.87/0.42
Ant	0.83/0.71	4.43/4.33	1.0/0.57
Cat	1.2/0.67	1.9/1.2	0.29/0.18
Bimba	0.76/0.37	2.98/1.62	1.66/0.11

To further evaluate the importance of using mesh saliency to improve the imperceptibility of the proposed method, we compare the obtained results with those obtained without using the saliency. Table 2 exhibits the imperceptibility performance in terms of MRMS, HD and MSDM without using the mesh saliency compared to the proposed method based on mesh saliency. According to Table 2, it can be seen that the proposed method gives good results which illustrates the imperceptibility improvement achieved using the saliency aspect in the watermark embedding.

Robustness. To evaluate the robustness of the proposed scheme, 3-D meshes have been undergone several attacks. For this purpose, a benchmarking system has been used [17]. The robustness of our scheme is tested under several attacks including noise addition, smoothing, quantization, cropping, subdivision and similarity transformations (translation, rotation and uniform scaling). Figure 7 shows the model Bimba after several attacks. To evaluate the robustness to noise addition attack, binary random noise was added to each vertex of 3-D models with four different noise amplitudes: 0.05%, 0.10%, 0.30% and 0.50%. According to Table 3, it can be seen that the proposed method is robust against noise addition four all the 3-D models.

For evaluating the resistance of the proposed scheme to smoothing attack, the 3-D models have undergone Laplacian smoothing proposed in [18] using 5, 10, 30 and 50 iterations while keeping the deformation factor $\lambda = 0.10$. Table 4 shows that our method is able to withstand smoothing operation. The robustness of the proposed scheme is evaluated against elements reordoring attack called also file attack. According to Table 5 the proposed scheme can resist to element reordoring. Quantization is also applied to the 3-D models to evaluate the robustness against this attack using 7, 8, 9, 10 and 11 bits. It can be concluded from Table 6 that our method shows good robustness against quantization regardless of the used 3-D mesh. The robustness of the proposed method is evaluated against similarity transformation in which 3-D models have undergone a random rotation, a random uniform scaling and a random translation. Table 7 sketches the obtained results in terms of correlation. It can be observed that our method can achieve high robustness against these attacks. Finally, the proposed scheme is

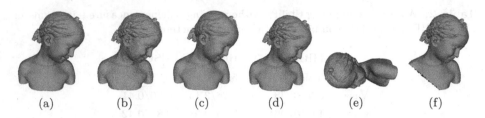

(a)   (b)   (c)   (d)   (e)   (f)

Fig. 7. Original Bimba and seven attacks versions: (a) Original Bimba, (b) noise addition 0.50%, (c) Smoothing $\lambda = 0.1$ with 5 iterations, (d) quantization 9 bits, (e) Similarity transformation, (f) Cropping ratio 10.0.

Table 3. Watermark robustness against additive noise measured in terms of correlation.

Noise intensity	Flower	Vase	Cup	Ant	Cat	Bimba
0.05%	0.97	1.0	0.97	0.98	0.98	1.0
0.10%	0.95	0.92	0.92	0.96	0.93	0.92
0.30%	0.89	0.87	0.83	0.86	0.89	0.90
0.50%	0.83	0.72	0.74	0.76	0.74	0.79

Table 4. Watermark robustness against Laplacian smoothing ($\lambda = 0.1$) measured in terms of correlation.

Number of iterations	Flower	Vase	Cup	Ant	Cat	Bimba
5	1.0	0.99	1.0	0.99	1.0	1.0
10	0.99	0.98	0.99	0.97	0.95	0.99
30	0.97	0.96	0.92	0.94	0.95	0.94
50	0.88	0.87	0.89	0.85	0.90	0.90

tested against subdivision attack including three schemes (loop, midpoint and sqrt3). The obtained results in Table 8 in terms of correlation exhibit the high robustness against subdivision. Cropping is considered to be one of the most damaging attack since it deletes a region from the 3-D mesh and thus the useful information will be lost. It can be observed from Table 9 that the proposed method is not enough robust to cropping attacks. In fact, if the deleted surface contains salient points, the extraction process will fail. In the future work, we will search a solution to the issue related to the robustness weakness against this attack.

Table 5. Watermark robustness against elements reordering measured in terms of correlation.

Elements reordering	Flower	Vase	Cup	Ant	Cat	Bimba
Element reordering 1	0.99	1.0	0.99	1.0	1.0	0.99
Element reordering 2	0.96	0.98	1.0	0.97	1.0	0.97
Element reordering 3	1.0	0.99	0.986	0.99	0.98	0.96

Table 6. Watermark robustness against quantization measured in terms of correlation.

Quantization	Flower	Vase	Cup	Ant	Cat	Bimba
11-bits	1.0	1.0	1.0	1.0	1.0	1.0
10-bits	1.0	0.99	0.99	0.99	0.98	1.0
9-bits	0.99	0.98	0.97	0.97	0.98	0.99
8-bits	0.93	0.90	0.91	0.92	0.93	0.98
7-bits	0.80	0.79	0.80	0.77	0.78	0.86

Table 7. Watermark robustness against similarity transformations measured in terms of correlation.

Similarity transformations	Flower	Vase	Cup	Ant	Cat	Bimba
Similarity transformation 1	0.99	0.92	1.0	0.94	1.0	0.98
Similarity transformation 2	0.94	0.95	1.0	0.97	1.0	0.99
Similarity transformation 3	0.97	0.98	0.99	1.0	0.98	0.94

Table 8. Watermark robustness against similarity transformations measured in terms of correlation.

Subdivision	Flower	Vase	Cup	Ant	Cat	Bimba
Loop iter 1	1.0	0.98	1.0	0.96	0.96	0.98
Midpoint iter 1	0.94	0.88	0.84	0.92	0.93	0.95
Sqrt3 iter 1	0.99	0.97	0.94	1.0	0.98	0.94

Table 9. Watermark robustness against cropping measured in terms of correlation.

Cropping	Flower	Vase	Cup	Ant	Cat	Bimba
10	0.53	0.57	0.65	0.63	0.59	0.52
30	0.46	0.34	0.39	0.46	0.34	0.27
50	0.28	0.12	0.19	0.24	0.22	0.21

Table 10. Imperceptibility comparison with Cho's [10], Rolland-Neviere's [8] and Son's [9] schemes measured in terms of MRMS and MSDM for Horse model.

Method	MRMS (10^{-3})	MSDM
[10]	3.17	0.3197
[8]	1.48	0.2992
[9]	2.90	0.3197
Our method	0.51	0.2683

Table 11. Robustness comparison with Cho's [10] and [7] schemes against additive noise in terms of correlation for Bunny and Venus models.

Model	Amplitude	[10]	[7]	Our method
Bunny	0.1%	0.72	1.0	1.0
	0.3%	0.72	0.91	0.94
	0.5%	0.66	0.80	0.86
Venus	0.1%	0.94	0.95	1.0
	0.3%	0.87	0.95	0.99
	0.5%	0.27	0.79	0.83

Table 12. Robustness comparison with Cho's [10] and [7] schemes against smoothing in terms of correlation for Bunny and Venus models.

Model	Number of iterations	[10]	[7]	Our method
Bunny	10	0.84	0.92	0.96
	30	0.60	0.85	0.92
	50	0.36	0.44	0.62
Venus	10	0.94	0.95	0.99
	30	0.63	0.93	0.97
	50	0.45	0.78	0.81

4.4   Comparison with Alternative Methods

To further evaluate the performance of the proposed scheme in terms of imperceptibility and robustness we compare it with Cho's [10,19], Zhan's et al. [7], Rolland-Neviere et al. [8] and Son's et al. [9] schemes. We note that for comparison purpose, we have tested the robustness of our method using the 3-D models Bunny, horse and Venus.

Table 13. Robustness comparison with Cho's [10] and [7] schemes against quantization in terms of correlation for Bunny and Venus models.

Model	Intensity	[10]	[7]	Our method
Bunny	9	0.73	1.0	1.0
	8	0.58	0.91	0.95
	7	0.17	0.58	0.65
Venus	9	0.87	1.0	1.0
	8	0.48	0.83	0.93
	7	0.07	0.73	0.83

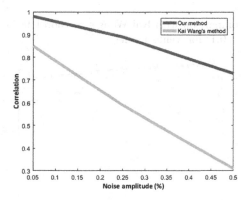

Fig. 8. Robustness comparison with Kai Wang's method [19] in terms of correlation against noise addition for Venus model.

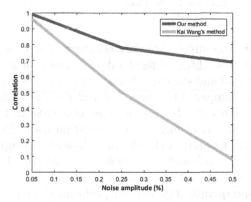

Fig. 9. Robustness comparison with Kai Wang's method [19] in terms of correlation against noise addition for Horse model.

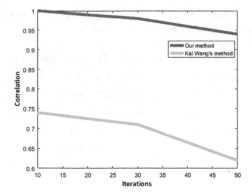

Fig. 10. Robustness comparison with Kai Wang's method [19] in terms of correlation against smoothing ($\lambda = 0.1$) for Venus model.

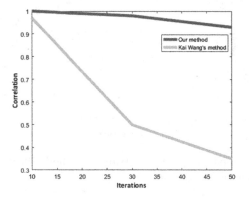

Fig. 11. Robustness comparison with Kai Wang's method [19] in terms of correlation against smoothing ($\lambda = 0.1$) for Horse model.

Table 10 exhibits the imperceptibility comparison with schemes in terms of MRMS and MSDM. The obtained results demonstrate the high imperceptibility of the proposed method and show its superiority to the alternative methods. The proposed method is compared to Cho's [10] and Zhan's [7] methods in terms of imperceptibility in terms of MRMS as well as robustness in terms of correlation against noise addition, smoothing and quantization using Bunny and Venus 3-D meshes. Tables 11, 12 and 13 sketch the robustness comparison in terms of correlation between our method and schemes [7] and [10]. It can be concluded from Tables 11, 12 and 13 that the proposed method is quite robust to additive noise, smoothing and quantization and outperforms the alternative methods. In addition, according to Figs. 8, 9, 10 and 11, it can be seen that the proposed method shows relatively high robustness to Kai Wang's method [19] in terms of correlation for noise addition and smoothing.

5   Conclusion

In this work, a blind and robust 3-D mesh watermarking method based on mesh saliency and SCS quantization for Copyright protection is proposed. The proposed method ensures both high robustness and imperceptibility by taking the full advantages of SCS quantization and mesh saliency. The robustness requirement is achieved by quantizing the vertex norms using SCS while the imperceptibility requirement is ensured by adjusting the watermark embedding according to the mesh saliency. The obtained results demonstrate that the proposed scheme yields a good tradeoff between the imperceptibility and robustness requirements. Moreover, experimental results show that in comparison with alternative techniques, the proposed method is able to withstand the majority of common attacks including smoothing, noise addition, quantization, similarity transformations, element reordering, subdivision, etc. Our future work will be focused on investigating the robustness weakness to cropping attack.

References

1. Hamidi, M., El Haziti, M., Cherifi, H., El Hassouni, M.: Hybrid blind robust image watermarking technique based on DFT-DCT and Arnold transform. Multimedia Tools Appl. **77**(20), 27181–27214 (2018)
2. Hamidi, M., El Haziti, M., Cherifi, H., Aboutajdine, D.: A robust blind 3-D mesh watermarking based on wavelet transform for copyright protection. In: 2017 International Conference on Advanced Technologies for Signal and Image Processing (ATSIP), pp. 1–6. IEEE (2017)
3. Wang, K., Lavoué, G., Denis, F., Baskurt, A.: Three-dimensional meshes watermarking: review and attack-centric investigation. In: Furon, T., Cayre, F., Doërr, G., Bas, P. (eds.) IH 2007. LNCS, vol. 4567, pp. 50–64. Springer, Heidelberg (2007). https://doi.org/10.1007/978-3-540-77370-2_4
4. Hamidi, M., Chetouani, A., El Haziti, M., El Hassouni, M., Cherifi, H.: Blind robust 3D mesh watermarking based on mesh saliency and wavelet transform for copyright protection. Information **10**(2), 67 (2019)
5. Nakazawa, S., Kasahara, S., Takahashi, S.: A visually enhanced approach to watermarking 3D models. In: 2010 Sixth International Conference on Intelligent Information Hiding and Multimedia Signal Processing (IIH-MSP), pp. 110–113. IEEE (2010)
6. Lee, C.H., Varshney, A., Jacobs, D.W.: Mesh saliency. In: ACM Transactions on Graphics (TOG), vol. 24, no. 3, pp. 659–666. ACM (2005)
7. Zhan, Y., Li, Y., Wang, X., Qian, Y.: A blind watermarking algorithm for 3D mesh models based on vertex curvature. J. Zhejiang Univ. Sci. C **15**(5), 351–362 (2014)
8. Rolland-Neviere, X., Doërr, G., Alliez, P.: Triangle surface mesh watermarking based on a constrained optimization framework. IEEE Trans. Inf. Forensics Secur. **9**(9), 1491–1501 (2014)
9. Son, J., Kim, D., Choi, H.-Y., Jang, H.-U., Choi, S.: Perceptual 3D watermarking using mesh saliency. In: Kim, K., Joukov, N. (eds.) ICISA 2017. LNEE, vol. 424, pp. 315–322. Springer, Singapore (2017). https://doi.org/10.1007/978-981-10-4154-9_37

10. Cho, J.-W., Prost, R., Jung, H.-Y.: An oblivious watermarking for 3-D polygonal meshes using distribution of vertex norms. IEEE Trans. Sig. Process. **55**(1), 142–155 (2007)

11. Song, R., Liu, Y., Martin, R.R., Rosin, P.L.: Mesh saliency via spectral processing. ACM Trans. Graph. (TOG) **33**(1), 6 (2014)

12. Taubin, G.: Estimating the tensor of curvature of a surface from a polyhedral approximation. In: ICCV, p. 902. IEEE (1995)

13. Eggers, J.J., Bauml, R., Tzschoppe, R., Girod, B.: Scalar costa scheme for information embedding. IEEE Trans. Sig. Process. **51**(4), 1003–1019 (2003)

14. Pérez-Freire, L., Comesaña, P., Pérez-González, F.: Information-theoretic analysis of security in side-informed data hiding. In: Barni, M., Herrera-Joancomartí, J., Katzenbeisser, S., Pérez-González, F. (eds.) IH 2005. LNCS, vol. 3727, pp. 131–145. Springer, Heidelberg (2005). https://doi.org/10.1007/11558859_11

15. Cignoni, P., Rocchini, C., Scopigno, R.: Metro: measuring error on simplified surfaces. In: Computer Graphics Forum, vol. 17, no. 2, pp. 167–174. Wiley Online Library (1998)

16. Lavoue, G., Gelasca, E.D., Dupont, F., Baskurt, A., Ebrahimi, T.: Perceptually driven 3D distance metrics with application to watermarking. In: SPIE Optics+ Photonics, p. 63120L. International Society for Optics and Photonics (2006)

17. Wang, K., Lavoue, G., Denis, F., Baskurt, A., He, X.: A benchmark for 3D mesh watermarking. In: Shape Modeling International Conference (SMI), pp. 231–235. IEEE (2010)

18. Taubin, G.: Geometric signal processing on polygonal meshes. In: Proceedings of the Eurographics State-of-the-art Reports, pp. 81–96 (2000)

19. Wang, K., Lavoué, G., Denis, F., Baskurt, A.: Hierarchical watermarking of semiregular meshes based on wavelet transform. IEEE Trans. Inf. Forensics Secur. **3**(4), 620–634 (2008)

A New Mechanism to Secure IPv6 Networks Using Symmetric Cryptography

Ali El Ksimi$^{(\boxtimes)}$ and Cherkaoui Leghirs

L@M, RTM Team, Faculty of Sciences and Technologies,
University Hassan 2 of Casablanca, Mohammedia, Morocco
ali.elksimi@yahoo.fr, cleghris@yahoo.fr

Abstract. Traditionally, configuring a network interface of a machine requires manual configuration and it's often a long and tedious job. With IPv6, this configuration is automated, introducing plug-and-play functionality to the network interface. Automatic configuration means that a machine gets all the information it needs to connect to an IPv6 LAN without any human intervention. The IPv6 address auto-configuration process includes creating a link-local address, verifying its uniqueness, and determining global unicast addresses. Checking the uniqueness of an IPv6 address is done by running an algorithm called DAD (Duplicate Address Detection) by the new node. This algorithm uses the multicast communications namely the messages neighbor solicitation and neighbor advertisement. However, this mechanism is not secure. In our paper, we propose a new algorithm to secure these multicast communications using symmetric cryptography. Our method shows its efficiency in terms of execution time and security level.

Keywords: IPv6 · DAD · Security · NS · NA · Multicast · Cryptography

1 Introduction

The network protocol mainly used today for Internet communications is the Internet Protocol (IP). The IPv4 protocol suffers from many weaknesses such as the insufficient address space nowadays. Indeed, the IPv4 addresses are 32 bits long, which represents about 4,3 milliards of possible IPv4 addresses. Following the explosion of network growth Internet and wastage of addresses due to the class structure, the number of IPv4 addresses has become insufficient. Another problem is the saturation of the routing tables in the main routers of the Internet. Although since 1993, many emergency measures have been taken, this only allows delaying its deadline. So, the Internet Engineering Task Force (IETF) launched work in 1994 to specify the Internet protocol that will replace IPv4, this protocol is IPv6 [1].

The Neighbor Discovery (NDP) [2] is the most important part in IPv6; it allows a node to integrate into the local network environment in which IPv6 packets are physically transmitted. Through to this protocol, it becomes possible to interact with the equipment connected to the same support (stations and routers). It is important to note that for a given node, the neighbors discovery does not consist in establishing an exhaustive list of the others connected to the link. Indeed, it is only to manage those

© Springer Nature Switzerland AG 2019
É. Renault et al. (Eds.): MSPN 2019, LNCS 11557, pp. 229–246, 2019.
https://doi.org/10.1007/978-3-030-22885-9_20

with whom it dialogues. This protocol performs the following functions: Address Resolution, Neighbour Unreachability Detection, Auto-configuration, and Redirect Indication. It uses five messages including Router Solicitation, Router Advertisement, Neighbor Solicitation, Neighbor Announcement and Indication redirection. The IPv6 StateLess Address AutoConfiguration (SLAAC) [3] of IPv6 is primarily based on the NDP process. This mechanism uses Duplicate address detection (DAD) [4] to verify the uniqueness of the addresses on the same link. However, it is vulnerable to attack and many solutions have been standardized to minimize this vulnerability such as SEcure Neighbour Discovery (SEND) [5], but, they are subject to certain limitations.

We base our study on SmObNet6 (Small Objects Network with IPv6) which is a generic term used to define network used to connect small communicating objects. The use of IPv6 protocol regarding communication, collecting and exchanging data between objects, represents a common point between these networks within the internet infrastructure. This paper treats the SLAAC phases and explains the problems associated with them. So, we propose a new algorithm based on symmetric encryption [6] in order to optimize secure IPv6 networks.

This paper is organized as follows: Sect. 2 presents a related work to our field when Sect. 3 describes some IPv6 functionalities, in particular, the DAD process. Section 4 shows the parameters and methodology following in this work and we present our algorithm in Sect. 4. Section 6 includes the algorithm implementation with evaluation, after we conclude this paper and addresses some prospects.

2   Related Work

Attacks on the IPv6 operations, especially on DAD process, become one of the interesting research fields. Several proposals have been made by researchers to address security issues in IPv6 DAD. Many authors have treated this problem.

In [7], the authors have proposed a scheme to secure IPv6 address which includes the modifications to the RFC 3972 standard by reducing the granularity factor of a sec from 16 to 8, and replacing RSA with ECC and ECSDSA, using SHA-256 [6] hash function. This method improves the address configuration performance, but it does not eliminate the address conflict.

In [8], the authors have presented a new algorithm for address generation. This mechanism has a minimal computation cost as compared to CGA. Nevertheless, this mechanism uses SHA-1 hash encryption which is vulnerable to collisions attacks.

In [9], the authors have utilized a novel approach for securing IPv6 link-local communication. They have used an alternative approach for the CGA and SEND protocols which still represent a limitation to the security level.

Another approach such as secure IPv6 address configuration protocol for vehicular networks [10] was proposed to ensure security in IPv6 without DAD process. However, this method is used only when the distance between a vehicle and its serving AP is one-hop.

In [11], the authors have proposed a new method to secure Neighbour Discovery Protocol in IPv6. This mechanism is based on SDN controller to verify the source of

NDP packets. However, this method is not efficient because it does not handle the detection of NDP attacks.

Another method was used in [12] to secure the DAD; it is called trust-ND. It is used to detect fake NA messages. However, the experiments show some limits of this method.

In [13], the authors have presented a technique for detecting neighbor solicitation spoofing and advertisement spoofing attacks in IPv6 NDP. However, this method can only detect NS spoofing, NA spoofing, and DoS attacks. The disadvantage of this method is that it does not detect other attacks like Duplicate Address Detection attacks.

In [14], the authors have proposed a new method to secure NDP attacks; this method is based on the digital signature. It detects the messages NS and NA spoofing and Dos attacks, router redirection and Duplicate Address Detection, but this mechanism is not complete.

In [15], the authors have presented a new method to secure IPv6-DAD process; however, this mechanism consumes a lot of execution time for generating NS and NA messages.

In [21], the authors have presented a novel approach to secure DAD process in IPv6 networks. They have used the SHA256 hash function to hide the target IPv6 address. The experimental results show a significant effect in term of Address Configuration Success Probability. However, this method consumes also a lot of execution time to generate NS and NA messages.

In this paper, we propose to study and evaluate the security in the NDP within the network based on IPv6 protocol. Indeed, we suggest a new method which could secure the attacks in the DAD process based on symmetric cryptography key. The results showed that DAD process could be optimized by introducing a new field which contains a random word decrypted with the secret key which is a part of the target address. Overall, this method showed a significant effect in terms of security and execution time.

3 The Autoconfiguration of IPv6 Addresses by the Random Method

The most common method is based on the modified IEEE identifier EUI-64, which itself is based on the IEEE 802 address, better known as the Media Access Control (MAC) address. The disadvantage of this method is that the IPv6 node will always have the same IID even if it changes its network prefix. As a result, it would be easy to identify the node in question despite its movements.

In our paper, we will use the random method to generate the IPv6 address.

The steps of the algorithm are as follows:

- When it starts, the IPv6 node randomly initiates a 64-bit variable named history value and backs it up;
- When the node needs an IID, first it generates an IID of type EUI-64 that it concatenates to the current value of history value;
- Then, it applies on the result the hash function MD5;

- The last 64 bits output are saved as new value for history value;
- It takes the first 64 bits out and sets the 7th bit of the first octet to 0;
- If this value corresponds to an IID value already used by the node or reserved, it starts the procedure again from its beginning; otherwise, it uses the calculated value as IID.

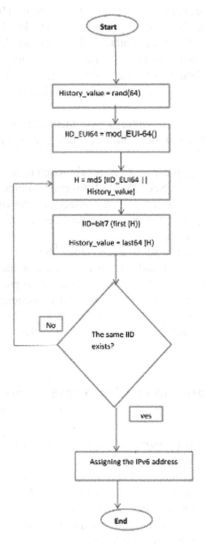

Fig. 1. The random method of IPv6 address generating

This method is summarized in Fig. 1, where rand (n) is a function randomly returning a value of n bits, mod_EUI-64 () is a function returning an IID of type EUI-64 modified, md5 (x) is a function applying the hash function MD5 to the value x, bit7

(x) is a function setting the 7th bit of x to 0, first64 (x) is a function returning the first 64 bits of the value x and last64 (x) is a function returning the last 64 bits of the x value.

4 Duplicate Address Detection

The Neighbor Discovery Protocol (NDP) mechanism provides IPv6 with some number of features essential for the proper IPv6 protocol functioning. The best known is the address resolution feature that matches what is ARP in IPv4. This protocol also offers other features. The one that will interest in our paper, Duplicate Address Detection (DAD), allows detect when two nodes want to use the same address and avoids the future collision by refusing the assignment of the address. This is equivalent to "gratuitous ARP" in IPv4. This feature is even more important, that in IPv6, new nodes can use the "stateless auto-configuration" and assign themselves an address (self-generated).

4.1 DAD Process

The Duplicate Address Detection mechanism applies to all type addresses unicast before they are assigned to network interfaces, regardless of whether they are manual, stateless or stateful. This feature can still be disabled by system administrators.

The Neighbor Discovery Protocol mechanism uses ICMPv6 type messages [2]. Under the DAD mechanism, we are only interested in two types of messages, the Neighbor Solicitation (NS) and the Neighbor Advertisement (NA). When resolving an address, the message Neighbor Solicitation is used to request the physical address of a node (e.g. MAC address) it wants to communicate by contacting it via IPv6 address. This message contains a target field that is populated with the node's IPv6 address that we want to contact. If this target exists, it responds with a message to the request sending node and contains, in one of its fields, an option with the physical address of this node regarding the network interface concerned. This association between the logical address and the physical address will then be kept in the neighbor cache table.

For the DAD mechanism, this request/response exchange is used more finely. The node does not appropriate the address it desires until the procedure has been completed satisfactorily; during this procedure, this address will be called "tentative". To be more precise, if the node receives traffic destined for a "temporary" address, it must not process it or respond to it. The procedure is to issue a Neighbor Solicitation message with as target its "temporary" address and in source address, the address with type "unspecified" (::). If someone answers, to this NS message with a Neighbor Advertisement message means that the address is already taken and a node already has this address, it is considered that the attempt to obtain an address fails: the node cannot get this address. There is no other attempt to get this address; the administrator must intervene on the node to configure it with another address. There is another case where we cannot get the address: when the node receives a message NS with as target address the "temporary" address that we want. This means that another node also performs a DAD procedure for the same address. In this case, neither of the two nodes performing the DAD mechanism on the same address will be able to obtain it.

The DAD mechanism is not infallible, especially if it occurs during the time when several nodes of the same network are temporarily "separated" (loss of connecting or dropping a link between the nodes) and that one or more of the nodes perform a DAD procedure. They can assign the same address without the collision detection procedure.

4.2   The Algorithm of DAD Process

For the node, the procedure starts by listening to the multicast group "all-nodes multicast" and the multicast group of the solicited-node ("solicited-node multicast"). The first allows it to receive address resolution requests ("Address Resolution ") for this address and the second will allow it to receive the messages sent by other nodes also making a DAD on this address. In order to listen to these, the node must send a Multicast Listener Discovery (MLD) [16] request; when a node triggers the DAD procedure, it sends a Neighbor Solicitation message, an ICMPv6 type message.

The header IPv6 contains the following fields:

- The source address of the IPv6 packet is the unspecified address (::);
- The destination address is the multicast address of the solicited-node ("Solicited-Node Multicast Address ") of the "tentative" address, that is the last three octets of the provisional address concatenated with the prefix FF02::1:FF00: 0/104.

When sending this NS message, we observe for the ICMPv6 header:

- The target address field is filled with the "tentative" address;
- The link layer option of the source is not used. So, two nodes can send the same identical NS message.

With stateless auto-configuration, it's important to note that if the DAD mechanism fails, then there is no further testing and a new address will have to be assigned otherwise, in particular, for addresses that will have been built automatically via the modified EUI-64 format.

The algorithm DAD is described as follows:

- The first step is to generate an IPv6 address with either autoconfiguration or other methods;
- In the second step, the node will be subscribed in multicast groups: all multicast nodes and solicited multicast node;
- After, there are three cases:
- A NA message is received: the tentative address is used as a valid address by another node. The tentative address is not unique and cannot be retained;
- A NS message from a neighbor is received as part of a DAD procedure; the tentative address is also a tentative address for another node. The tentative address cannot be used by any other node;
- Nothing is received after one second (default value): the tentative address is unique, it passes from the provisional state to a valid one and it is assigned to the interface.

Figure 2 shows the DAD algorithm.

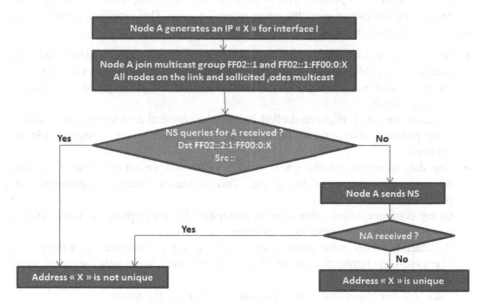

Fig. 2. The flowchart of the DAD process

4.3 The Attack on DAD Process

An attack on the DAD mechanism was identified in [10], the attack is composed as follows: the attacker will deceive the DAD mechanism and make it succeed in one of the two cases where it fails so that the victim cannot claim an address. Since there is a finite number of tries to get an address, the DAD always ends up failing, it's a DoS attack [11]. For the attack to be feasible the attacker must be able to listen on the network any query necessary to perform the DAD procedure (e.g. the NS messages with the unspecified address as the source address are characteristics of the DAD procedure); this implies being able to join the multicast group "Solicited-Node". He then has two choices; he can send an NS message with, as source address, the unspecified address and, as the target address, the address of the victim or an NA message with, as the target address, the "tentative" address of the victim. He can thus prevent the arrival of new nodes having no address yet. The effectiveness of the attack depends strongly on the type of links because it is necessary that the attacker can receive the first NS sent by the victim and that he can answer them. Indeed the attacker must be able to join the multicast group "Solicited-Node", which is not easy in the case of a level 2 point-to-point technology, for example, ADSL.

4.4   Vulnerabilities of Multicast Communications

In IPv6 multicast DAD process, groups are identified by a group address and any node in the network can join or leave the group when it wishes. This simplicity, which is the power of multipoint routing, presents however vulnerabilities:

- IPv6 multicast does not support the notion of the closed group. Indeed, multicast addresses are public: joining a group or leaving a group is an operation that does not require special permissions. This allows any node to join a group and receive messages for it;
- Access to the group is not controlled: an intruder can send data to the group without being part of it, disrupt the multipoint session, and possibly cause congestion in the network;
- The data intended for the group can cross several unsecured channels before reaching all members of the group. This increases listening opportunities to potential intruders;
- Group communications offer more opportunities for intercepting communications, proportional to the number of participants;
- A vulnerable point in the group implicates the safety of all members of the group;
- The large-scale publication of the group's identity and address helps intruders focus their attacks;
- Attackers can impersonate the legitimate members of the group.

To counteract these attacks, group communication requires security services such as authentication, data privacy, confidentiality of the traffic flow.

4.5   Security Needs in Multicast

Multicast requires the set of security mechanisms in a unicast communication in addition to some needs inherent to its nature which is the group communication. These needs can be divided into three main parts:

A. Authentication

All participants in a multicast session must self-authenticate before joining the group. Authentication [17] may be restricted to group members: sources and receivers, or possibly extended to the routing infrastructure: designated routers.

Among other authentication mechanisms, the certification scheme with a third authority can be used.

B. Integrity

This ability ensures that the multicast stream reaches the recipients without falsification. This option is usually provided by cryptographic, hash and digital signature mechanisms [18].

C. Confidentiality

This confidentiality [19] must be provided at several levels:

- Past privacy (backward confidentiality): We can imagine that a hacker can store the multicast stream for a time interval $[t_0, t]$, join the group at time t to acquire the keys needed to decrypt this stream "past". Past privacy alters such a hacking scheme by, for example modifying decryption keys for the stream, once a new member joins the group;
- Forward Confidentiality: A system with this ability prevents any member excluded from the multicast group at time t from having the keys necessary for decrypting the multicast stream at times $t + \mu$. This usually results in a modification of these keys and then their redistribution to the remaining members;
- Group Privacy: Only authenticated members must have the keys to decrypt multicast messages.

5 Symmetric Key Cryptography

Symmetric cryptography, also called secret key (as opposed to asymmetric cryptography), is the oldest form of encryption. It can both encrypt and decrypt messages using the same key.

A symmetric encryption algorithm transforms a clear message M with a key secret K. The result is an encrypted message E (M).

There are two categories of symmetric cryptography: block encryption, in which the message to be encrypted is processed by blocks of data (e.g. 64 bits or 128 bits) (DES, AES, blowfish…), and stream encryption or the message which is processed bit by bit (RC4, Bluetooth E0/1, GSM A5/1…).

The general idea of block ciphering is:

1. Replace characters with a binary code;
2. Cut this string into blocks of given length;
3. Encrypting a block by "adding" it bit by bit to a key;
4. Move some bits of the block;
5. Repeat a number of times operation 3. This is called a round;
6. Go to the next block and return to point 3 until the entire message is encrypted.

In our paper, we have used AES as encryption and decryption algorithm.

In this section, we present the description of our algorithm which makes it possible to secure the target address used in NS message in the DAD process.

6 Proposed Algorithm

In this section, we present the description of our algorithm which makes it possible to secure the target address used in NS message and NA based on AES algorithm.

6.1   The Comparison Between AES and RSA

The Table 1 shows the characteristics of AES and RSA:

Table 1. The characteristics of AES and RSA

	AES	RSA
Key size	128, 192, 256 bits	>1024 bits
Algorithm	Symmetric algorithm	Asymmetric algorithm
Encryption	Faster	Slower
Decryption	Faster	Slower
Power consumption	LOW	High

Our method is called New-Secured-DAD. It uses two new message types, namely, NSNew-Secured-DAD and NANew-Secured-DAD.

6.2   The Steps of New-Secured-DAD

The steps of our algorithm are:

- Generation step (Step 1): In the first step, the new node will generate an IPv6 address using the random method. Then the tentative IPv6 address is used as a secret key (ks) for the encryption and decryption steps;
- Encryption step (Step 2): In this step, the new node sending the NS message and the existing nodes use a random function to generate a number n;
- Insertion step (Step 3): A new field will be added in the NSNew-Secured-DAD and NANew-Secured-DAD messages. This field is composed of the random number n generated in step 2 and the encryption of the random number E (n);
- Sending step (Step 4): NSNew-Secured-DAD and NANew-Secured-DAD messages will be sent to FF02::1:FFXX:XXXX/104, where X represents the last 24-bit of generated IPv6 address;
- Message authentication step (Step 5): In this step, the nodes will verify the NSNew-Secured-DAD and NANew-Secured-DAD messages.
    - ✓ For NS verification, the existing node who will receive the NSNew-Secured-DAD message, it checks the existing of the new field in NSNew-Secured-DAD message, if it does not exist; NSNew-Secured-DAD message should be rejected. Otherwise, and the mechanism will proceed;
    - ✓ For NA message verification, at the first, each NANew-Secured-DAD message without the new field will be rejected; moreover, the existing node decryption must match the random number in the new field.

If no NA message is received after 3 s, the temporary address will be defined as unique and the new node uses it for its configuration.

After node MN2 receives $NS_{DAD\_Hide\_Target}$, it removes B::1:1 from its address pool and determines that the hash value of B::1:1 is equal to the "Hash_64" field in $NS_{DAD\_Hide\_Target}$. Thus, node MN2 replies with a $NA_{DAD\_Hide\_Target}$. If Node MN2 has another address IP_Z with a hash value of "edce7a8659a73312" (i.e. the last 64 bits also match the "Hash_64" field), then node MN2 must reply again with $NA_{DAD\_Hide\_Target}$.

Each node can have several addresses and centralized random address space to increase the probability of address conflict.

6.3   Workflow of New-Secured-DAD Mechanism

When there is a node recently joined the IPv6 link-local network intents to generate a new IPv6 address for its own purpose. First of all, it must make sure that no other node on the same link uses that address already. For this, the node must execute the DAD process. First, the new node will generate an IPv6 address as a tentative IPv6 using the random method of IPv6 addressing [20]. Then, it generates a random number (n)s and encrypt it E(n)s via using the tentative IPv6 address as a secret key for encryption.

Subsequently, the random number (n)s and the encryption number E(n)s will insert into $NS_{New-Secured-DAD}$. The new node should send the $NS_{New-Secured-DAD}$ message to Solicited -node multicast group FF02::1:FFXX:XXXX based on the last 24 bit of the tentative IPv6 address, Fig. 3 shows $NS_{New-Secured-DAD}$ /$NA_{New-Secured-DAD}$ message format.

Ethernet header	Dest MAC (33:33:FF:XX:XX:XX)
	Src MAC (Sender/Receiver MAC)
	Type (0x0808)
IPv6 header	Src IPv6 address (::)
	Dest IPv6 address (FF02::1:FFXX:XXXX)
	Next header (0X3a)
ICMPv6 header	Type 200 For $NS_{New-Secured-DAD}$, 201 for $NA_{New-Secured-DAD}$
	Target address (::)
	Options ICMPv6
	New secured field: (n)	E(n)

Fig. 3. The $NS_{New-Secured-DAD}$ and $NA_{New-Secured-DAD}$ message format

All the existing nodes on the same link that joined the same address FF02::1:FFXX: XXXX will receive the $NS_{New-Secured-DAD}$ message. Firstly, receiving nodes will use its IPv6 address attempting to decrypt the encryption number n, then compare the decryption number $D(E(n)s)_R$ with the random number $(n)_S$:

$$D(E(n)s, IPv6)r = (n)s \qquad (1)$$

If the last equality is verified, the receiving node sends a $NA_{New-Secured-DAD}$ message to the new node. Before sending the NANew-Secured-DAD message, should generate a random number $(n)_R$ and encrypt its IPv6 and insert them to $NA_{New-Secured-DAD}$. This method will completely prevent any attacker to catch the IPv6 and perform any kind of attacks because the IPv6 address is not sent.

New nodes joined the group FF02::1:FFXX:XXXX are going to receive the NANew-Secured-DAD message, as the result, the new node will verify the NA message while the other nodes should discard it. The new node verifies if the NANew-Secured-DAD message contains the new field otherwise the new node will discard it and consider the message came from illegitimate node. If the new field exists, the verification process will proceed through decrypt the encryption number, then compare the decryption word $D(E(n)_R)_S$ with the random number $(n)_R$:

$$D(E(n)r, IPv6s)s = (n)r \qquad (2)$$

If this equality is verified, the address is considered non-unique and the new node generates another address, otherwise the new node rejects the message NA. If after 3 s the new node does not receive an NA message, it can use the temporary address as its IPv6 address.

The algorithm used to encrypt and decrypt the message is the AES symmetric cryptography algorithm.

The flowchart in Fig. 4 shows our algorithm:

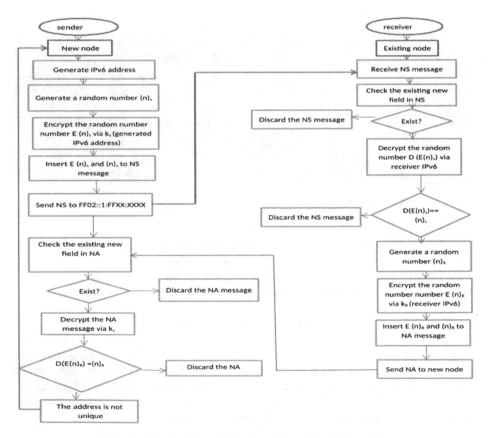

Fig. 4. The flowchart of the New-Secured-DAD algorithm

7 Analysis of Proposed New-Secured-DAD Technique

7.1 Security Analysis of Tentative IPv6 Address

The tentative IPv6 address represents the important information in DAD process in IPv6 link-local network. In standard DAD, the new node multicasts the tentative IPv6 address by sending NS messages to FF02::1. All the nodes will, therefore, receive NS messages including the attacker. Since the attacker can obtain the tentative IPv6 address, it can claim that this tentative IPv6 address is not unique by sending fake NA messages, which prevents the new node from joining the IPv6 network. In the New-Secured-DAD process, the tentative IPv6 address can be hidden using a random number. In this case, the attacker will not be able to obtain the tentative IPv6 address and perform its attack.

7.2 Security Analysis of Probability of Collision Attack

If B is bandwidth in Gbyte on the network, the messages size for $NS_{New\text{-}Secured\text{-}DAD}$ and $NA_{New\text{-}Secured\text{-}DAD}$ is M bytes and T is the time is seconds, Eq. (1) will calculate how many messages N the attacker can send at most:

$$N = \frac{B}{M} * T \tag{3}$$

Example:

B = 10 Gbyte, M = 102 bytes and T = 3 s
N = (10 * 1024 * 1024) * 3/102 = 308 405

Where (308 405) is the number of messages that can be sent by the attacker on the LAN within three seconds.

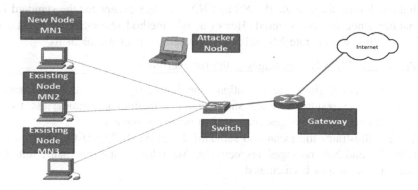

Fig. 5. The network topology

8 Simulations and Results

8.1 Network Topology

The network environment includes a gateway router, an Ethernet switch, a new node (MN1), two existing nodes (MN2 and MN3) and an attacker. Figure 5 shows the network topology. The simulated network is a LAN network.

Each node can have several addresses and centralized random address space to increase the probability of address conflict.

8.2 Processing Time Analysis

An analysis of the execution time for generating and verifying NS and NA messages at sender and receiver nodes is given in this section. Moreover, a comparison of the obtained results with all the existing mechanisms' results is made to prove the efficiency of New-Secured-DAD security technique.

- Generating NS and NA messages at the sender node

Both NS and NA messages will be sent by the sender node to complete the DAD process in IPv6 link-local network. For New-Secured-DAD technique, each sender node should generate a random number with its required fields and attach it to each of the NS and NA messages. The measurement of processing time PT in the sender node is done by subtracting ending time te with starting time ts of the message generation process as shown below in Eq. (3):

$$PT = te - ts \tag{5}$$

10 scenarios were realized for each message (NS and NA). The execution time to generate NS and NA messages is illustrated in Figs. 6 and 7, respectively.

Based on the simulation results, it is obvious that all the existing mechanisms needed much time to generate the NS and NA message except for the standard DAD mechanism since it's not secured. However, our method (New-Secured-DAD) consumes less time to generate NS and NA compared to other mechanisms.

- Verifying NS and NA messages at the receiver node

Figures 8 and 9 show the execution time for verifying NS and NA messages, respectively. The results obtained show that the method consumes less time for checking NS and NA messages compared to other mechanisms.

Table 2 illustrates the mean and standard deviation (STDVE) for generating and verifying NS and NA messages, respectively. Accordingly, the processing time of the mechanisms' messages is calculated.

Table 2. Execution time for generating NS and NA messages at the sender and receiver nodes

Execution time (ms)				
NDP messages	Generating messages		Verifying messages	
	NS	NA	NS	NA
Standard DAD				
Mean	0,59472	0,7786	0,052892	0,04788
STDVE	0,04795238	0,17508461	0,00059421	0,00090037
HSec-Target-DAD				
Mean	4,55836	93,616052	1,92908	1,82908
STDVE	0,17445503	0,2130023	0,02345941	0,02345941
New-Secured-DAD				
Mean	1,56837	1,61003	0,14531	0,09288
STDVE	0,28086091	0,18975245	0,00346328	0,002214
SeND				
Mean	40,57246	83,44244	46,94133	47,35326
STDVE	0,2926556	0,26982376	0,03358002	0,02051645

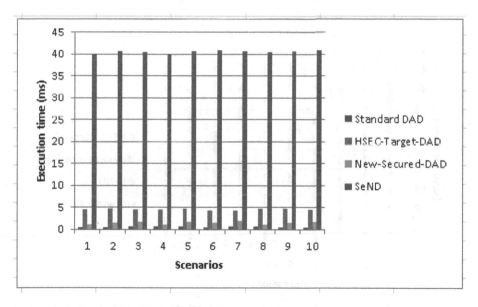

Fig. 6. Execution time for generating NS message at the new node (sender)

Based on Table 2, it is noticeable that the existing mechanisms' processing time such as SeND and HSEC-Target-DAD is considerably high compared with the standard process of Standard-DAD. Whereas, New-Secured-DAD consumes less processing time compared with other existing mechanisms. Based on the overall results,

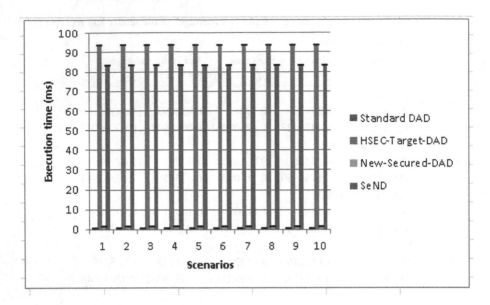

Fig. 7. Execution time for generating NA message

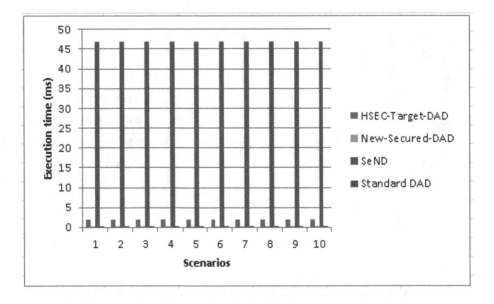

Fig. 8. Execution time for verifying NS message at the receiver node.

the proposed technique can clearly reduce the level of complexity issues, i.e., the processing time of NS and NA messages' generation and verification between nodes during DAD process in IPv6 link-local network.

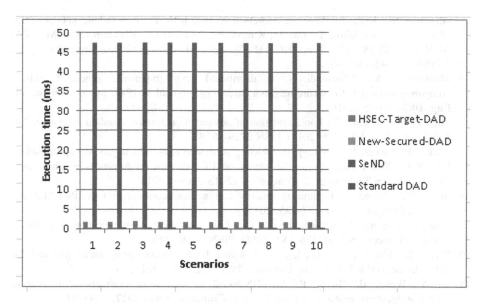

Fig. 9. Execution time for verifying NA message at the receiver node.

9 Conclusion and Perspectives

In order to ensure that all configured addresses are likely to be unique on a given IPv6 link, the nodes execute a Duplicate Address Detection algorithm. Nodes must execute the algorithm before assigning addresses to an interface. However, this process is not secured.

In this paper, we have developed a new mechanism to secure the DAD process in IPv6 network. This mechanism is based on the symmetric cryptography. The algorithm used for encrypting and decrypting the message is AES.

The simulation results show that our algorithm consumes less time for generating and verifying NS and NA messages compared to other mechanisms like SeND.

Although IPv6 node communications are limited to NDP and DAD protocols when IPv6 is not officially deployed, there are still attacks that can affect network performance by exploiting only these two protocols as we have been able to study. Our future work will be focalized on other parameters security.

References

1. Deering, S., Hinden, R.: Internet Protocol, Version 6 (IPv6) Specification. IETF, RFC 8200, July 2017
2. Ahmed, A.S.A.M.S., Hassan, R., Othman, N.E.: IPv6 Neighbor Discovery Protocol Specifications, Threats and Countermeasures: A Survey (2017). ISSN 2169-3536
3. Gont, F., Cooper, A., Thaler, D., Liu, W.: Recommendation on Stable IPv6 Interface Identifiers. IETF, RFC 8064, February 2017

4. Alisherov, F., Kim, T.: Duplicate address detection table in IPv6 mobile networks. In: Chang, C.-C., Vasilakos, T., Das, P., Kim, T.-h., Kang, B.-H., Khurram Khan, M. (eds.) ACN 2010. CCIS, vol. 77, pp. 109–115. Springer, Heidelberg (2010). https://doi.org/10. 1007/978-3-642-13405-0_11

5. Moslehpour, M., Khorsandi, S.: A distributed cryptographically generated address computing algorithm for secure neighbor discovery protocol in IPv6. Int. J. Comput. Inf. Eng. **10**(6), 10–15 (2016)

6. Pitchaiah, M., Daniel, P.: Implementation of advanced encryption standard algorithm. Int. J. Sci. Eng. Res. **3**(3), 3–5 (2012). ISSN 2229-5518

7. Shah, J.L., Parvez, J.: IPv6 cryptographically generated address: analysis and optimization. In: AICTC 2016 Proceedings of the International Conference on Advances in Information Communication Technology & Computing, 12–13 August 2016

8. Shah, J.L., Parvez, J.: Optimizing security and address configuration in IPv6 SLAAC. Procedia Comput. Sci. **54**, 177–185 (2015)

9. Shah, J.L.: A novel approach for securing IPv6 link local communication. Inf. Secur. J. Glob. Perspect. **25**(1–3), 136–150 (2016). ISSN 1939-3555

10. Wang, X., Mu, Y., Han, G., Le, D.: A secure IPv6 address configuration protocol for vehicular networks. Wirel. Pers. Commun. **79**(1), 721–744 (2014)

11. Lu, Y., Wang, M., Huang, P.: An SDN-based authentication mechanism for securing neighbor discovery protocol in IPv6. J. Secur. Commun. Netw. **2017**, 1–9 (2017)

12. Praptodiyono, S., et al.: Improving Security of Duplicate Address Detection on IPv6 Local Network in Public Area (2016). ISSN 2376-1172

13. Barbhuiya, F.A., Bansal, G., Kumar, N., et al.: Detection of neighbor discovery protocol based attacks in IPv6 network. Netw. Sci. **2**(3–4), 91–113 (2013)

14. Hassan, R., Ahmed, A.S., Osman, N.E.: Enhancing security for IPv6 neighbor discovery protocol using cryptography. Am. J. Appl. Sci. **11**(9), 1472–1479 (2014)

15. El Ksimi, A., Leghris, C.: Towards a New Algorithm to Optimize IPv6 Neighbor Discovery Security for Small Objects Networks (2018). hindawi.com

16. Sridevi: Implementation of multicast routing on IPv4 and IPv6 networks. Int. J. Recent Innov. Trends Comput. Commun. **5**, 1455–1467 (2017). ISSN 2321-8169

17. Cunjiang, Y., Dawei, X., Li, J.: Authentication analysis in an IPV6-based environment. IEEE, December 2014

18. Nia, M.A., Sajedi, A., Jamshidpey, A.: An Introduction to Digital Signature Schemes. IEEE (2014)

19. Chittimaneni, K., Kaeo, M., Kaeo, M.: Operational Security Considerations for IPv6 Networks. Internet-Draft, 27 October 2014

20. Narten, T., Draves, R., Krishnan, S.: Privacy extensions for stateless address autoconfig- uration in IPv6 (2007)

21. El Ksimi, A., Leghris, C.: An enhancement approach for securing neighbor discovery in IPv6 networks. In: Renault, É., Boumerdassi, S., Bouzefrane, S. (eds.) MSPN 2018. LNCS, vol. 11005, pp. 54–69. Springer, Cham (2019). https://doi.org/10.1007/978-3-030-03101-5_6

Deep Neural Networks for Indoor Localization Using WiFi Fingerprints

Souad BelMannoubi[1,2]([envelope]) and Haifa Touati[1,2]

[1] Hatem Bettaher IResCoMath Research Unit, Gabès, Tunisia
souad.belmannoubi@gmail.com, haifa.touati@cristal.rnu.tn
[2] Faculty of Science of Gabes, University of Gabes, Gabès, Tunisia

Abstract. In this paper, we propose a novel Wi-Fi positioning method based on Deep Learning. More specifically, we investigate a Stacked AutoEncoder-based model for global location recognition from WiFi fingerprinting data. Stacked AutoEncoder works very well in learning useful high-level features for better representation of input raw data. For our proposed model, two trained unsupervised autoencoders were stacked, then the whole network was trained globally by adding a Softmax output layer for classification. The experimental results show that our Deep Learning based model performs better than SVM and KNN machine learning approaches in a large multi-floor building composed of 162 rooms. Our model achieves an accuracy of 85.58% and a test time that does not exceed 0.26 s.

Keywords: Indoor localization · Fingerprinting · RSSI · WiFi · Deep Neural Networks · Stacked AutoEncoders

1 Introduction

Nowadays, physical environment incorporates massive and varied information options, for instance, seismic waves, motion, light, temperature and so on. It is necessary to acquire the information from numerous varied options for a greater comprehension of the environment. In this context Wireless Sensor Network (WSN) is a simple to employ infrastructure that enables collecting this kind of abundant information. A WSN includes spatially dispersed autonomous sensors to monitor the physical environment also to cooperatively cross their data via a network to a primary node or base station. In many applications, an event detected by a sensor is only useful if the information relating to its geographical location is provided. This is the case of monitoring forest fires or enemy troops in a military context. Without this information, these applications would not make sense. For this reason most sensor network operations are typically based on the location [1].

In most large scale systems, it is financially unfeasible to use Global Positioning System (GPS) hardware in each node. Moreover, GPS service may not be available in the observed environment (e.g., indoor). Consequently, several

© Springer Nature Switzerland AG 2019
É. Renault et al. (Eds.): MSPN 2019, LNCS 11557, pp. 247–258, 2019.
https://doi.org/10.1007/978-3-030-22885-9_21

indoor localization methods based on Angle Of Arrival (AOA) [2], Time Of Arrival (TOA) [3] and WiFi fingerprinting [4] have been adopted to ensure efficient indoor localization. Recently, WiFi fingerprint-based localization is widely used as it doesn't require extra infrastructures. In fact, since WiFi networks are ubiquitous in public buildings and private residences, such as office blocks, shopping malls, and airports, WiFi information can be exploited to provide rough position estimates without additional costs of special infrastructure. Hence, the Received Signal Strength Indicator (RSSI) data is commonly used for fingerprinting by many existing indoor localization systems for its high availability in almost all of mobile devices, although RSSI fingerprints are coarse-grained. Fingerprints-based indoor localization, consists of two phases, as illustrated in Fig. 1.

– *The offline phase* is mainly for database construction by collecting and preprocessing survey data of pre-established reference positions.

– *The online phase* in which the real-time data sensed by a mobile device is used to estimate its position.

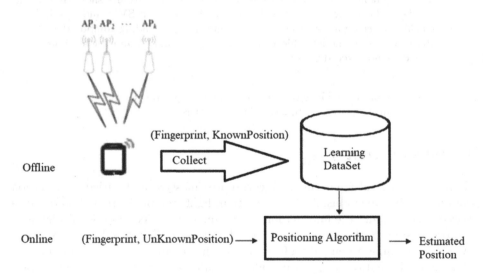

Fig. 1. Fingerprint-based Wi-Fi positioning system

Recently, the area of learning approaches is attracting widespread interest by producing remarkable research in almost every aspect of artificial intelligence. Machine learning methods, such as the KNearest- Neighbor (KNN) scheme [5], Artificial Neural Networks (ANN) based method [6,7], and Support Vector Machines (SVM) [8], can be used to extract the core features from the data and train the learning model, thus obtaining better localization performance and reducing the computational complexity in the online phase.

However, the variation of RSSIs due to the fluctuating nature of wireless signal, such as multipath fading and attenuation by static or dynamic objects like walls or moving people is the major problem for accurate fingerprint-based localization. Moreover, it is necessary to collect more Reference Points (RPs) for accurate positioning especially when the environment turns to be large, thus the built fingerprint database tends to be tremendous. Consequently, the challenge in wireless positioning is how to extract reliable features and find good mapping function from massive RPs with widely fluctuating RSSI signals. The aforementioned methods essentially belong to shallow learning architectures which have limited modeling and representational power when dealing with such big and noisy data problem.

To extract complex structure and build internal representation from such rich data, human information processing mechanisms suggest the use of a Deep Learning architecture with multiple layers of nonlinear processing stages [9]. Deep Learning simulates the hierarchical structure of human brain by processing data from low level to high-level and gradually producing more and more semantic concepts. Deep Neural Networks (DNNs) have been applied to tackle such kinds of problems with notable success, beating state-of-the-art techniques in certain areas such as vision [10,11], audio [12,13] and robotics [14,15].

One of these deep architecture-based models is Stacked AutoEnoder (SAE), which is created by hierarchically connecting hidden layers to learn hierarchical embedding in compressed representations. Autoencoders [20] are widely used to obtain latent representations capturing sufficient information to reconstruct the input data. These representations are efficiently used for pre-training deep neural networks (DNN) [21]. SAE-based deep learning approaches demonstrate interesting results in term of classification accuracy, in different domains such as medicine [22], biology [23], image processing [24], motions [25], music [26] and speech [27].

In this paper, we propose to use DNN, more specifically a Stacked AutoEncoder-based model, to resolve our indoor localization classification problem using WiFi fingerprints. This choice is guided by the ability of Stacked AutoEncoders to reduce feature space dimension and assess the scalability of the proposed DNN solution especially for large buildings with many floors and rooms.

The rest of this paper is organized as follows: Sect. 2, gives a brief review of the prior literature. Then, Sect. 3 details our SAE-based localization solution. Next, Sect. 4 describes our experimental environment and discusses the obtained results. Finally, Sect. 5 concludes this work.

2   Literature Review of Deep Neural Networks Solutions for Indoor Localization

The architecture of a Deep Neural Network (DNN) has the ability to automatically learn features with higher levels of abstractions as well as complex mappings from input to output. Recently, several research projects have been launched to use the deep learning approach in order to enhance indoor localization accuracy.

Wang et al. present in [16] a system called DeepFi that utilizes a Restricted Boltzmann Machines (RBM) model over fingerprinting data to locate indoor positions based on Channel State Information (CSI). As many other fingerprinting techniques, their model consists of offline training and online localization phases. In the off-line training phase, they employ deep learning to train all the weights as fingerprints based on the previously stored CSI. For the positioning localization phase, they use a probabilistic method based on the radial basis function to obtain the estimated location.

In [17], Wang et al. implement CiFi, a Deep Convolutional Neural Networks (DCNN) based approach for indoor localization with commodity 5GHz WiFi. Leveraging a modified device driver, they extract phase data of CSI, which is used to estimate the Angle of Arrival (AoA). Then, they create estimated AoA images as input to a DCNN, to train the weights in the offline phase. The location of a mobile device is predicted using the trained DCNN and the new CSI AoA images.

The main limitation of these two approaches is that CSI information collection requires the use of specialized hardware which is not available on today mobile devices. Due to this limitation, it is not feasible to implement these techniques on smartphones for example.

In [18], the authors propose a four-layer DNN that uses WiFi fingerprints to generate a coarse positioning estimate, which, in turn, is refined to produce a final position estimate by a Hidden Markov Model (HMM). The performance of the proposed indoor localization system is evaluated in both indoor and outdoor environments which are divided into hundreds of square grids. The main limitation of this approach, is that HMM predictions can be prone to error accumulation since predictions are based on the previous position acquired through the DNN.

In [19], the authors investigate the application of Deep Belief Networks (DBNs) with two different types of Restricted Boltzmann Machines for indoor localization and evaluate the performance of their approaches using data from simulation in heterogeneous mobile radio networks using ray tracing techniques. This approach uses custom UWB beacons which yields to very high implementation cost.

In summary, recent DNN-based localization proposals either need additional hardware or lack accuracy in some specific cases. Hence the need of an accurate DNN-based solution that doesn't require any additional implementation or infrastructure cost, still exists.

3   Proposed Model

Recently, Deep Neural Networks (DNNs) are demonstrating great success on tackling classification problems in different domains. The requirement is that a large database of training samples has to be available. Hence the built fingerprint database tends to be tremendous and the processing will be more complex. Therefore, it is difficult to propose a reduced higher level features for machine learning approaches. Fortunately, we can use stacked autoencoders [20] for this task and provide raw measurements at DNN input. In this section, firstly, we present the general architecture of an AutoEncoder, then we detail our DNN model with the proposed Stacked AutoEncoder (SAE) for the indoor localization classification problem.

3.1   The AutoEncoder Model

AutoEncoders (AE) are parts of neural network methods that are used to reduce the dimensionality of the input data by learning the reduced representation of the original data. It is a kind of unsupervised learning structure that owns three layers: input layer, hidden layer and output layer as shown in Fig. 2.

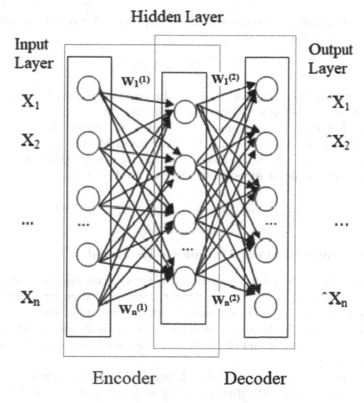

Fig. 2. AutoEncoder architecture

The process of an autoencoder training consists of two parts: the encoder and the decoder part as presented in Fig. 2.

The encoder computes a hidden representation of X made of a vector h of size m (number of hidden units) as follows:

$$h = \sigma(W^{(1)}X + b^{(1)}) \tag{1}$$

Where $W^{(1)}$ is a $m \times n$ weight matrix and $b^{(1)}$ is a m dimensional bias vector. $\sigma(.)$ is the activation function for the hidden layer units. For traditional activation functions (*sigmoid* and *hyperbolic tangent* functions), the gradients decrease quickly with training error propagating to forward layers. The *Rectified Linear Units (ReLU)* activation function has received extensive attention in recent years, since its gradient will not decrease with the independent variables increasing. Thus, the network with ReLU does not suffer from gradient diffusion or vanishing. That's why we choose ReLU (2) as an activation function for the hidden layer units of our model.

$$f_r(x) = max(0, x) \tag{2}$$

The decoder attempts to reconstruct the input vector X from the hidden vector h to obtain the output vector $\hat{X}$:

$$\hat{X} = \sigma(W^{(2)}h + b^{(2)}) \tag{3}$$

where the reconstructed vector $\hat{X}$ is a n-dimensional vector, $W^{(2)}$ is a $m \times n$ weight matrix and $b^{(2)}$ is a n dimensional bias vector.

During learning, the autoencoder attempts to reduce the reconstruction error l between X and $\hat{X}$ by using the traditional Mean Square Error (MSE) $(l_{MSE}(X, \hat{X}) = ||X - \hat{X}||^2)$ for minimizing the total reconstruction error l_{MSE} with respect to the parameters set $\theta = W^{(1)}, b^{(1)}, W^{(2)}, b^{(2)}$:

$$l_{MSE}(\theta) = \frac{1}{d}\Sigma l_{MSE}(X, \hat{X}) = \frac{1}{d}\Sigma||X - \hat{X}||^2 \tag{4}$$

3.2   The Proposed Stacked AutoEncoder Model

The Stacked Autoencoder is a deep neural network consisting of multiple layers of basic AE, forming a deep multi-layer encoder and decoder architecture in which the outputs of each layer is wired to the inputs of the successive layer.

For classification problems, one can use a SAE as a dimensionality reduction technique, where the outputs of the last encoder are used as input features for the classification.

In this paper, we construct a two layers SAE which consists of two basic AE to efficiently reduce the dimensionality of input vector from 206 networks to 150 and 100 features. The architecture of the proposed SAE model with a classification layer is shown in Fig. 3. For simplicity, we didn't show the decoder parts of each basic AE in the figure.

The training process of our SAE model is composed of two parts:

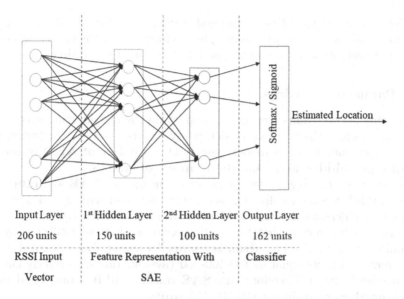

Fig. 3. The proposed stacked AutoEncoder model

- *Unsupervised pre-training*: Each layer is trained separately, which has input and hidden representation. In the pre-training process, the label samples are not needed, so we say the pre-training step is unsupervised.
- *Supervised fine tuning*: Once we complete the pre-training of all layers, a Sigmoid (5) or a Softmax (6) output layer with Cross Entropy cost (7) function was added.

$$Sigmoid(x_i) = \frac{1}{1 + e^{-x_i}} \tag{5}$$

$$Softmax(x_i) = \frac{1 + e^{-x_i}}{\sum_{j=0}^{k} e^{x_j}}, i = [0..k] \tag{6}$$

$$J(w) = -1/N \sum_{i=1}^{N} [yi * \log(zi) + (1 - yi) \log(1 - zi)] \tag{7}$$

Where N is the number of samples, yi is the calculated position and zi is the estimated one.

In this way, the network was globally fine tuned with a supervised algorithm to predict the location.

4   Experimental Results

4.1   Experimental Data

To test the efficiency of our Stacked AutoEncoder indoor localization model, real experiments are realized in a WLAN building with 4 floors and 162 rooms. Each location is mapped to a 206-dimensional RSSI fingerprint. In all cases, a set of 5156 fingerprints are used to evaluate the performance of the model, where 70% of the data set are used for training and 30% are used for testing.

4.2   Parameters Settings

The setting of the parameters had an impact on the classification success rate. Therefore, to find the accurate model, many experiments are conducted to fix the basic parameters of our model, namely **the number of AE**, **the number of units per hidden layer** and **the number of epochs**.

We start by choosing the two parameters: **number of AE** and **number of units**. Table 1 reports localization accuracies obtained with 2 and 3 AutoEncoders with different combination of units number (150, 100 and 50).

These results confirm that localization accuracy is widely affected by layer and units numbers. The best result is obtained when applying 2 AutoEncoders with number of units equal to 150-100-150 (average rate of correctly classified data reaches 78.99%). Therefore, **our SAE model will be composed of two AutoEncoders containing 150-100-150 units**.

Table 1. Choosing the number of layers and number of units parameters

Number of AE	2	2	2	3
Number of units	150-50-150	150-100-150	100-50-100	150-100-50-100-150
Accuracy	77.44%	**78.99%**	77.18%	76.79%

The next parameter to fix is the **number of epochs**, different epochs number (20, 40, 60, 80, 100 and 120 epochs) were compared in order to determine which one has the best performances. Results in Table 2 show clearly that using 100 epochs gives the best rate of correctly classified data, namely 85.58%.

Hence, according to the results of the tests carried out, we choose to set the **number of epochs to** 100 to build our SAE model.

Table 2. Choosing the number of epochs parameter

Number of epochs	20	40	60	80	100	120
Accuracy	78.99%	81.97%	83.97%	84.87%	**85.58%**	84.16%

4.3   SAE Model Testing

In this phase, the model already created in the previous phase will be tested. To predict the correct location, a Softmax or Sigmoid function can be applied as a classifier in the final layer. Hence, we test our SAE model with a Softmax output

Table 3. Parameters values for SAE-based indoor localization.

DNN parameter	Value
Number of epochs	100
Batch size	10
Dropout	0.2
SAE hidden layers	150-100-150
SAE activation	Rectified Linear Unit (ReLU)
SAE optimizer	Adamax
SAE loss	Mean Squared Error (MSE)
Classifier	Softmax or sigmoid
Classifier optimizer	Adamax
Classifier loss	Categorical crossentropy

layer and a Sigmoid output layer. Table 3 summarizes the parameters settings used to test our SAE with Softmax and SAE with Sigmoid models.

Using these parameters, we compare our proposed SAE-based models to two classical machine learning based models, namely SVM and KNN. For comparisons, we used SVM with polynomial kernel since our preliminary experiments show that a polynomial kernel achieves better accuracy than an RBF kernel. The models are compared according to two metrics: "accuracy" and "test time". These comparisons are given by Table 4.

Results in Table 4 show that there is not a big difference for the test time between SAE with Softmax and SAE with Sigmoid. However, using a **Softmax** as a classifier is better for the accuracy.

Compared to machine learning approaches, the results of the evaluation show that the Stacked AutoEncoder model clearly achieves better accuracy (85.58%) than KNN (77.98%) and SVM (80.52%) models. In addition, test time evaluation shows that the SAE-based model has the fastest test time (0.26 s) compared to KNN (4.93 s) and SVM (13.8 s) that need much more time for the localization task.

Table 4. Output layer classifier

Model	SAE + Softmax	SAE + Sigmoid	SVM	KNN
Accuracy	**85.58%**	83.97%	80.52%	77.98%
Test time	**0.26 s**	0.25 s	13.8 s	4.93 s

Finally, to understand why our SAE-based localization model accuracy does not exceed 85.58%, we analyses experimental results versus the building topology and the APs positions. We concluded that, this accuracy limitation can be explained by the reduced size of some zones (the dimensions of some rooms of the used building are very small), besides the APs emplacement impacts the predicting success rate. Our analysis of the space accuracy results, shows that the model is mistaken on the neighboring small rooms, since the values of RSSI are often close in these cases.

The choice of the SAE architecture was the strength of this work, since the unsupervised pre-training tends to avoid local minima and increase the network's performance stability [21]. In addition, the AEs are able to extract a deep hierarchical representation of the learning data, which simplifies and reduces the complexity of the learning task. This affects the performance of the model during the test phase and leads to a reduced test duration, that does not exceed 0.26 s.

5   Conclusion

In this paper, we proposed a WiFi fingerprinting indoor localization model using a Deep Neural Network approach, based on a Stacked AutoEncoder (SAE) for feature space reduction. Most of current classification methods used to resolve the localization problem are based on supervised learning. However, the application of an unsupervised pre-training greatly reduces the error on test sets, that increase the stability of network performance. Experimental results, in a multi-floors building composed of 162 rooms, show that our proposed solution reaches a localization accuracy of 85.58%, which clearly outperforms the KNN and SVM machine learning methods. Likewise, it achieves a very reduced testing time that does not exceed 0.26 s.

In a future work, we will focus on using deep learning architecture that takes into account the hierarchical nature of large-scale indoor localization.

References

1. Liu, H., Darabi, H., Banerjee, P., Liu, J.: Survey of wireless indoor positioning techniques and systems. IEEE Trans. Syst. Man Cybern. Part C: Appl. Rev. **37**(6), 1067–1080 (2007)
2. Rong, P., Sichitiu, M.L.: Angle of arrival localization for wireless sensor networks. In: IEEE Sensor and Ad Hoc Communications and Networks (2006)
3. Guvenc, I., Chong, C.C.: A survey on TOA based wireless localization and NLOS mitigation techniques. IEEE Commun. Surv. Tutor. **11**(3), 107–124 (2009)
4. Barsocchi, P., Chessa, S., Ferro, E., Furfari, F., Potorti, F.: Context driven enhancement of RSS-based localization systems. In: 2011 IEEE Symposium on Computers and Communications (ISCC), pp. 463–468, 28 June–1 July 2011 (2011)
5. Bahl, P., Padmanabhan, V.: RADAR: an in-building RF-based user location and tracking system. In: IEEE INFOCOM, vol. 2, pp. 775–784 (2000)
6. Laoudias, C., Kemppi, P., Panayiotou, C.: Localization using radial basis function networks and signal strength fingerprints in WLAN. In: IEEE GLOBECOM, pp. 1–6 (2009)

7. Nerguizian, C., Despins, C., Affes, S.: Geolocation in mines with an impulse response fingerprinting technique and neural networks. IEEE Trans. Wirel. Commun. **5**(3), 603–611 (2006)
8. Chriki, A., Touati, H., Snoussi, H.: SVM-based indoor localization in wireless sensor networks. In: IWCMC, pp. 1144–1149 (2017)
9. Deng, L.: Three classes of deep learning architectures and their applications: a tutorial survey. APSIPA Trans. Sig. Inf. Process. (2012). https://doi.org/10.1017/atsip.2013.9
10. Zhang, W., Zhang, Y., Ma, L., Guan, J., Gong, S.: Multimodal learning for facial expression recognition. Pattern Recognit. **48**(10), 3191–3202 (2015)
11. Krizhevsky, A., Sutskever, I., Hinton, G.E.: Imagenet classification with deep convolutional neural networks. In: Advances in Neural Information Processing Systems, pp. 1097–1105 (2012)
12. Mohamed, A.-R., Dahl, G.E., Hinton, G.: Acoustic modeling using deep belief networks. IEEE Trans. Audio Speech Lang. Process. **20**(1), 14–22 (2012)
13. Dahl, G.E., Yu, D., Deng, L., Acero, A.: Context-dependent pre-trained deep neural networks for large-vocabulary speech recognition. IEEE Trans. Audio Speech Lang. Process. **20**(1), 30–42 (2012)
14. Sermanet, P., Hadsell, R., Scoffier, M., Muller, U., LeCun, Y.: Mapping and planning under uncertainty in mobile robots with long-range perception. In: IEEE/RSJ International Conference on Intelligent Robots and Systems, IROS 2008, Nice, France, pp. 2525–2530. IEEE (2008)
15. Hadsell, R., et al.: Learning long-range vision for autonomous off-road driving. J. Field Robot. **26**(2), 120–144 (2009)
16. Wang, X., Gao, L., Mao, S., Pandey, S.: DeepFi: deep learning for indoor fingerprinting using channel state information. In: 2015 IEEE Wireless Communications and Networking Conference (WCNC), pp. 1666–1671. IEEE (2015)
17. Wang, X., Wang, X., Mao, S.: CiFi: deep convolutional neural networks for indoor localization with 5 GHz Wi-Fi. In: IEEE International Conference on Communications (ICC), May 2017
18. Zhang, W., Liu, K., Zhang, W., Zhang, Y., Gu, J.: Deep neural networks for wireless localization in indoor and outdoor environments. Neurocomputing **194**, 279–287 (2016)
19. Luo, J., Gao, H.: Deep belief networks for fingerprinting indoor localization using ultrawideband technology. Int. J. Distrib. Sensor Netw. **12**(1), 5840916 (2016)
20. Hinton, G.E., Salakhutdinov, R.R.: Reducing the dimensionality of data with neural networks. Science **313**(5786), 504–507 (2006)
21. Erhan, D., Bengio, Y., Courville, A., Manzagol, P.-A., Vincent, P., Bengio, S.: Why does unsupervised pre-training help deep learning? J. Mach. Learn. Res. **11**, 625–660 (2010)
22. Xu, J., et al.: Stacked sparse autoencoder (SSAE) for nuclei detection on breast cancer histopathology images. IEEE Trans. Med. Imaging **35**(1), 119–130 (2015)
23. Camacho, F., Torres, R., Ramos-Pollán, R.: Feature learning using stacked autoencoders to predict the activity of antimicrobial peptides. In: Roux, O., Bourdon, J. (eds.) CMSB 2015. LNCS, vol. 9308, pp. 121–132. Springer, Cham (2015). https://doi.org/10.1007/978-3-319-23401-4_11
24. Maria, J., Amaro, J., Falcao, G., Alexandre, L.A.: Stacked autoencoders using low-power accelerated architectures for object recognition in autonomous systems. Neural Process. Lett. **43**, 1–14 (2015)

25. Zhou, X., Guo, J., Wang, S.: Motion recognition by using a stacked autoencoder-based deep learning algorithm with smart phones. In: Xu, K., Zhu, H. (eds.) WASA 2015. LNCS, vol. 9204, pp. 778–787. Springer, Cham (2015). https://doi.org/10.1007/978-3-319-21837-3_76

26. Sarroff, A.M., Casey, M.: Musical audio synthesis using autoencoding neural nets. In: Proceedings ICMCISMCI 2014, Athens, Greece, 14–20 September 2014 (2014)

27. Chao, L., Tao, J., Yang, M., Li, Y.: Improving generation performance of speech emotion recognition by denoising autoencoders. In: The 9th International Symposium on Chinese Spoken Language Processing (ISCSLP), pp. 341–344 (2014)

A New Secure Cellular Automata Cryptosystem for Embedded Devices

Youssef Sbaytri[1(✉)], Saiida Lazaar[1], Hafssa Benaboud[2], and Said Bouchkaren[1]

[1] Mathematics, Computer Sciences and Applications Team
(ERMIA) ENSA of Tangier, University of AbdelMalek Essaadi, Tétouan, Morocco
yusef.sbitri@gmail.com, slazaar@uae.ac.ma, saidbouchkaren1@hotmail.com
[2] IPSS, FSR, University Mohammed V, Rabat, Morocco
hafssa.benaboud@um5.ac.ma

Abstract. Cryptography is one of the essential methods used to warrant the security of sensitive data stored into devices or exchanged between different entities. Many cryptosystems have been defined; those designed for embedded systems must take in consideration the resource-limited devices. In this paper, we propose a new secret key encryption algorithm that supports 64-bits block size with 128-bits keys size. We utilize irreversible Elementary Cellular Automata to generate the sub keys and two-dimensional reversible Cellular Automata to realize substitutions and permutations. The implemented encryption algorithm is analyzed using diffusion and confusion tests. The acquired results show that the proposed cryptosystem exhibits significant high avalanche effect which improves the security level. The paper gives a comparison of avalanche effect, CPU time and memory usage for our proposed cryptosystem and AES-128.

Keywords: Embedded systems · Secret key · Cellular Automata · Avalanche effect · AES-128

1 Introduction

The use of embedded devices in network communications will be more involved. Their main objective is to provide information and services everywhere and everytime, hence they must communicate with each other through communication channels accessible to potential attackers. They should ideally provide security functions such as data confidentiality, data integrity, and authentication. Data confidentiality protects sensitive information from undesired eavesdroppers. Data integrity ensures that the information has not been changed illegitimately. And authentication verifies that the information is sent and received by appropriate entities.

Cryptography is the process used to ensure the confidentiality of data. In general it is based on some mathematical functions used for encryption and decryption. The cryptographic algorithms can be classified into two main types:

© Springer Nature Switzerland AG 2019
E. Renault et al. (Eds.): MSPN 2019, LNCS 11557, pp. 259–267, 2019.
https://doi.org/10.1007/978-3-030-22885-9_22

Symmetric algorithms and asymmetric algorithms. A symmetric algorithm uses one secret key, known as 'Symmetric Key', to encode and decode the information, while an asymmetric algorithm incorporates two cryptographic keys to implement data security.

In this paper, we are interested in symetric cryptographic algorithms and we propose a new lightweight encryption/decryption algorithm to contribute to the security of information generated by embedded systems. The choice of a cryptosystem design for embedded systems or IoT devices focus on optimizing many essential implementation-based criteria, including space, power, and throughput. At the same time, these primitives must also satisfy the basic security requirements against well-known attacks.

In recent years, many cryptosystems, including block ciphers and stream ciphers, have been proposed, especially after the recent NIST's announcement of a lightweight cryptography project [4], which detailed the essential implementation-based criteria must be respected by such design, including the block size, the key size, simpler rounds, simpler key schedule and minimal implementation. To design our proposed cryptosystem for embedded devices, we use Cellular Automata (CA). The chaotic properties of a CA have been exploited by several researchers to design high performance encryption algorithms.

The remainder of the paper is organized as follows. In Sect. 2, we discuss some related work of lightweight cryptography proposed for embedded devices and IoT devices. Section 3 describes our proposed encryption and decryption algorithms by using CA. In the last section, we test the security of the algorithm with some avalanche tests. We conclude by a conclusion and perspectives.

2 Related Work

The inherent parallelism of CA cells and its clarity and its principle of cellule-interconnections make it more suitable for design of a low-implementation-cost cryptosystems. Authors in [12] presented a CA-base cryptosystem designed for Embedded System. In order to meet such conflicting demands, they applied a series of transforms (linear CA, affine CA, non-Affine CA, key mixing) of increasing complexity in successive levels. Another work has been proposed in [13] which gives a lightweight symmetric block key cryptosystem using CA, called Lightweight CA-based Symmetric-key Encryption (LCASE). LCASE meets the same specification as AES satisfying the base security criteria (confusion and diffusion). This block cipher supports 128-bits block size with 128,192 and 256-bits keys according to AES structure. In [14], the authors suggested a lightweight CA-based cryptosystem, the algorithm uses a key of 128-bits and evolving into 12 rounds. To increase complexity, they used different modules such as bit-permutation, inverse bit-permutation, Non-Reversible CA, Reversible CA. In [15,16], autors defined a new fast cryptosystem based on reversible and irreversible CA that supports a key of size 256-bits, they demostrated its efficiency by comparing its performance with AES-256 bits. A novel symmetric key cryptosystem using Asynchronous CA was discussed in [17], where the autors proposed a block cipher that supports a block of 64-bit. The confusion and diffusion analysis of this cryptosystem were achieved. However, the size of proposed key (32000-bit) makes it unsuitable for embedded systems. In [18], autors defined a symmetric key encryption based on non-complemented CA and hybrid CA, they analysed the security of the their proposed cryptosystem by using some statistical test.

3   Proposed Encryption/Decryption Algorithms

Our proposed cryptosystem uses reversible two-dimensional CA for encryption-decryption process and irreversible Elementary CA (ECA) for sub keys generation. It is also built on periodic boundary CA of dimension two (PB_CA2D). Before describing our algorithms, we recall some characteristics of used CA.

3.1   Elementary CA and Two Dimensional CA

A CA A is a quadruple $A = (S, N, d, f)$ where S is a finite set of possible states, N is the cellular neighbourhood, $d \in \mathbb{Z}^+$ is the dimension of A, f is the local cellular interaction rule, also referred to as the transition function.

ECA are the simplest one-dimensional CA with only two states $\{0, 1\}$, two nearest-neighbours (left, right): $d = 1$, $S = \{0; 1\}$, $N = (-1; 0; 1)$ and $f : S^3 \rightarrow S$. There are 256 ECA because the number of different local rules is $2^{2^3} = 256$.

The evolution of an ECA can be described by a table specifying the state of each cell in the next generation depend only on the state of its two nearest neighbours and its current state. A simple illustration is given in the table below (Table 1).

Table 1. ECA of rule 30

x	111	110	101	100	011	010	001	000
f(x)	0	0	0	1	1	1	1	0

Two-dimensional CA has almost of properties as ECA. The most know neighbourhoods are: The Von Neumann and Moore neighbourhoods (Fig. 1), consisting of two states $\{0, 1\}$, central cell and four neighbours for the first one and eight for the second. In Moore neighbourhood used in our cryptosystem, the next state of each cell depends on its current state and the eight cells in its nearest neighbourhood. Figure 2 shows all the rules of two-dimensional CA.

3.2   Periodic Boundary Cellular Automata (PB CA)

A periodic boundary CA is the one in which the extreme cells are connected to each other [10].

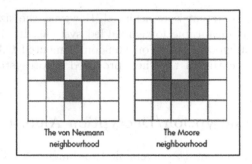

Fig. 1. The von Neumann and Moore neighbourhoods

64	128	256
32	1	2
16	8	4

Fig. 2. Two dimensional CA rule convention

3.3 Proposed Encryption/Decryption Cryptosystem

The following parameters are required for our algorithm:

- Key size: 128-bits;
- Plain text block size: 64-bits;
- Number of rounds: 10;
- Round key size: 64-bits.

Encryption Algorithm: Algorithm 1

```
Encrypt_Block (block, Key)
        SubKeys [10]   <-- GenerateSubKeys(Key)
        for i from 0 to 10 do
                state  <-- block_to_state (block, 8, 8)
                state  <-- oddSubBits (state)
                state  <-- PB_CA2D (32, state)
                state  <-- PB_CA2D (128, state)
                block  <-- state_to_block (state)
                block  <-- AddSubKey (block, SubKeys [i])
        End for
        Return block
End
```

The encryption procedure is described above. Initially, a GenerateSubkeys operation as presented in Algorithm 3 is needed. It is performed by using a key

"Key" of size 128-bits as entry parameter and it generates ten sub-keys of size 64-bits. This function is used in both processes, encryption and decryption.

After generating the ten sub keys, the plain text is converted into 8×8 state where each cell containing 1 bit. Next, we apply a non-linear CA substitution (oddSubBits). After the previous steps we apply two permutations (PB_CA2D) to the state by using PB CA rules (32,128). Finally, we apply a simple XOR between the working state and the round key.

Decryption Algorithm: Algorithm 2

```
Decrypt_Block (block, Key)
        SubKeys [10]  <--  GenerateSubKeys (Key)
        for i from 10 down to 0 do
                block  <--   AddSubKey (block, SubKeys[i])
                state  <--  block_to_state (block, 8, 8)
                state  <--  PB_CA2D (2, state)
                state  <--  PB_CA2D (8, state)
                state  <--  InvOddSubBits (state)
                block  <--  state_to_block (state)
        End for
        Return block
End
```

In the decryption algorithm, we call the same function GenerateSubkeys already used in encryption process, then we start the round by an XOR between the block and the round key, next we apply the inverse of the two PB CA 32 and 128 (PB CA 2, and PB CA 8), the last step of round is an inverse of substitution OddSubBits (InvOddSubBits).

Sub Keys Generator Algorithm: Algorithm 3.
The objective of this function is the generation of ten subkeys, the process starts with a key of 128-bits running into ten rounds; each round evolves according to the following steps:

- **Step 1**: The initial Key "Key" is divided into two sub-keys of 64-bits (left-subkey, right-subkey).
- **Step 2**: The left-subkey and the right-subkey are divided into two sub-blocks of size 32-bits.
- **Step 3**: Successive XOR operations are applied between the sub-blocks, and the result of each operation is passed into a specific ECA to generate a new sub-block.
- **Step 4**: Concatenation of the results obtained in "Step 3" to generate two sub-keys of size 64-bits.
- **Step 5**: The two sub-keys generated in "Step 4" are concatenated to get a new key of size 128-bits, this key will be using as the initial key of the next round.

The same steps are applied in each round until the generation of ten subkeys (64-bits).

4   Security Analysis

4.1   Avalanche Effect Test (Diffusion Test)

Avalanche effect is an important characteristic to ensure the security of an encryption algorithm. This property can be seen when changing one bit in plaintext and then watching the change in the outcome of at least half of the bits in the ciphertext. To realize this test, we use a chosen plaintext; we encrypt it with our proposed algorithm and with AES-128. Next, a successive one-bit-change operation are applied in distinct position of the plaintext, in every bit-change operation the two changed plaintext are encrypted simultaneously with our algorithm and with AES-128. Therefore, we calculate the avalanche effect between the cipher of initial plaintext and the cipher of changed plaintext. Figure 3 illustrates the results of the performed tests, it demonstrates an average of avalanche effect percentage corresponding to 51.30% for our proposed algorithm and 50.69% for AES-128. These results indicate that the new proposed algorithm gives better results on the avalanche effect than AES-128.

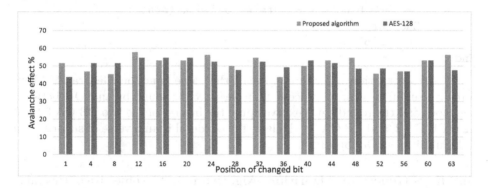

Fig. 3. Avalanche effect % versus one-bit change in different position in plaintext

4.2   Confusion Test

The confusion test refers to make the correlation between the key and the ciphertext as complex as possible, it is observed as the number of bits changed in the ciphertext in comparison with the number of bits changed in key bits. To realize this test, we keep the plaintext unchanged while one bit will be changed in the key in a distinct position on each test, we realized the same test by using our proposed algorithm and AES-128 and we compare the result of each encryption algorithm. Figure 4 shows the result of the performed tests. We remark that the average of changing rate for our algorithm corresponds to 51.36% while the average of changing rate for AES-128 is 50.82%. The results demonstrate that the proposed algorithm has good confusion compared to AES-128.

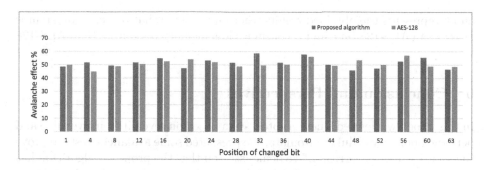

Fig. 4. Changing rate % versus one-bit change in different position in key

5 Performance Analysis

The performance of our block cipher and AES-128 bits is experimented on a windows 10 laptop of processor i5 CPU 2.6 GHz. The two algorithms were implemented in Python. The aims of this test is to compare the encryption CPU time and Memory usage of the two algorithms over different plain text size, the Figs. 5

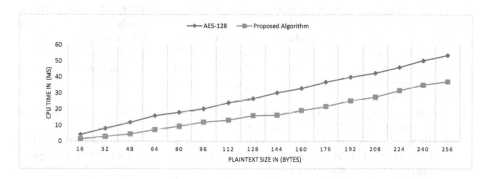

Fig. 5. CPU time of our proposed algorithm and AES-128 bits

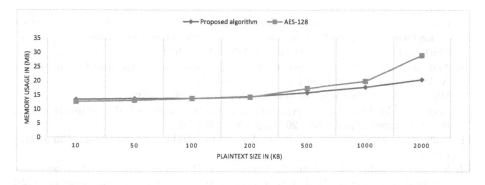

Fig. 6. Memory usage of our proposed algorithm and AES-128 bits

and 6 represents the obtained results where we observe that our cryptosystem is faster than AES-128 bits, and it consumes less memory ressources than AES-128 bits.

6 Conclusion and Perspectives

In this paper, we defined a new cryptosystem based on reversible, irreversible and periodic boundary cellular automata. We presented some avalanche tests to prove the security of our algorithm. We demonstrated that the proposed algorithm has better avalanche effect than AES-128. It's also more secure against brute force attack due to the size of the key (128 bits). It contains both linear functions (permutations) and nonlinear functions (substitutions), which ensure a good security level of cryptography. In addition to the above results, a future work will introduce NIST (National Institute of Standards and Technology) statistical tests to evaluate the randomness of our algorithm.

References

1. Pande, A., Zambreno, J.: A chaotic encryption scheme for real-time embedded systems: design and implementation. Telecommun. Syst. **52**(2), 551–561 (2013)
2. Wollinger, T., Guajardo, J., Paar, C.: Cryptography in embedded systems: an overview. In: Proceedings of the Embedded World 2003 Exhibition and Conference, Design & Elektronik, Nuernberg, Germany, pp. 735–744, 18–20 February 2003
3. Hatzivasilis, G., Floros, G., Papaefstathiou, I., Manifavas, C.: Lightweight authenticated encryption for embedded on-chip systems. Inf. Secur. J. Glob. Perspect. **25**(4–6), 151–161 (2016)
4. McKay, K.A., Bassham, L., Sönmez Turan, M., Mouha, N.: Report on lightweight cryptography, NIST.IR.8114, March 2017
5. Wolfram, S.: Cryptography with cellular automata. In: Williams, H.C. (ed.) CRYPTO 1985. LNCS, vol. 218, pp. 429–432. Springer, Heidelberg (1986). https://doi.org/10.1007/3-540-39799-X_32
6. Das, D., Ray, A.: A parallel encryption algorithm for block ciphers based on reversible programmable cellular automata. J. Comput. Sci. Eng. **1**(1), 82–90 (2010)
7. Pal Choudhury, P., Sahoo, S., Chakraborty, M.: Characterization of the evolution of nonlinear uniform cellular automata in the light of deviated states. Int. J. Math. Math. Sci. (2011). https://doi.org/10.1155/2011/605098
8. Neumann, J.V.: Theory of Self-Replicating Automata. Edited and Completed by A. W. Burks. University of Illinois Press (1966)
9. Wolfram, S.: A New Kind of Science. Wolfram Media (2002)
10. Singh, A., Mishra, S.S.: Crytpographic algorithm using cellular automata rules. Int. J. Comput. Appl. **3**(4) (2014). ISSN 2250-1797
11. Toffoli, T., Margolus, N.: Cellular Automata Machines. MIT Press, Cambridge (1987)
12. Sen, S., Hossain, S.I., Islam, K., Chowdhuri, D.R., Chaudhuri, P.P.: Cryptosystem designed for embedded system security. In: International Conference on VLSI Design (VLSI 2003). IEEE (2003). 1063-9667/03

13. Tripathy, S., Nandi, S.: LCASE: lightweight cellular automata-based symmetric-key encryption. Int. J. Netw. Secur. **8**(2), 243–252 (2009)
14. Reddy, S., Kumar, M.S.: Light weight cellular automata computations and symmetric key for achieving efficient cryptography. Int. J. Emerg. Eng. Res. Technol. **3**(12) (2015)
15. Bouchkaren, S., Lazaar, S.: A new cryptographic scheme based on cellular automata. In: El Oualkadi, A., Choubani, F., El Moussati, A. (eds.) Proceedings of the Mediterranean Conference on Information & Communication Technologies 2015. LNEE, vol. 381, pp. 663–668. Springer, Cham (2016). https://doi.org/10.1007/978-3-319-30298-0_74
16. Bouchkaren, S., Lazaar, S.: A fast cryptosystem using reversible cellular automata. Int. J. Adv. Comput. Sci. Appl. **5**(5), 207–210 (2014)
17. Sethi, B., Das, S.: On the use of asynchronous cellular automata in symmetric-key cryptography. In: Mueller, P., Thampi, S.M., Alam Bhuiyan, M.Z., Ko, R., Doss, R., Alcaraz Calero, J.M. (eds.) SSCC 2016. CCIS, vol. 625, pp. 30–41. Springer, Singapore (2016). https://doi.org/10.1007/978-981-10-2738-3_3
18. Parashar, D., Roy, S., Dey, N., Jain, V., Rawat, U.S.: Symmetric key encryption technique: a cellular automata based approach. In: Bokhari, M.U., Agrawal, N., Saini, D. (eds.) Cyber Security. AISC, vol. 729, pp. 59–67. Springer, Singapore (2018). https://doi.org/10.1007/978-981-10-8536-9_7

An ElGamal-Like Digital Signature Based on Elliptic Curves

Leila Zahhafi$^{(\boxtimes)}$ and Omar Khadir

Laboratory of Mathematics, Cryptography, Mechanics and Numerical Analysis, Fstm,
University Hassan II of Casablanca, Mohammedia, Morocco
`leila.zahhafi@gmail.com`, `khadir@hotmail.com`

Abstract. In this work, we present a new variant of the ElGamal digital signature scheme. We ameliorated the signature equation to make it more secure against current attacks. The method is based on the elliptic curves notion. We analyze the complexity and security of the protocol.

Keywords: Digital signature · Elliptic curves · ElGamal signature · Discrete logarithm

1 Introduction

The security in information technology is an important topic on scientific research. Cryptography presents a solid way to ensure the transfer of information with secret and confidential content upon insecure network. It also allows internet users to make all their online transactions and operations safely with any form of mobile computing. In addition, automating several common actions has increased the need for effective methods to verify user's identity.

Digital signature is a practical tool for ensuring identity of the signer and integrity of the signed document. Any signature protocol is based on mathematical notions often used in cryptography as factoring large numbers and discrete logarithm problem [22].

Among the basic methods known on the digital signature we quote the work of Rivest, Shamir and Adleman [19] published in 1978. This protocol is based on the problem of factoring large number to solve the polynomial equation: $x^a = b \bmod n$ where: a and b are two integers, n is a large composite number and x is the unknown. Then, Rabin [18] created in 1979 a new system for encryption and signing messages. Its method is also based on the problem of factoring large numbers as others schemes [8,9,15,16,21]. In 1984, ElGamal [7] proposed a new digital signature scheme based on the discrete logarithm problem. This method gave rise to several variants as [5,14,20,23,24]. In this paper, we use the elliptic curves method to create a new signature scheme.

In fact, using elliptic curves in cryptography was initiated by Koblitz [11] and Miller [13] since 1985. The hardness of arithmetic operations in the elliptic curves makes protocols based on this approach more solid. Several public-key

© Springer Nature Switzerland AG 2019
É. Renault et al. (Eds.): MSPN 2019, LNCS 11557, pp. 268–275, 2019.
https://doi.org/10.1007/978-3-030-22885-9_23

cryptographic protocols are based on elliptic curves as crypto-systems that allow coding and decoding secret messages safely like [2]. And among the more important digital signature schemes we mention the elliptic curve digital signature algorithm (ECDSA) [10] and the elliptic curve ElGamal digital signature [17] with its variants as [1].

In this work, we present a new alternative of the elliptic curve ElGamal digital signature scheme. We ameliorated the basic signature equation in order to reenforce the signature system.

The paper is structured as follow: We present in the second section the elliptic curves notion. Section three details the basic elliptic curves ElGamal digital signature protocol. We describe in the next section our main contribution and we finish by a conclusion in section five.

We denote by $x \equiv y\,[n]$ if n divides the difference $x - y$ with: x, y and n are three integers.

We start by introducing the basic elliptic curves method.

2   Overview of the Elliptic Curves Method

Using the elliptic curves method [11] in cryptography was proposed by Koblitz [11] and Miller [13] since 1985. This notion employing several algebraic properties improves existing cryptographic primitives, such as reducing the size of the using keys, or constructing new cryptographic primitives that were not known before.

2.1   Group Law

Consider (E) an elliptic curve defined on a finite filed F_q with a characteristic different of 2 and 3 in order to write (E) in the simplified form of the Weierstrass.

In this section, we give an explicit method to calculate the addition of two points in the curve (E).

Let q be a large prime integer, (a, b) integers smaller than q and $\mathcal{O}$ an imaginary point at infinity. The equation of the elliptic curve (E) is as follow:

$$y^2 \equiv x^3 + bx + c \,[q] \tag{1}$$

Let $P_1 = (x_1, y_1)$, $P_2 = (x_2, y_2)$ and $P_3 = (x_3, y_3)$ be points of (E) with P_1, $P_2 \neq \mathcal{O}$ and $P_1 + P_2 = P_3$.

1. If $x_1 \neq x_2$ then:
   $x_3 = m^2 - x_1 - x_2$ and $y_3 = m(x_1 - x_2) - y_1$. Such that: $m = \dfrac{y_2 - y_1}{x_2 - x_1}$.
2. If $x_1 = x_2$ and $y_1 \neq y_2$ then $P_3 = \mathcal{O}$
3. If $P_1 = P_2$ and $y_1 \neq 0$ then:
   $x_3 = m^2 - 2x_1$ and $y_3 = m(x_1 - x_3) - y_1$. Such that: $m = \dfrac{3x_1^2 + a}{2y_1}$.
4. If $P_1 = P_2$ and $y_1 = 0$ then $P_3 = \mathcal{O}$.

And for all point P in (E) we have: $P + \mathcal{O} = P$

2.2   The Discrete Logarithm Problem

Let G be a group and $\alpha \in G$. The discrete logarithm in G is to solve the following equation:

$$y = \alpha^x \tag{2}$$

Where x is the unknown parameter.

In the case where $G = (E)$ an elliptic curve, the discrete logarithm problem is to find α that verifies:

$$Q = \alpha P \tag{3}$$

Such that Q and P are points in (E).

We describe in the next section the basic ElGamal signature with elliptic curves.

3   ElGamal Elliptic Curves

In the first, we fix a secure hash function h as SHA3 [6].

The signer starts by choosing a prime integer and an elliptic curve (E) defined by the following equation:

$$y^2 \equiv x^3 + bx + c \; [p] \tag{4}$$

In the next, the signer selects a point G belonging to (E) with the order q. He fixes its secrete key $\alpha < q$ and calculates $A = \alpha G$. His public keys are (a, b, p, q, G, A).

To sign the message m, the signer has to solve the following equation:

$$h(m)G = r_1 A + sR \tag{5}$$

Such that: $R = (r_1, r_2)$ and s are the unknowns.

To solve Eq. (5), the signer chooses arbitrary an integer $k \leq q - 1$, then he computes $R = kG = (r_1, r_2)$ and he finds the integer s as follow:

$$s \equiv \frac{h(m) - r_1\alpha}{k} \; [q] \tag{6}$$

So, the signature for the message m is the pair (R, s).

The verifier downloads the signature sent by the signer. He can check the validity of the data received as follow:

He calculates $V_1 = r_1 A + sR$ and $V_2 = h(m)A$. If $V_1 = V_2$ then the signature is valid.

We show in the following section our main contribution.

4 Our Contribution

4.1 Description of the Protocol

Let (E) be an elliptic curve defined by the following equation:

$$y^2 \equiv x^3 + bx + c \ [p] \tag{7}$$

The signer selects a point $G \in E$ with the order q. He chooses the secrete key $\alpha < q$ and calculates $A = \alpha G$. His public keys are (a, b, p, q, G, A).

To sign the message m, the signer has to solve the following equation:

$$h(m)G + x_1 A + y_1 X = sY \tag{8}$$

Such that: $X = (x_1, x_2)$, $Y = (y_1, y_2)$ and s are the unknowns.

To solve Eq. (8), the signer chooses arbitrary two integers $k, l \leq q - 1$, then he computes $X = kG = (x_1, x_2)$ and $Y = lG = (y_1, y_2)$, then he finds the integer s as follow:

$$s \equiv \frac{h(m) + \alpha x_1 + k y_1}{l} \ [q] \tag{9}$$

So, the signature for the message m is the triplet (X, Y, s).

The verifier downloads the signature sent by the signer. He can checks the validity of the data received as follow:

He calculates $V_1 = h(m)G + x_1 A + y_1 X$ and $V_2 = sY$. If $V_1 = V_2$ then the signature is valid.

Correctness of the Algorithm

The validity of our signature amounts to find $V_1 = V_2$.

We have: $V_1 = h(m)G + x_1 A + y_1 X$ and $V_2 = sY$ such that $s \equiv \frac{h(m) + \alpha x_1 + k y_1}{l}$ $[q]$. So, $V_2 = sY = \frac{h(m) + \alpha x_1 + k y_1}{l} Y$. As $Y = lG$, we get $V_2 = (h(m) + \alpha x_1 + k y_1)G = h(m)G + \alpha x_1 G + k y_1 G$. Since $\alpha G = A$ and $kG = X$ we obtain: $V_2 = h(m)G + x_1 A + y_1 X = V_1$. So, the result is proved.

Example 1. Let's take the elliptic curve (E) defined by the following equation:

$$y^2 \equiv x^3 + 23x + 34 \ [1429] \tag{10}$$

The signer selects $G = (875, 1317)$ a point belonging to the curve (E). The order of G is $q = 497$. Then he chooses its secrete key $\alpha = 351$. So, the public key is: $A = \alpha G = (479, 644)$.

Now, suppose that the signer wants to sign a message m that verifies: $h(m) = 213$. He starts by fixing $k = 123$ and $l = 334$. Then he calculates: $X = kG = (968, 1300)$ and $Y = lG = (94, 720)$.

Using its private key, he finds: $s \equiv \frac{h(m) + \alpha x_1 + k y_1}{l} \equiv 168$ $[q]$. The final signature is: $S = (X(968, 1300), Y(94, 720), 168)$.

By receiving the signature S, the verifier can check its validity as follow: He computes $V_1 = h(m)G + x_1 A + y_1 X = (1331, 434)$ and $V_2 = sY = (1331, 434)$. As $V_1 = V_2$, the verifier accepts the received signature.

4.2 Security Analysis

The security of our signature method is based on the difficulty of solving a discrete logarithm problem. We discuss in this paragraph some possible attacks.

Attack 1: Discovering the signer's private key is one of the most dangerous attacks that threaten the efficiency of any digital signature system. Knowing all public parameters of the signer (a, b, q, A), the attacker cannot compute the secrete key α. Indeed, he's confronted to the elliptic curve discrete logarithm problem: $A \equiv \alpha G[q]$ that implies $\sqrt{\log q \log \log q}$ operations as it's mentioned by Adleman in [3].

Attack 2: The basic Eq. (8) of our signature method presents three unknown variables: Points X, Y and the integer s. If the attacker tries to fix arbitrary two variables and find the third then he will be confronted to one of this three cases:

1. If he fixes the points X and Y:

$$sY = h(m)G + x_1 A + y_1 X \qquad (11)$$

He will be confronted to the ECDLP.
2. If he fixes the point X and the integer s:

$$sY = h(m)G + x_1 A + y_1 X \qquad (12)$$

There is not a known method that allows to find the point Y using Eq. (11) in a polynomial time.
3. If he fixes the point X and the integer s:

$$y_1 X = sY - h(m)G - x_1 A \qquad (13)$$

As the previous case, there is not a known method that allows to find the point X using Eq. (12) in a polynomial time.

4.3 Complexity Analysis

Let $T_{FM}, T_{FD}, T_{FS}, T_h, T_{PM}, T_{PA}$ and T_{PD} be times to execute respectively a field multiplication, field division, field squaring, hash function, point multiplication, point addition and a point doubling.

   To calculate a point multiplication: kP where k is an integer and P a point, we need computing $\log(k)$ point additions and doublings (for more details see [4, 11]) using for example the algorithm of Double-and-add.

   The point addition requires 9 field multiplications and 1 field squaring. And the point doubling necessitates 3 field multiplications and 4 field squaring.

   We assume that $T_{FS} = O((\log n)^3)$ and $T_{FM} = O((\log n)^2)$, (see [12]). Let T_K, T_S, T_V be respectively complexities of keys production, signing and signature verification. We describe their values as follow:

1. To sign a given message m, the signer needs to perform one point multiplication to construct it public key.

$$
\begin{aligned}
T_K &= T_{PM} \\
&= \log(\alpha)(T_{PA} + T_{PD}) \\
&= \log(\alpha)(9T_{FM} + T_{FS} + 3T_{FM} + 4T_{FS}) \\
&= \log(\alpha)(12T_{FM} + 5T_{FS}) \\
&= \log(\alpha)(12O((\log q)^2) + 5O((\log q)^3))
\end{aligned}
$$

2. The signer executes two point multiplications, two field multiplications and one hash function to generate a valid signature.

$$
\begin{aligned}
T_S &= 2T_{PM} + 2T_{FM} + T_h \\
&= (\log(k) + \log(l))(T_{PA} + T_{PD}) + 2T_{FM} + T_h \\
&= (\log(k) + \log(l))(9T_{FM} + T_{FS} + 3T_{FM} + 4T_{FS}) + 2T_{FM} + T_h \\
&= (\log(k) + \log(l))(12T_{FM} + 5T_{FS}) + 2T_{FM} + T_h \\
&= (\log(k) + \log(l))(12O((\log q)^2) + 5O((\log q)^3)) + 2O((\log q)^2) + T_h
\end{aligned}
$$

3. The verifier checks the correctness of the received signature after four point multiplications, two point additions and one hash function.

$$
\begin{aligned}
T_V &= 4T_{PM} + 2T_{PA} + T_h \\
&= (\log(x_1) + \log(y_1) + \log(s) + \log(h(m)))(T_{PA} + T_{PD}) + 2T_{PA} + T_h \\
&= (\log(x_1) + \log(y_1) + \log(s) + \log(h(m)))(9T_{FM} + T_{FS} + 3T_{FM} \\
&\quad + 4T_{FS}) + 2(9T_{FM} + T_{FS}) + T_h \\
&= (\log(x_1) + \log(y_1) + \log(s) + \log(h(m)))(12T_{FM} + 5T_{FS}) \\
&\quad + 2(9T_{FM} + T_{FS}) + T_h \\
&= (\log(x_1) + \log(y_1) + \log(s) + \log(h(m)))(12O((\log q)^2) + 5O((\log q)^3)) \\
&\quad + 2(O((\log q)^2) + O((\log q)^3)) + T_h
\end{aligned}
$$

So, the total complexity T_t of our signature method is as follow:

$$
T_t = T_K + T_S + T_V
$$

5   Conclusion

In this paper, we used the elliptic curves to propose a new signature scheme inspired from the ElGamal method. We have suggested a signature equation with three unknown variables to make it more difficult for attackers. We have also exploited the hash functions in the protocol to guarantee the authenticity of the signed message.

References

1. Abid, O., Ettanfouhi, J., Khadir, O.: New digital signature protocol based on elliptic curves. Int. J. Cryptogr. Inf. Secur. (IJCIS) **2**, 13–19 (2012)
2. Abid, O., Khadir, O.: Adaptation of a cryptosystem based on the arithmetic of finite fields to elliptic curves. Libertas Math. **38**, 59–68 (2018)
3. Adleman, L.: A sub exponential algorithmic for the discrete logarithm problem with applications to cryptography. In: Foundations of Computer Science (1979)
4. Bernstein, D.J., Lange, T.: Faster addition and doubling on elliptic curves. In: Kurosawa, K. (ed.) ASIACRYPT 2007. LNCS, vol. 4833, pp. 29–50. Springer, Heidelberg (2007). https://doi.org/10.1007/978-3-540-76900-2_3
5. Lee, C.-Y., Lai, W.-S.: Extended DSA. J. Discrete Math. Sci. Cryptogr. **11**(5), 545–550 (2008). https://doi.org/10.1080/09720529.2008.10698206
6. Dworkin, M.J.: SHA-3 Standard: Permutation-Based Hash and Extendable-Output Functions. Federal Information Processing Standards (NIST FIPS) – 202 (2015)
7. ElGamal, T.: A public key cryptosystem and a signature scheme based on discrete logarithm problem. IEEE Trans. Info. Theory **31**, 469–472 (1985)
8. Fiat, A., Shamir, A.: How to prove yourself: practical solutions to identification and signature problems. In: Odlyzko, A.M. (ed.) CRYPTO 1986. LNCS, vol. 263, pp. 186–194. Springer, Heidelberg (1987). https://doi.org/10.1007/3-540-47721-7_12
9. Guillou, L.C., Quisquater, J.-J.: A practical zero-knowledge protocol fitted to security microprocessor minimizing both transmission and memory. In: Barstow, D., et al. (eds.) EUROCRYPT 1988. LNCS, vol. 330, pp. 123–128. Springer, Heidelberg (1988). https://doi.org/10.1007/3-540-45961-8_11
10. Johnson, D., Menezes, A., Vanstone, S.: The elliptic curve digital signature algorithm (ECDSA). Int. J. Inf. Secur. **1**, 36–63 (2001)
11. Koblitz, N.: Elliptic curve cryptosystems. Math. Comput. **48**(177), 203–209 (1987)
12. Menezes, A.J., van Oorschot, P.C., Vanstone, S.A.: Handbook of Applied Cryptography, p. 72 (1996)
13. Miller, V.S.: Use of elliptic curves in cryptography. In: Williams, H.C. (ed.) CRYPTO 1985. LNCS, vol. 218, pp. 417–426. Springer, Heidelberg (1986). https://doi.org/10.1007/3-540-39799-X_31
14. National Institute of Standard and Technology (NIST). FIPS Publication 186, DSA, Department of Commerce (1994)
15. Okamoto, T.: Provably secure and practical identification schemes and corresponding signature schemes. In: Brickell, E.F. (ed.) CRYPTO 1992. LNCS, vol. 740, pp. 31–53. Springer, Heidelberg (1993). https://doi.org/10.1007/3-540-48071-4_3
16. Paillier, P.: Public-key cryptosystems based on composite degree residuosity classes. In: Stern, J. (ed.) EUROCRYPT 1999. LNCS, vol. 1592, pp. 223–238. Springer, Heidelberg (1999). https://doi.org/10.1007/3-540-48910-X_16
17. Rabah, K.: Elliptic curve ElGamal encryption and signature schemes. Inf. Technol. J. **4**, 299–306 (2005)
18. Rabin, M.O.: Digital signatures and public-key functions as intractable as factorization. Technical report MIT/LCS/TR-212 (1978)
19. Rivest, R., Shamir, A., Adeleman, L.: A method for obtaining digital signatures and public key cryptosystems. Commun. ACM **21**, 120–126 (1978)
20. Schnorr, C.P.: Efficient signature generation by smart cards. J. Cryptol. **4**, 161–174 (1991)
21. Shamir, A.: Identity-based cryptosystems and signature schemes. In: Blakley, G.R., Chaum, D. (eds.) CRYPTO 1984. LNCS, vol. 196, pp. 47–53. Springer, Heidelberg (1985). https://doi.org/10.1007/3-540-39568-7_5

22. Shor, P.W.: Polynomial-time algorithms for prime factorization and discrete logarithms on a quantum computer. SIAM J. Comput. **26**, 1484–1509 (1997)
23. Zahhafi, L., Khadir, O.: A digital signature scheme based simultaneously on the DSA and RSA protocols. Gulf J. Math. **6**(4), 37–43 (2018)
24. Zahhafi, L., Khadir, O.: A secure variant of Schnorr signature using the RSA algorithm. J. Univ. Math. **1**(4), 104–109 (2018)

Author Index

Printed in the United States
By Bookmasters